I0795662

IMAGES
of Rail

THE RAHWAY VALLEY RAILROAD

IMAGES
of Rail

THE RAHWAY VALLEY RAILROAD

Donald A. Maxton

ARCADIA PUBLISHING

ISBN 978-0-7385-1008-8

Published by Arcadia Publishing
Charleston, South Carolina

Printed in the United States of America

Library of Congress Catalog Card Number: 2002100081

For all general information contact Arcadia Publishing at:
Telephone 843-853-2070
Fax 843-853-0044
E-mail sales@arcadiapublishing.com
For customer service and orders:
Toll-Free 1-888-313-2665

Visit us on the Internet at www.arcadiapublishing.com

This book is dedicated to
Dennis, Don, Doug, Jim, and Steve.

Research and art consultant: Gregory R. Suriano

Contents

ACKNOWLEDGMENTS

The Rahway Valley Railroad has a rich history, but it required a determined search to locate and gather the information, photographs, postcards, advertisements, documents, and other material included in this book. I thank the following individuals and organizations, who generously provided time, assistance, information, advice, and access to their precious collections of Rahway Valley memorabilia: Ben Anthony, Museum of Erie GE History; Bill Burke; Doug Chieff; Susan and Alan Coen; Tom Dolan; Christine Faucher; Virginia Faulkner; Jon Franz; Paul Harvan; Jeff Jargosch; Michael Kaplonski; Kenilworth Historical Society; Richard King; Steven Lynch; Nancy Nett; Patricia Pagnetti, Roselle Park Historical Society/Roselle Park Museum; Robert Pennisi; Carl G. Perelman; Ronald F. Pietranowicz; Elizabeth Plowe; Judy Pommett; James Price; John Sheppard; Steamtown National Historic Site; Summit Historical Society; *Trains* magazine; George Weiss; Chris Wolff; and Norman W. Woolley.

Special thanks go to Mary E. McCoy for kindly sharing the outstanding collection of her late husband, John J. McCoy; Edward H. Weber for his photographs and memories; and fellow Rahway Valley Railroad aficionados Scott Schnipper and Bruce Trampler for providing encouragement along with their collections.

This book was made possible in part by a 2001 HEART Grant from the Union County Board of Chosen Freeholders, Alexander Mirabella, Chairman.

INTRODUCTION

The Rahway Valley Railroad (RV), what railroaders call a short line, was active in Union and Essex Counties from 1897 to 1992, when it was formally abandoned. It played a key role in developing this busy part of New Jersey by providing freight and passenger service to Roselle Park, Kenilworth, Springfield, Summit, Union, and Maplewood.

The RV traced its roots to a little pike called the New York & New Orange Railroad (NY&NO), formed by a group of businessmen developing the area of New Orange (now Kenilworth). In those less hectic days before automobiles and trucks became commonplace, the NY&NO became a convenient means for the transportation of goods and people in a mostly rural Union County.

The Rahway Valley and its predecessors provided convenient passenger service at a time when travel was not an easy endeavor. In its time the railroad carried students to Upsala College, then based in Kenilworth; vacations visiting the New Jersey shore; golfers heading for the links at Baltusrol Golf Club in Springfield; families on church excursions or outings to local picnic groves; munitions plant workers during World War I; and many more.

It even enjoyed a brief period of Hollywood-style glamour, when early filmmakers used the railroad and surrounding area as a setting for silent Westerns. Over the years, the Rahway Valley became a familiar neighbor, and many residents can still recall the nostalgic site of a Rahway Valley train working its way through the neighborhood and the friendly waves of the crew.

The number of passengers gradually declined, and there was little need for the service by 1919, which the Rahway Valley subsequently discontinued. But the Rahway Valley soldiered on. Through its vital links with larger railroads crisscrossing Union County—the Central Railroad of New Jersey, the Lehigh Valley Railroad, and (later) the Delaware, Lackawanna & Western Railroad—it provided a bustling freight service, picking up and delivering goods to local businesses and shipping out their finished products to markets throughout the nation. It also offered a steady source of employment for many area residents over the years, although the staff and crew rarely exceeded 20 people at any one time.

The Rahway Valley transported a host of important commodities, including lumber and stone for constructing residences and businesses; coal for heating homes and factories; raw materials for manufacturing pharmaceuticals; metals and plastics for fabricators; chemicals for industry; food products; and paper for school supplies. The parcels of land adjacent to the Rahway Valley tracks evolved into vibrant industrial neighborhoods.

Success did not come easy, and the Rahway Valley operated on a shoestring for many years. President and general manager George A. Clark recounted those days of struggle to author John

T. Cunningham in 1950: "Plenty of times I went down to Trenton in those days and got down on my knees to the tax men. We didn't know from day to day if we were going to make it. We didn't even have the money to meet our payroll when we started."

By 1934, the Rahway Valley had turned an actual net profit, right in the middle of the Great Depression. It would continue to operate in the black for many years, which was no small achievement for a tiny short line competing with the growing trucking industry for a share of the freight-forwarding market.

Much of the Rahway Valley's success during this period can be credited to the combined experience, determination, and business savvy of Roger A. Clark and his son George and to their dedicated, hardworking train crews. The Clarks left the forests and short lines of the Pacific Northwest in 1920 to manage the Rahway Valley. Clark once said to Cunningham, "I don't believe in losing money. I don't lose money. Those trucks are hurting us more and more, but we're figuring out ways to meet them." The feisty short line—only 15.3 miles long, including freight sidings, and one of the shortest in the country—competed successfully for many years and became one of the nation's most profitable railroads.

As the 20th century progressed, trucks began to make more serious inroads on the Rahway Valley's freight business. By the mid-1970s, when seasoned railroader Bernard J. Cahill became president and general manager, much of the railroad's business was seasonal. There was a high turnover of businesses in the area as well, making it more difficult for the line to establish long-term relationships with customers. Cahill kept the Rahway Valley up and running as best he could.

In 1986, the Rahway Valley was unable to renew its liability insurance, and the Delaware Otsego Corporation, a growing regional carrier, took over operations. Later that year, Delaware Otsego purchased the short line and continued to run it until 1992, when only one shipper remained on the once flourishing line.

Although it is no longer in service, the Rahway Valley Railroad is not forgotten. Until the early 1950s, its trains were powered by a succession of steam locomotives. The last one, No. 15, is seen by thousands of visitors every year at the Steamtown National Historic Site in Scranton, Pennsylvania, and has been used for special excursions. The Rahway Valley's two colorful diesel locomotives, Nos. 16 and 17, are now on display at the Whippany Railway Museum, Whippany, New Jersey. The Rahway Valley right of way is now owned by the New Jersey Department of Transportation. Sections of the line were rebuilt from 2001 to 2007, and the Rahway Valley may someday be reactivated for freight service.

One

New Orange and Kenilworth: Rahway Valley Genesis

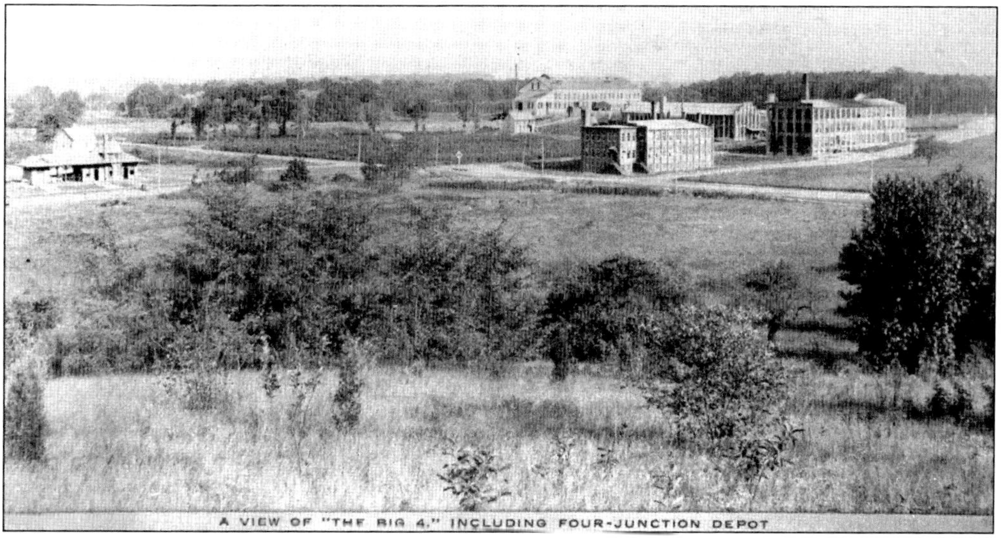

Here is a vintage view of the original "Big Four" factories of the New Orange Industrial Association at New Orange, now the intersection of Boulevard and Market Streets in Kenilworth. The association, formed by a group of businessmen in Elmira, New York in 1894, planned to develop the area that is now Kenilworth for industry and residences. The association's early factories were the Circular Loom Company, the Ricca Manufacturing Company, the New Orange Decorative Leather Company, and the Charles E. Wright Company. A rail line was needed for the enterprise to succeed so the New York & New Orange Railroad was formed in June, 1897. The New Orange depot stands at the upper left of this photograph taken from the southeast slope of Tin Kettle Hill in the summer of 1901. (Courtesy of the Kenilworth Historical Society.)

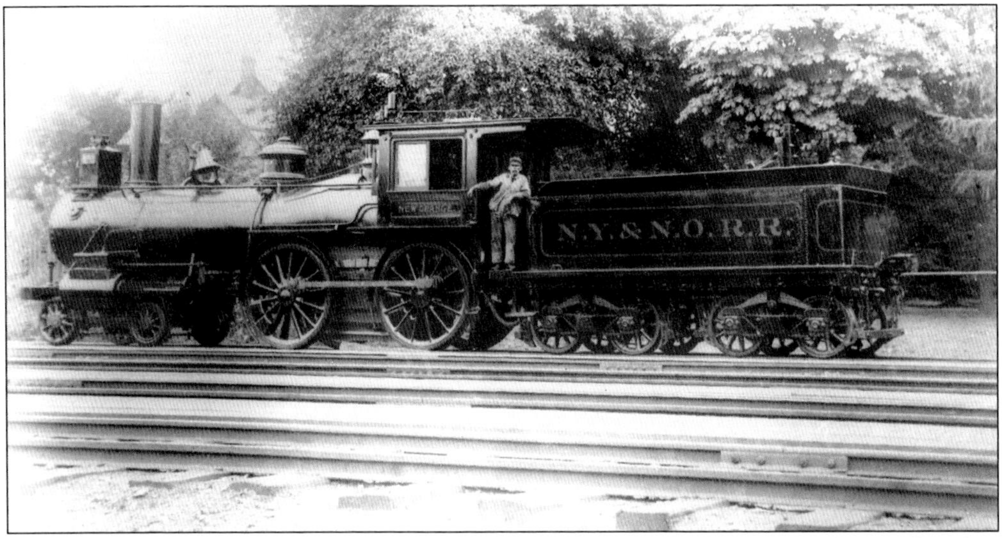

New York & New Orange No. 1 was a tall-stacked, American 4-4-0 purchased secondhand in 1898. Duane Kimball, an engineer from the Central Railroad of New Jersey, was hired to ready the locomotive for service. J. Wallace Higgins, a local civil engineer, planned the railroad's initial four miles of track, from Roselle Park to New Orange. (Photograph by Warren Crater, courtesy of Mary E. McCoy.)

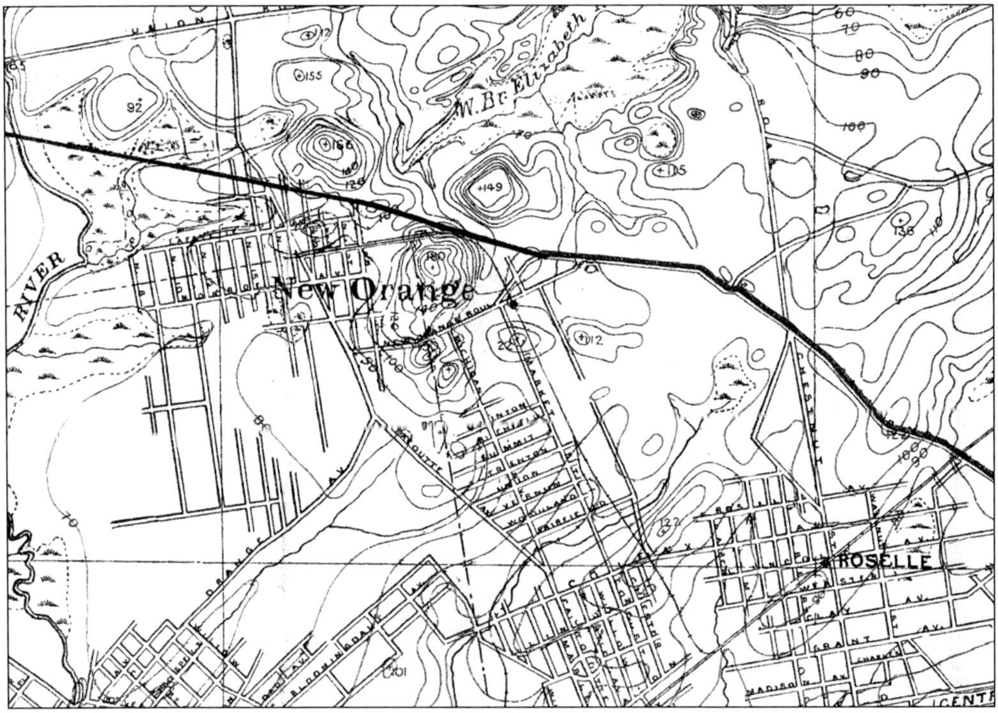

This early map provides a glimpse of New Orange and the surrounding area before New Orange became Kenilworth. The map shows the tracks of the New York & New Orange Railroad, connections with the Central Railroad of New Jersey and the Lehigh Valley Railroad, and the New York & New Orange Railroad station on Boulevard. (Collection of Donald A. Maxton.)

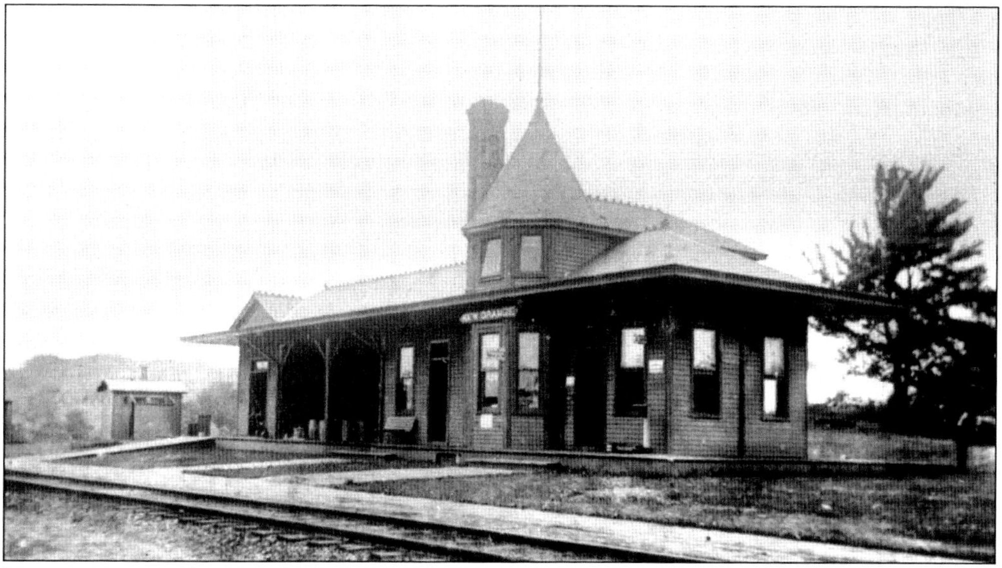

Here is a 1902 photograph of the New Orange Station of the New Orange Four Junction Railroad. This Victorian-style structure, designed by J. Wallace Higgins, chief engineer for the railroad, was constructed in the late 1890s. By the time this photo was taken the railroad had become the "New Orange Four Junction Railroad" (NOFJ) after the NY&NO fell into foreclosure in 1901. The backers of the NY&NO quickly organized the NOFJ to take over railroad operations. (Courtesy of Mary E. McCoy.)

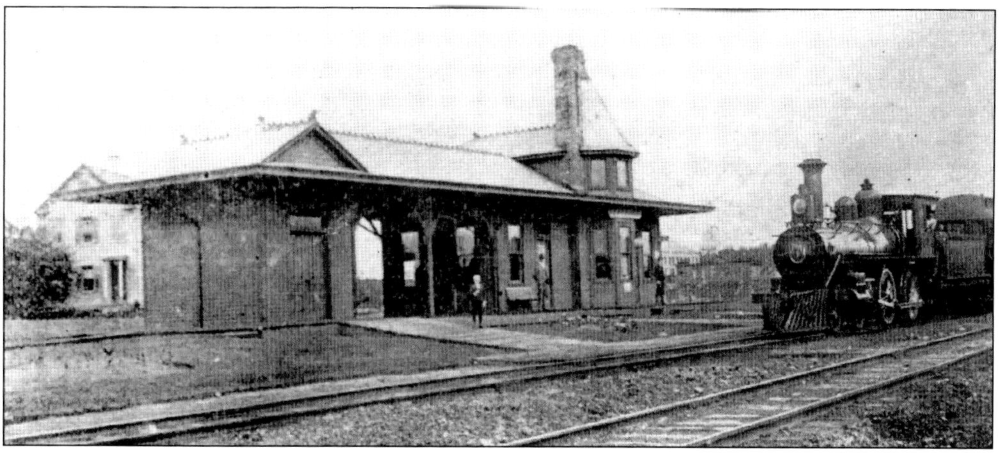

Several passengers watch a locomotive heading up a passenger train pull into the New Orange Station in the early 1900s. Kenilworth's first telegraph and telephone were located in the station. (Courtesy of the Kenilworth Historical Society.)

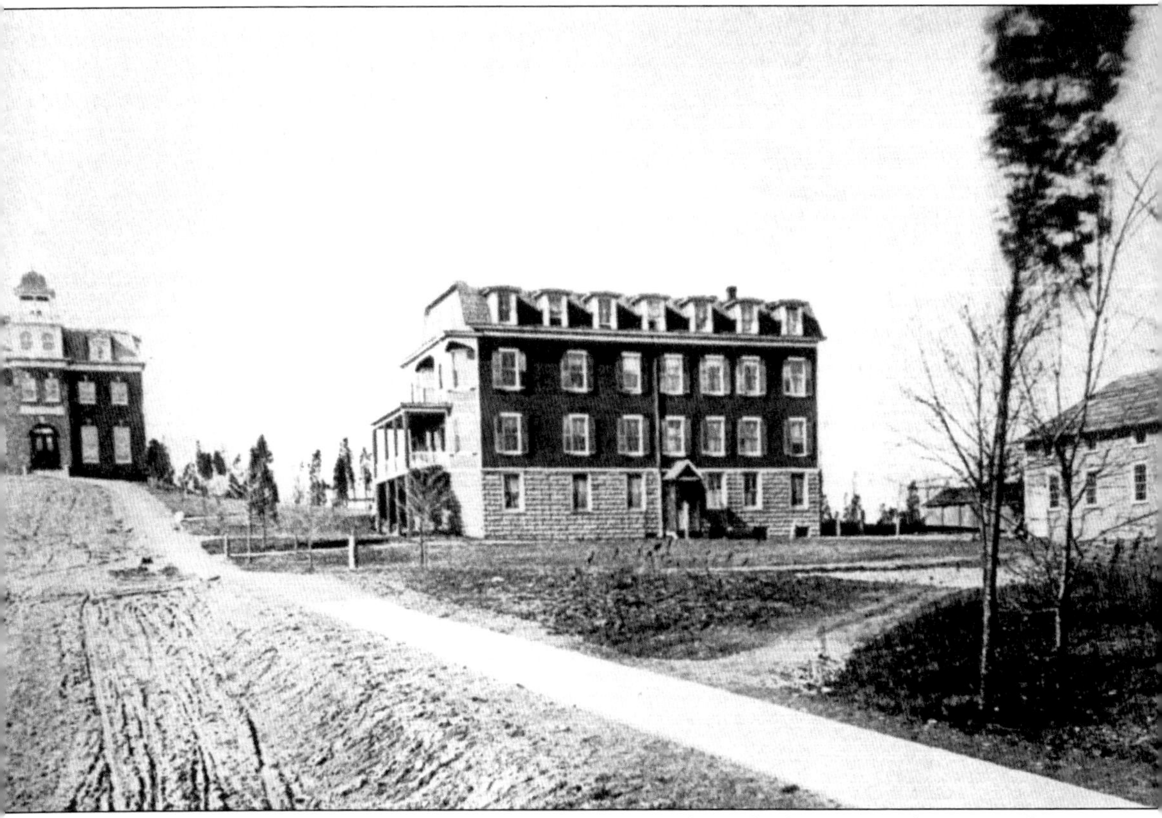

Upsala College students were among the passengers who rode the New York & New Orange, New Orange Four Junction, and Rahway Valley Railroads during the early years of the 20th century. This c. 1900 view of the campus show Old Main (Upsala's main building) on the left and the Ark (which housed dormitory rooms, science classrooms, and a dining hall). The campus site was provided at no cost by the New Orange Industrial Association, along with a $100,000 endowment, and served as Upsala's home until 1924, when the college moved to East Orange, New Jersey. When the college moved this hill was leveled to make room for residential housing. Before long, this quiet area evolved into a vibrant community. (Photograph by J. Fieldman, courtesy of Upsala College Library.)

RAHWAY VALLEY RAILROAD

TIME TABLE IN EFFECT APRIL 10, 1906

STATIONS	*WEEK DAY TRAINS*											*SUNDAYS*			
	2	4	6	10		16	18	20	22	24	26	102	104	106	108
Leave Springfield	AM	AM	AM	AM	PM	PM	PM	PM	PM	PM	PM*	AM	AM	PM	PM
Springfield	6 30	7 25	8 47	10 22		2 47	3 42	4 40		6 32	10 10	8 02	9 52	1 47	4 37
Katemiller	6 32	7 28	8 50	10 25		2 50	3 45	4 52		6 35	10 12	8 05	9 55	1 50	4 40
Doty	6 34	7 31	8 53	10 28		2 53	3 48	4 55		6 38	10 14	8 08	9 58	1 53	4 43
Kenilworth, Warren Street	6 36	7 33	8 55	10 30		2 55	3 50	4 57	5 27	6 40	10 17	8 10	10 00	1 55	4 45
Kenilworth, Central Station	6 38	7 35	8 57	10 33		2 58	3 52	4 59	5 30	6 43	10 19	8 13	10 03	1 58	4 48
Michigan Ave.	6 41	7 38	9 00	10 36		3 00	3 55	5 02	5 33	6 46	10 23	8 16	10 06	2 01	4 51
Aldene	6 44	7 41	9 03	10 39		3 04	3 58	5 06	5 36	6 49	10 27	8 19	10 09	2 04	4 54
Roselle–Roselle Pk. **C. R. R. of N. J.**	6 53	7 50	9 07	10 51		3 11	4 06	5 11	5 45	7 31	10 37	8 22	10 12	2 08	5 03
Elizabeth " "	6 58	7 56	9 12	10 56		3 17	4 12	5 18	5 52	7 37	10 43	8 28	10 19	2 15	5 10
Elizabethport " "		8 07		11 01		3 22	4 17	5 22	6 00	7 42	10 49	8 34	10 25	2 21	5 15
Newark, Broad Street " "	7 26	8 37	9 38			4 14	5 16	5 50	6 17				11 18	2 36	6 33
Jersey City " "	7 18	8 14	9 32	11 17		3 40	4 36	5 42	6 36	8 05	11 13	8 58	10 53	2 44	5 40
West 23rd St. " "	7 40	8 43	10 10	11 40		4 10	4 58	6 10	7 10	8 35	11 34	9 20	11 15	3 10	6 15
Liberty St. " "	7 30	8 25	9 45	11 30		3 53	4 47	5 55	6 52	8 17	11 25	9 10	11 05	2 55	5 55

*Saturday only

This timetable, re-created from a tattered original, shows the scope of the passenger service available on the Rahway Valley Railroad in the spring of 1906. Connections were available to Elizabeth, Newark, Jersey City, and New York City through an agreement with the Central Railroad of New Jersey. Connections were made at the Central's Aldene station in Roselle Park. At this time on the Rahway Valley Railroad mainline, there were station stops in Springfield (near Mountain Avenue) and Kenilworth (Warren Street, Central Station, and Michigan Avenue). There were also two stops in Union: Doty and Katemiller. A year later, Doty and Katemiller were renamed Union and Arion, respectively.

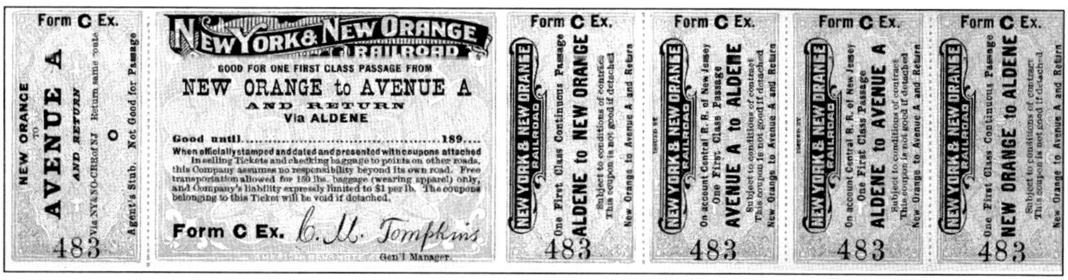

This New York & New Orange passenger ticket provided first-class round-trip service from New Orange to Avenue A in Bayonne through a connection with the Central Railroad of New Jersey at Aldene. (Collection of Donald A. Maxton.)

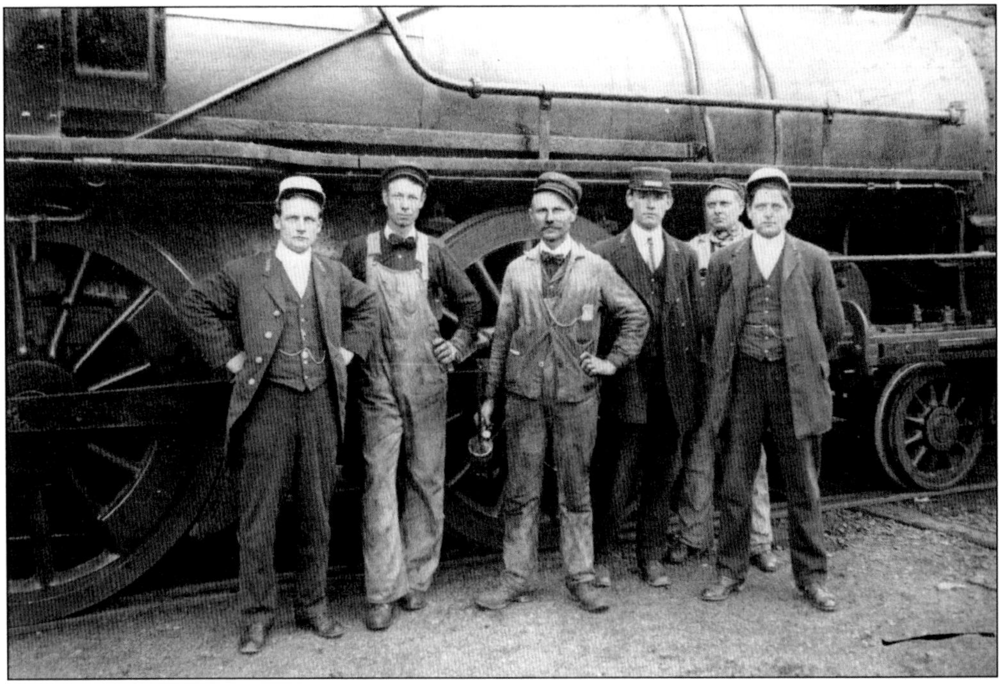

A Rahway Valley passenger crew poses next to Locomotive No. 3 at Kenilworth. From left to right are Jack Shallcross, conductor; Glenn Halladay, fireman; Mike Tiroley, engineer; Charlie Lang; and Joe Shallcross, Summit Station Agent. New Orange became Kenilworth on May 13, 1907. When the New Orange Industrial Association's real estate venture failed, the land was divested to Kenilworth Realty. (Courtesy of Mary E. McCoy.)

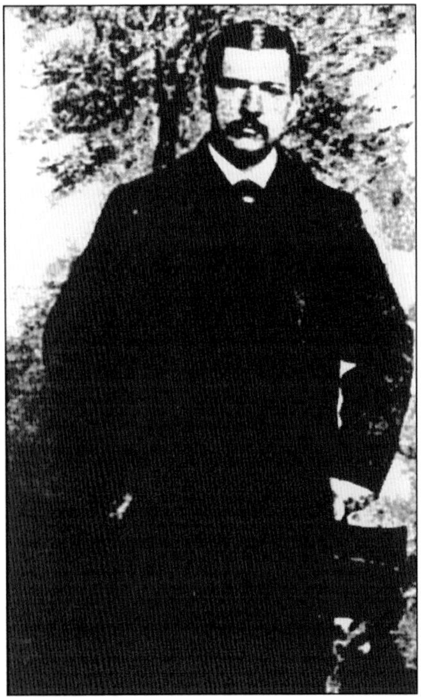

After the failure of the New Orange Industrial Association, the New Orange Four Junction Railroad attempted to make it on its own and extend toward Summit, but the NOFJ never made it that far. Along with some business associates, Louis Keller—wealthy publisher of the *Social Register of New York* and a founder of Baltusrol Golf Club in Springfield—chartered the Rahway Valley Railroad in 1904, purchased the New Orange Four Junction Railroad in 1905, and consolidated the two companies. The railroad's new name was probably chosen because the line crossed and generally followed the course of the Rahway River. Consolidated with the New Orange Four Junction Railroad in 1905, Keller brought new life to the railroad by extending it all the way to Summit, as called for in the original charter. For convenience, he built a station close to the golf club. Keller's golfing friends from New York no longer had to rely on a horse and carriage or bicycle to reach the links. Reportedly, they referred to the railroad as "Keller's Baltusrol and Pacific." (Collection of Donald A. Maxton.)

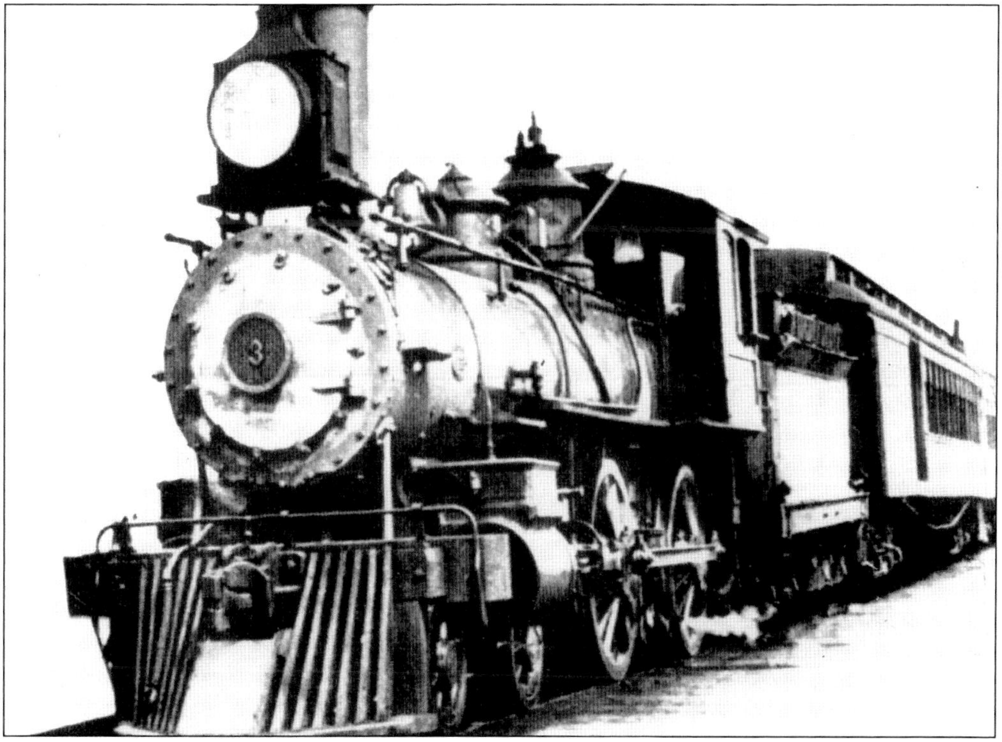

NY & NORR No. 3 pulls a passenger coach in this early photograph. (Courtesy of Mary E. McCoy.)

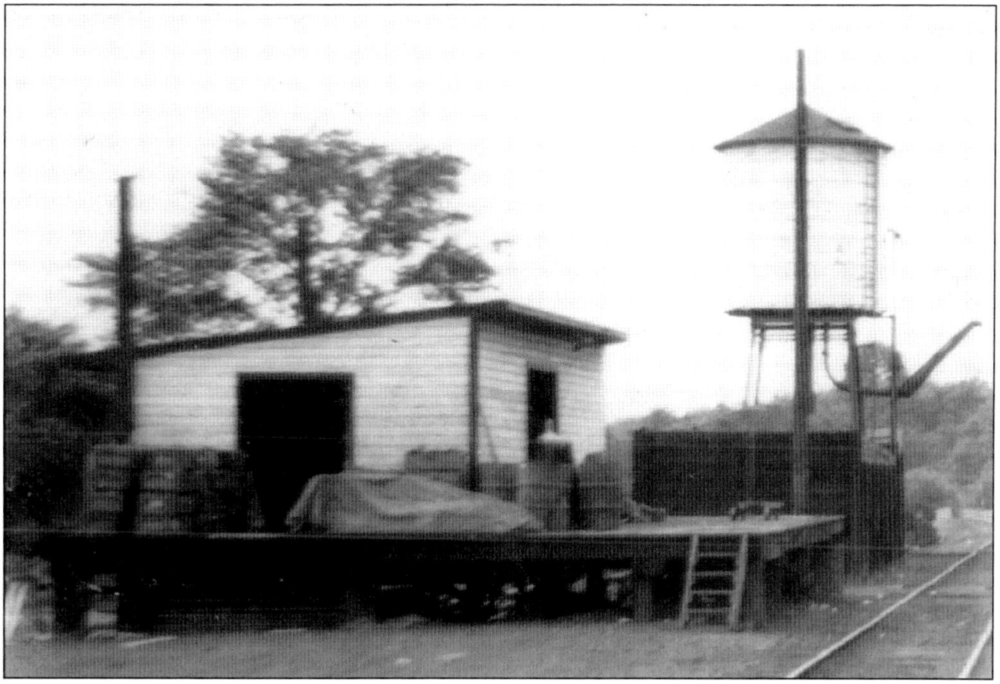

This photograph shows part of the Kenilworth terminal, including a loading platform, a storage shed, and the Rahway Valley Railroad's water tank. (Photograph by Bill Burke.)

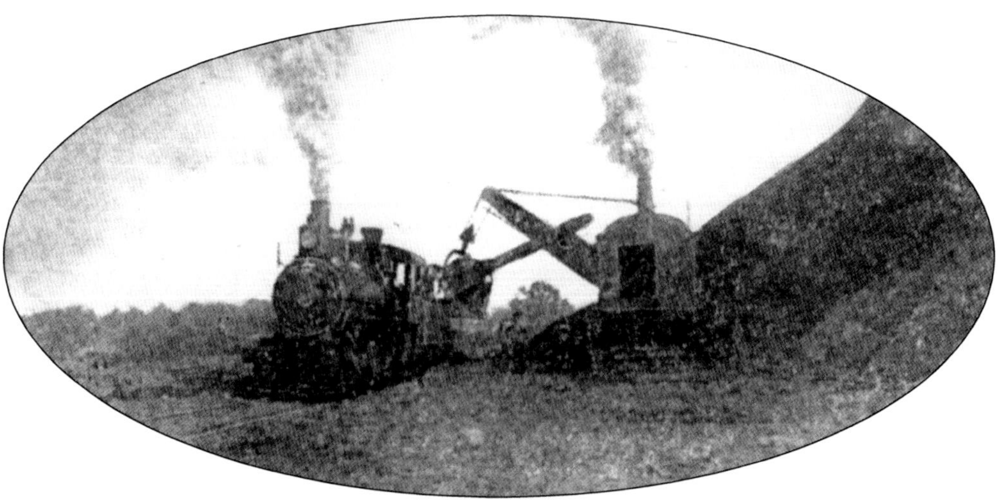

A steam shovel cuts into a slope of 186-foot Tin Kettle Hill, filling a gondola coupled to a locomotive. (Courtesy of Mary E. McCoy.)

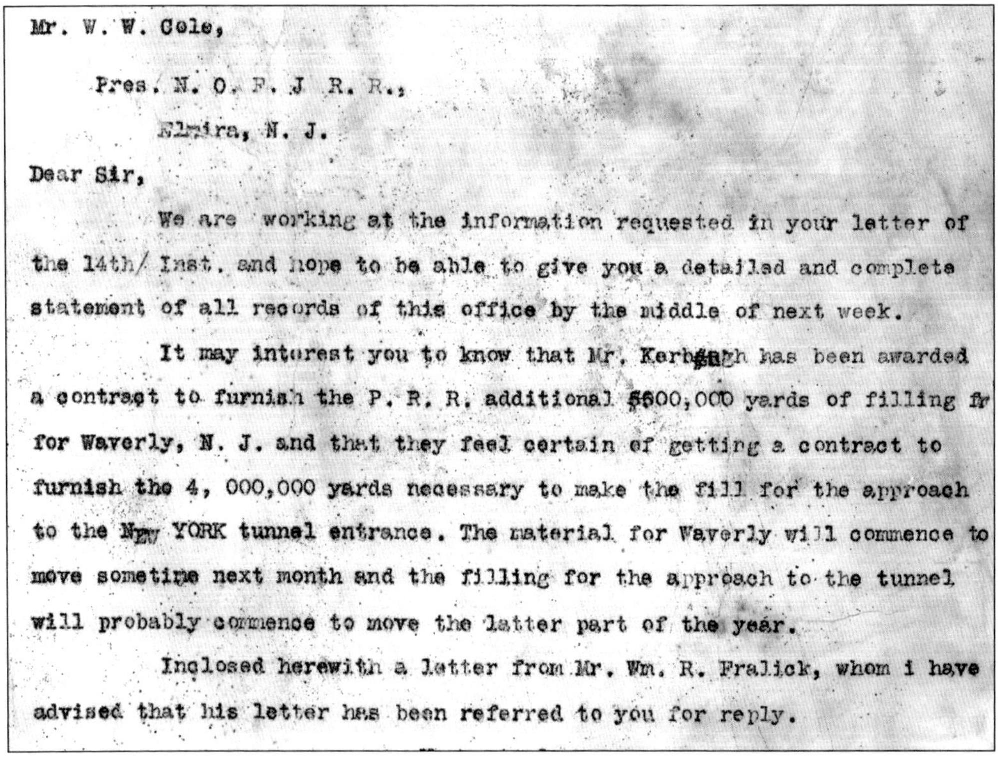

Mr. W. W. Cole,

Pres. N. O. F. J R. R.,

Elmira, N. J.

Dear Sir,

We are working at the information requested in your letter of the 14th/ Inst. and hope to be able to give you a detailed and complete statement of all records of this office by the middle of next week.

It may interest you to know that Mr. Kerbaugh has been awarded a contract to furnish the P. R. R. additional $600,000 yards of filling fr for Waverly, N. J. and that they feel certain of getting a contract to furnish the 4, 000,000 yards necessary to make the fill for the approach to the New YORK tunnel entrance. The material for Waverly will commence to move sometime next month and the filling for the approach to the tunnel will probably commence to move the latter part of the year.

Inclosed herewith a letter from Mr. Wm. R. Fralick, whom i have advised that his letter has been referred to you for reply.

The New Orange Four Junction Railroad experienced a big boost in activity (and revenue) when the soil of Tin Kettle Hill was sold to provide fill for the marshes near Jersey City and elevate the tracks of the Pennsylvania Railroad for its approach to the New York City tunnel. This May 20, 1903 letter, from a superintendent on the project to president William W. Cole, survived the 1974 fire at the Kenilworth Station. It reports how the Pennsylvania Railroad placed an order for an additional 4.6 million yards of fill and discusses the timetable for filling in the marshes. (Courtesy of Mary E. McCoy.)

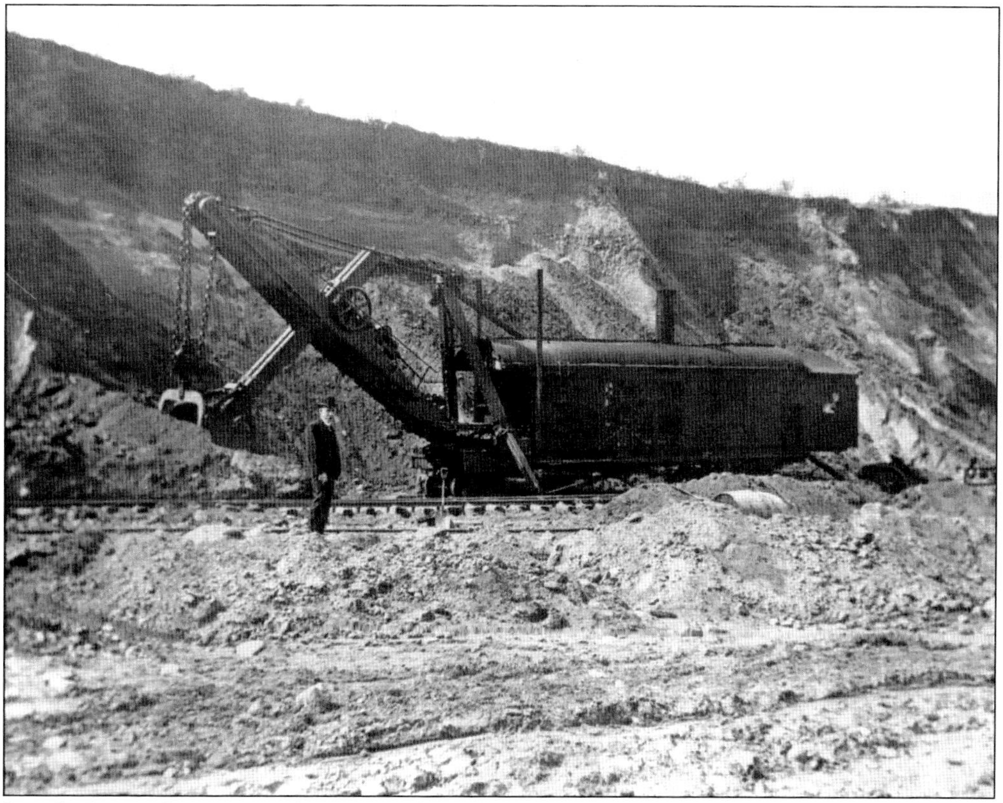

Joseph Gow, a foreman on the Tin Kettle Hill removal job, poses by a massive steam shovel. It took more than three years to remove and transport the soil to the marshes. The New Orange Four Junction Railroad moved thousands of cars during these years, as it continued to conduct its passenger service. (Courtesy of Mary E. McCoy.)

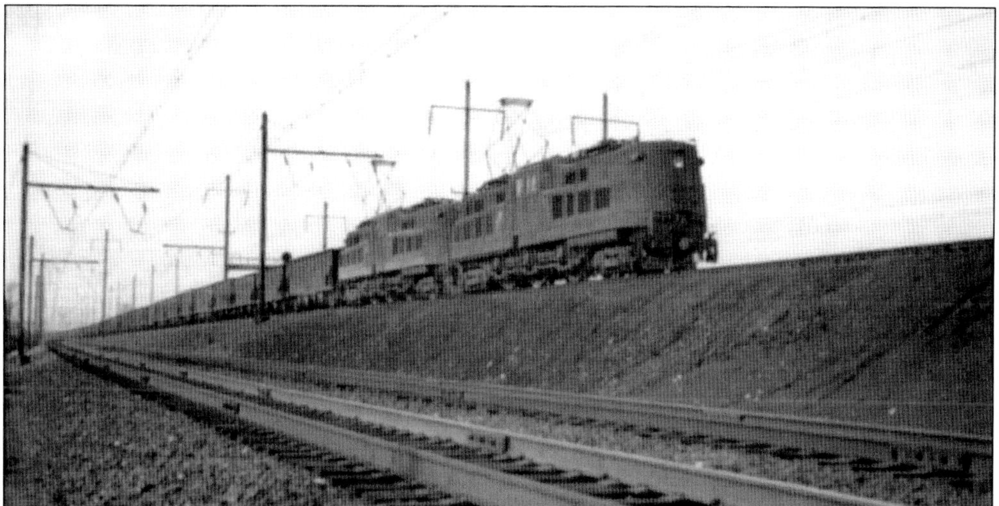

A Pennsylvania Railroad train glides over the embankment composed of soil from Kenilworth's Tin Kettle Hill. (Courtesy of Mary E. McCoy.)

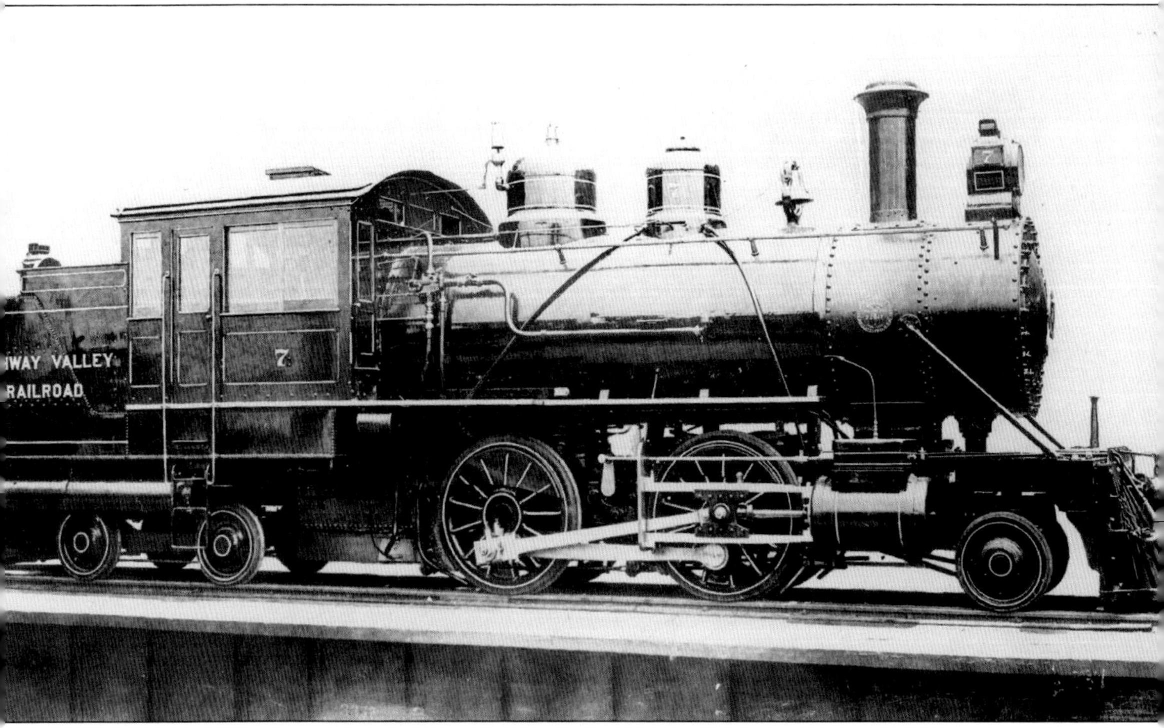

Here is a handsome photograph of RV No. 7, a 2-4-4 tank engine built by the Baldwin Locomotive Works in 1908. This engine, which had a coal box instead of a tender, worked reliably on the Rahway Valley Railroad's steep grades and tight curves. The engine was reportedly sold off in 1917. (Photograph by Joseph LaVella, courtesy of Mary E. McCoy.)

In this early-1900s photograph, Joe Shallcross poses with a maintenance of way crew on the tail end of a passenger coach. Standing on the tracks are, from left to right, Leo Scramuzzino; unidentified; Luciano Vitale; and ? Serpi. The railroad employed many Italian immigrants in the early 20th century. The Vitales were the first Italian Americans to settle in New Orange, and many of their descendants still live in the area. (Courtesy of Mary E. McCoy.)

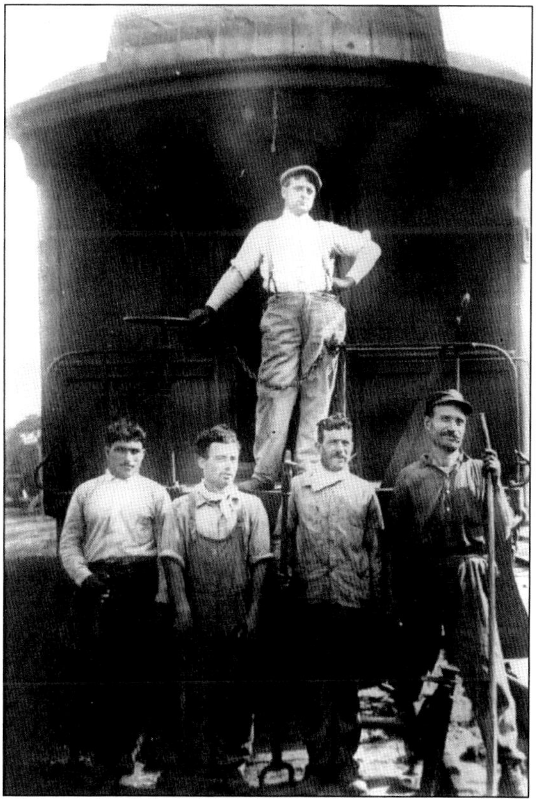

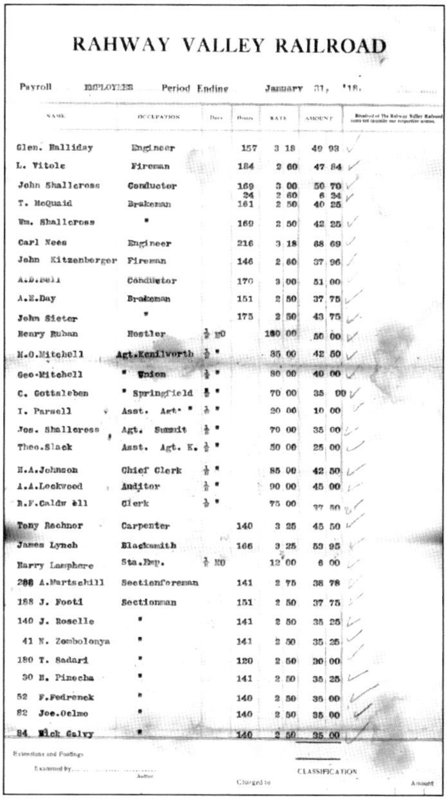

RAHWAY VALLEY RAILROAD

Payroll EMPLOYEES Period Ending January 31, '18.

NAME	OCCUPATION	Days	Hours	RATE	AMOUNT
Glen. Halliday	Engineer		157	3 18	49 93
L. Vitole	Fireman		184	2 60	47 84
John Shallcross	Conductor		169	3 00	50 70
			24	2 60	6 24
T. McQuaid	Brakeman		161	2 50	40 25
Wm. Shallcross	"		169	2 50	42 25
Carl Nees	Engineer		216	3 18	68 69
John Kitzenberger	Fireman		146	2 60	37 96
A.D.Bell	Conductor		170	3 00	51 00
A.E.Day	Brakeman		151	2 50	37 75
John Sieter	"		175	2 50	43 75
Henry Ruban	Hostler	½ MO		100 00	50 00
M.O.Mitchell	Agt.Kenilworth	½ "		85 00	42 50
Geo.Mitchell	" Union	½ "		80 00	40 00
C. Gottsleben	" Springfield	½ "		70 00	35 00
I. Parsell	Asst. Agt. "	½ "		20 00	10 00
Jos. Shallcross	Agt. Summit	½ "		70 00	35 00
Theo.Slack	Asst. Agt. K.	½ "		50 00	25 00
H.A.Johnson	Chief Clerk	½ "		85 00	42 50
A.A.Lockwood	Auditor	½ "		90 00	45 00
R.F.Caldwell	Clerk	½ "		75 00	37 50
Tony Rechnor	Carpenter		140	3 25	45 50
James Lynch	Blacksmith		166	3 25	53 95
Harry Lamphere	Sta.Emp.	½ MO		12 00	6 00
288 A.Martschill	Sectionforeman		141	2 75	38 78
188 J. Footi	Sectionman		151	2 50	37 75
140 J. Roselle	"		141	2 50	35 25
41 N. Zombolonya	"		141	2 50	35 25
180 T. Sadari	"		120	2 50	30 00
30 B. Pinecha	"		141	2 50	35 25
52 F.Fedrenck	"		140	2 50	35 00
82 Joe.Oelmo	"		140	2 50	35 00
84 Nick Galvy	"		140	2 50	35 00

Extensions and Footings

Examined by........................ Auditor

CLASSIFICATION

Charged to Amount

A Rahway Valley payroll dated January 31, 1918, shows that wages ranged from an hourly rate of 25¢ for sectionmen to $32^1/_2$¢ for carpenters and blacksmiths. Blacksmith James Lynch worked 166 hours during this pay period, earning $53.95. These were pretty fair wages at the time. (Courtesy of Mary E. McCoy.)

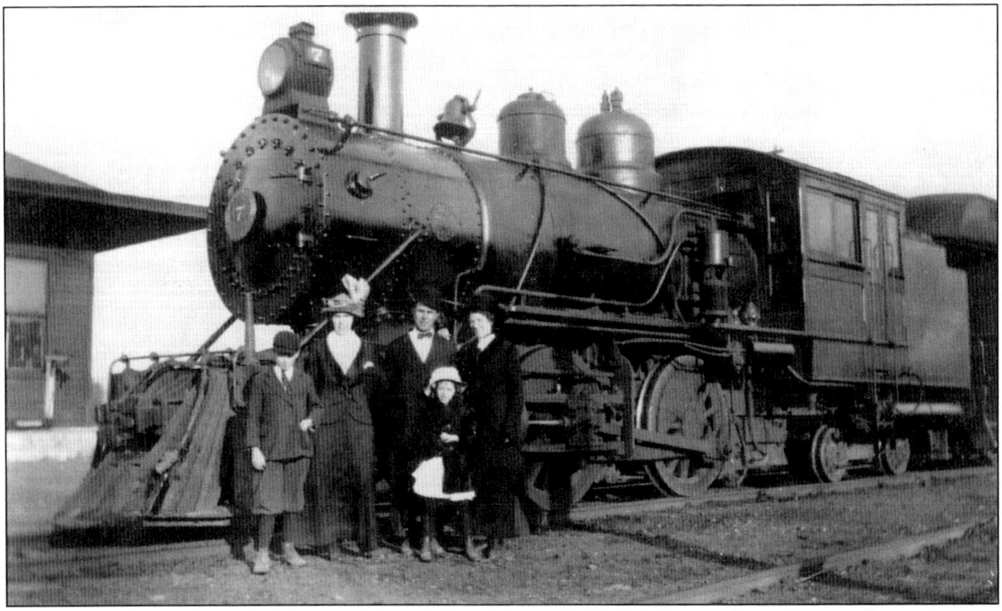

Well dressed for an outing, a family poses in front of RV No. 7 at Kenilworth. Popular passenger destinations included picnic groves along the Rahway Valley Railroad, such as Miller's Grove in Kenilworth, Petrilla's Grove in Kenilworth, and Farcher's Grove in Union. People came from New York, Jersey City, Bayonne, and Newark to enjoy a day in the country. (Courtesy of the Roselle Park Historical Society.)

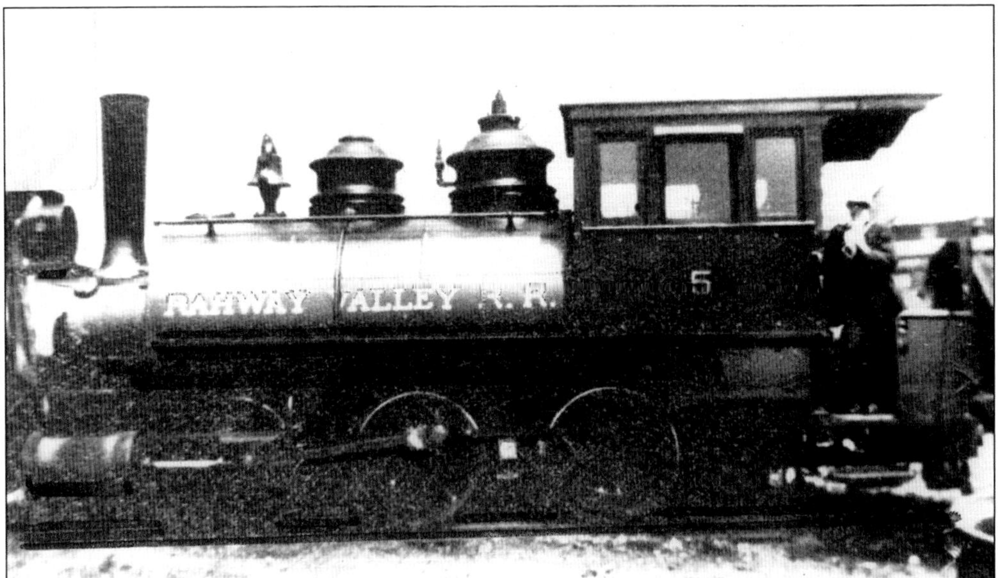

RV No. 5, a 0-6-0T saddle tank engine known as "Dinkey," was built by the Baldwin Locomotive Works in 1882 for the Jersey Central. The railroad purchased this locomotive in 1905. This engine was not powerful enough to haul long trains up the steep four percent grade to Summit. (Courtesy of Mary E. McCoy.)

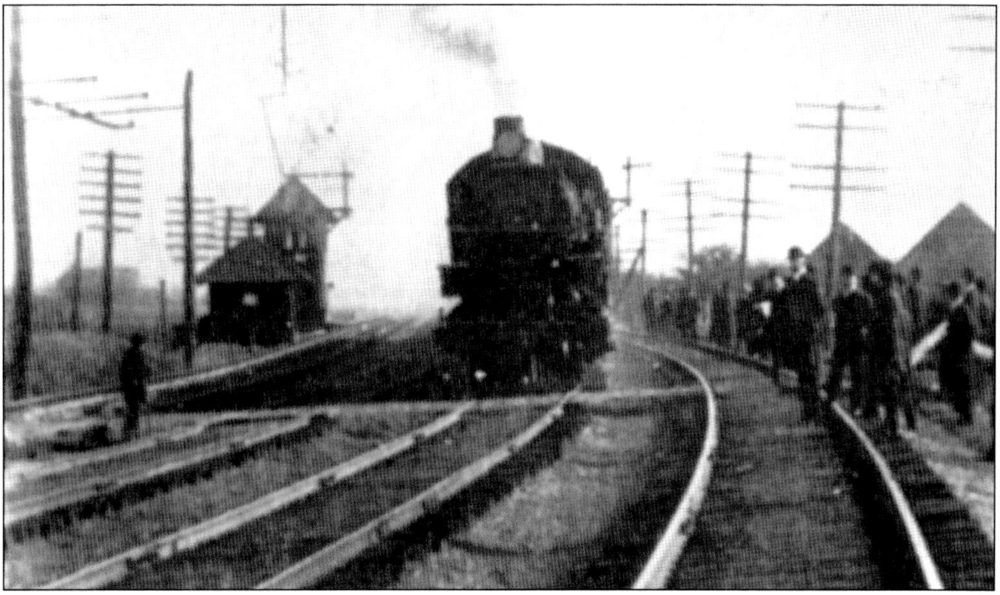

The motion picture industry ushered in a lively period of activity in Kenilworth and along the Rahway Valley Railroad. The surrounding countryside proved to be an ideal setting for silent Westerns, including *The Switchman's Daughter* and *The Midnight Flyer*, both produced by the Edison Biograph Company. Apparently, photographs of actual filming on the Rahway Valley Railroad have not survived. This still is from *The Empire State Express*, another Biograph film.

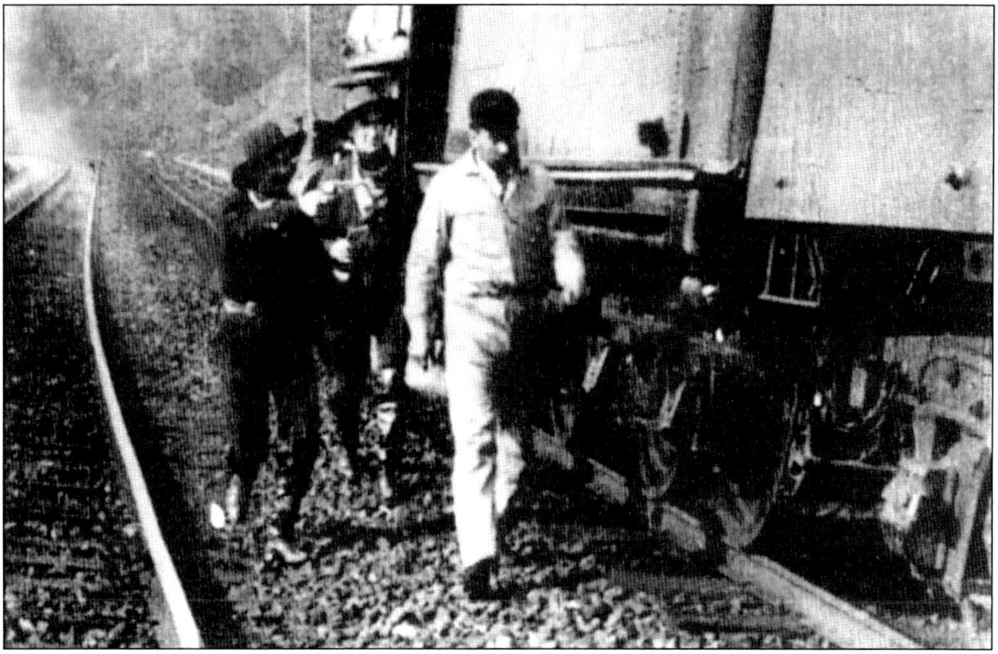

Railroad workers enjoyed a $1-a-day bonus from the movie companies for participating in the silent films, as well as lunch and free beer. According to longtime master mechanic Carl Nees, one day an explosion of film chemicals put an end to filmmaking on the Rahway Valley Railroad. Four actors were injured in the accident, and the windows of the Kenilworth Station were blown out. This scene from *The Great Train Robbery* was filmed in Dover, New Jersey.

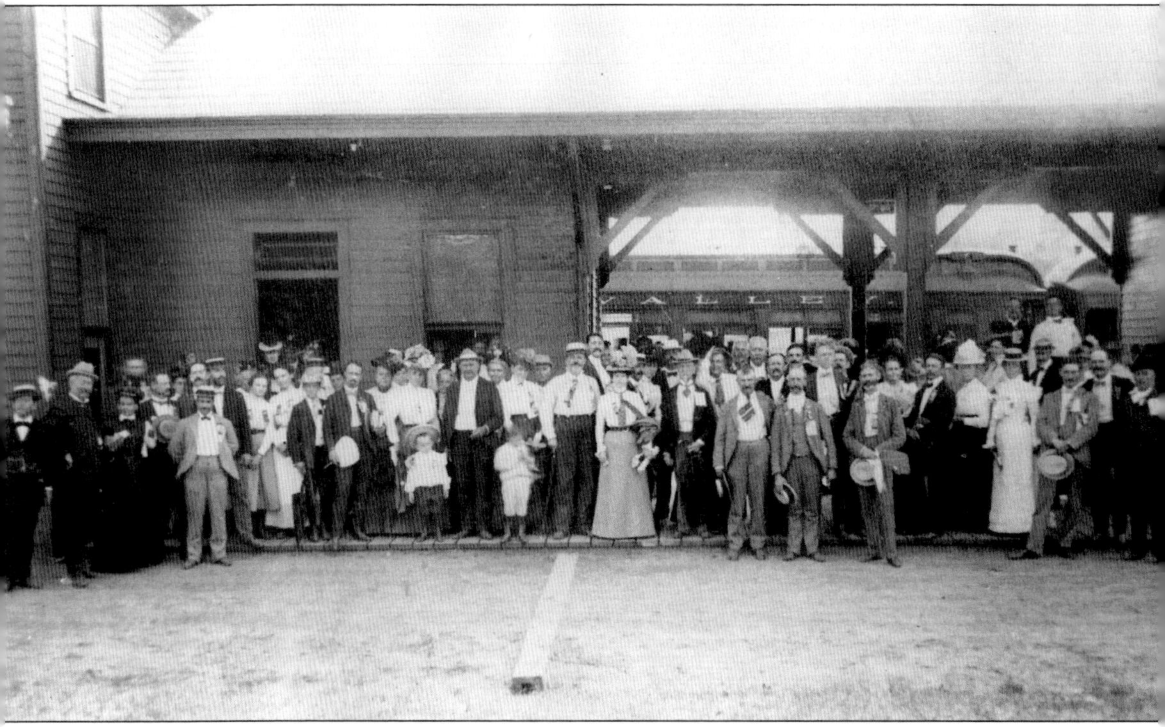

A large group of delegates to the New York Conference of Augustana Lutheran Church poses in this 1910 photograph of the Rahway Valley station in Kenilworth. Two passenger coaches are visible in the background. (Courtesy of the Kenilworth Historical Society.)

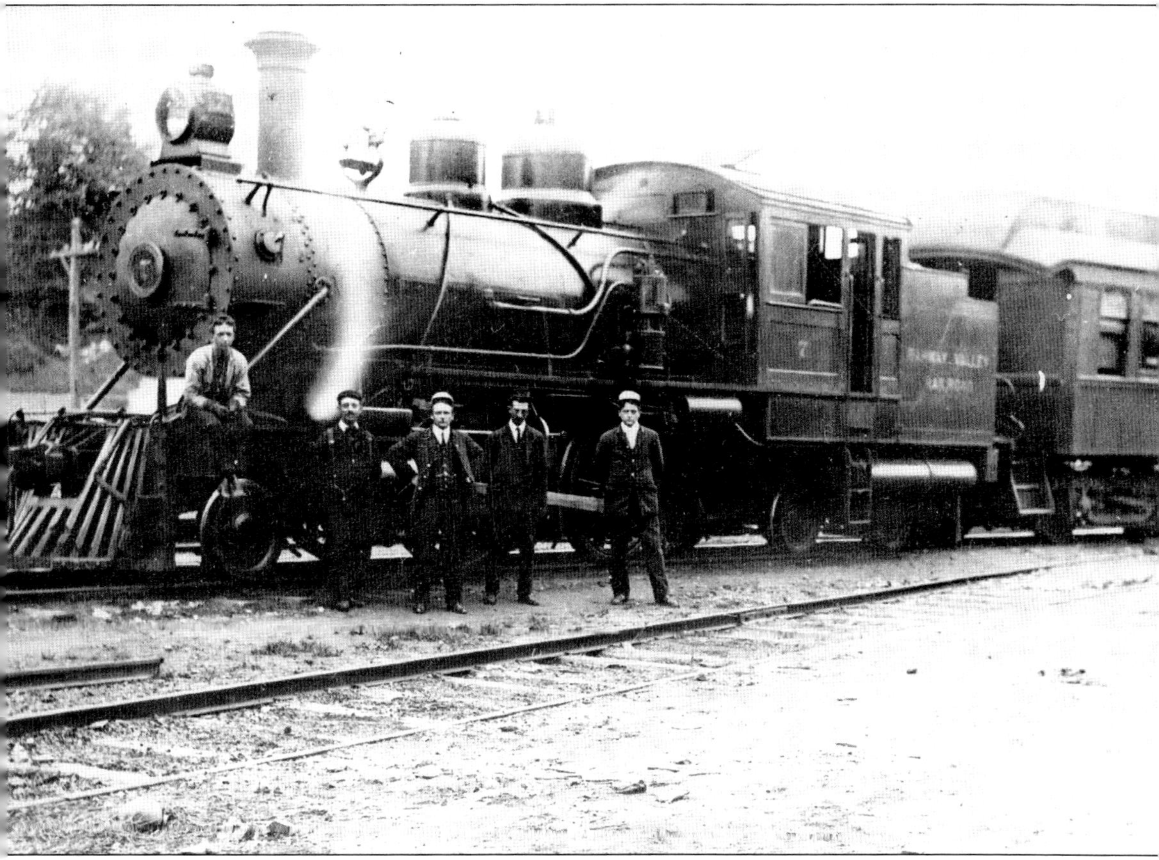

A Rahway Valley passenger train crew poses next to RV No. 7 in 1910. The railroad operated as a deficit operation until the World War I period, when a number of industries sprouted up along the railroad. These included the American Can Company, the American Laundry and Machine Company, and two munitions plants (one in Kenilworth and the other on the Unionbury Branch). The Rahway Valley Railroad carried thousands of workers to local factories and plants around the clock during the war years. (Courtesy of Mary E. McCoy.)

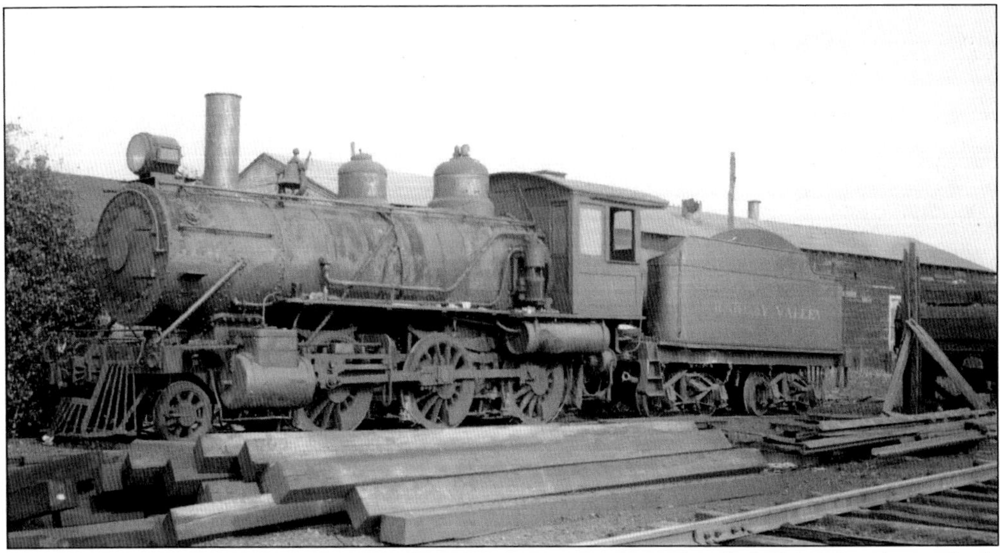

RV No. 11 sits in retirement at Kenilworth on August 17, 1934. A 2-6-0, Mogul-type built in 1904 by the Baldwin Locomotive Works, it was purchased from the Grafton and Upton Railroad in 1920. It was scrapped two years after this photograph was taken. (Courtesy of Mary E. McCoy.)

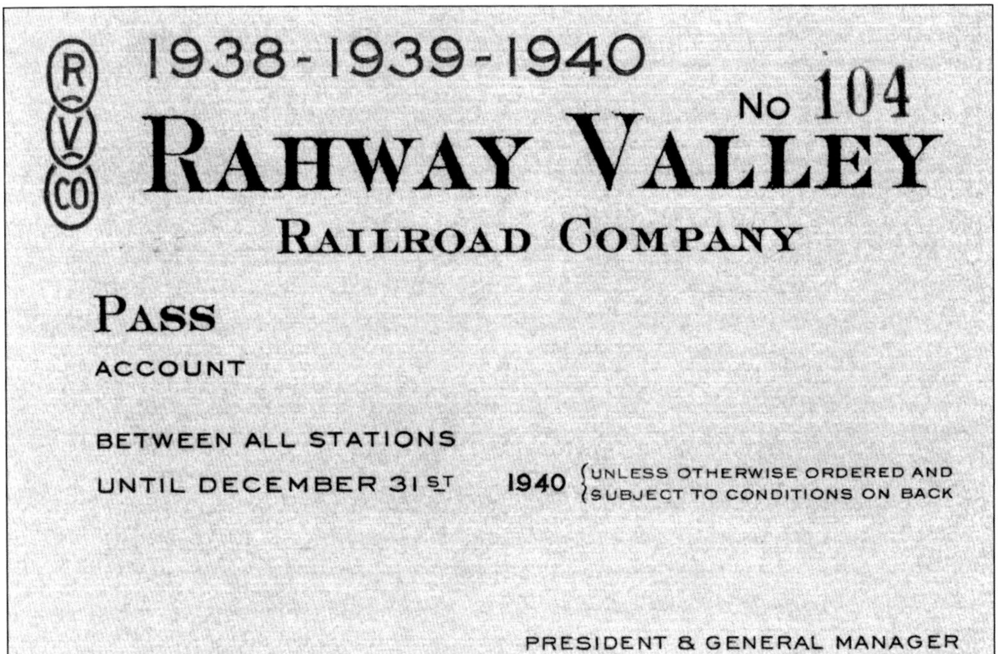

R V CO

1938-1939-1940

No 104

RAHWAY VALLEY

RAILROAD COMPANY

PASS

ACCOUNT

BETWEEN ALL STATIONS

UNTIL DECEMBER 31ST 1940 {UNLESS OTHERWISE ORDERED AND SUBJECT TO CONDITIONS ON BACK

PRESIDENT & GENERAL MANAGER

This Rahway Valley pass was good for a period of three years between all stations on the short line. (Courtesy of Mary E. McCoy.)

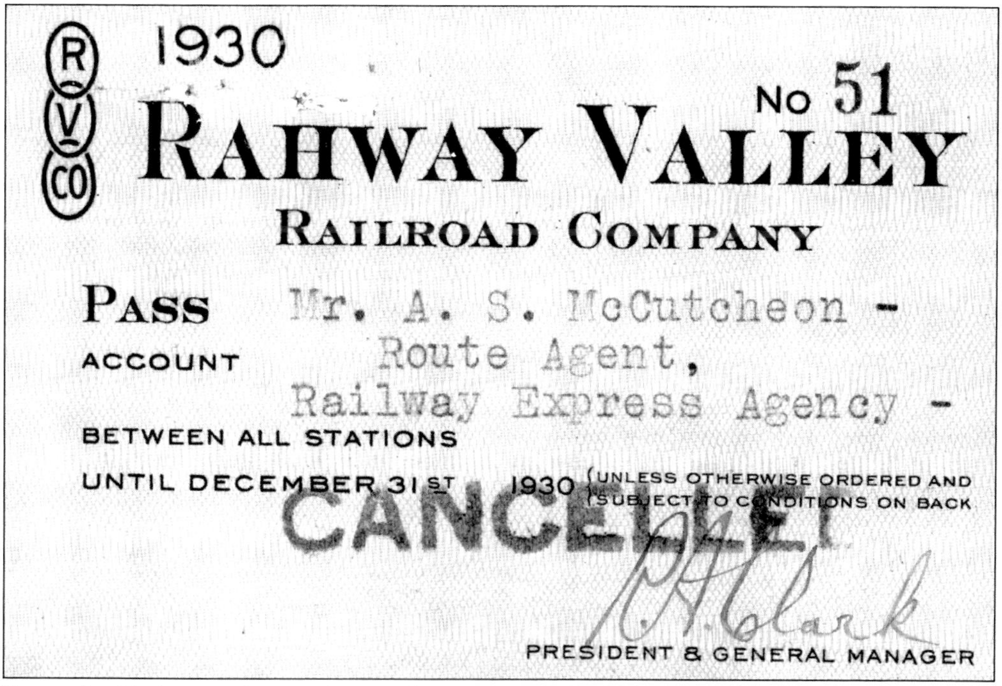
RVCO

1930

No 51

RAHWAY VALLEY

RAILROAD COMPANY

PASS Mr. A. S. McCutcheon -

ACCOUNT Route Agent,

Railway Express Agency -

BETWEEN ALL STATIONS

UNTIL DECEMBER 31ST 1930 {UNLESS OTHERWISE ORDERED AND SUBJECT TO CONDITIONS ON BACK

CANCELLED

R. A. Clark

PRESIDENT & GENERAL MANAGER

Roger A. Clark, president and general manager of the Rahway Valley Railroad, signed this one-year railroad pass in 1930 for A.S. McCutcheon, a Railway Express Agency route agent. (Courtesy of Mary E. McCoy.)

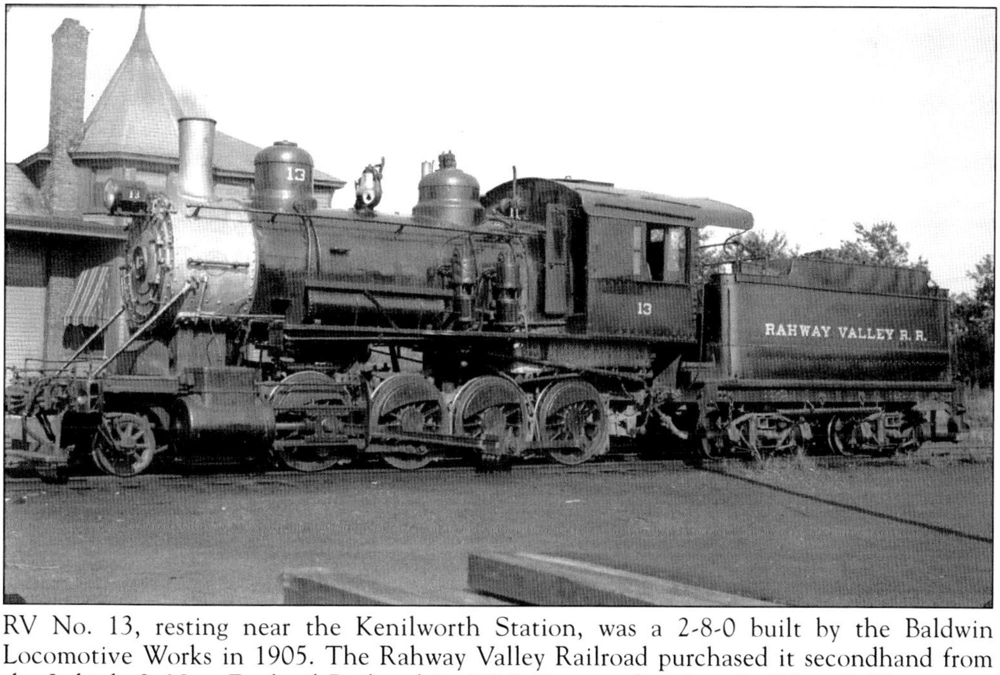

RV No. 13, resting near the Kenilworth Station, was a 2-8-0 built by the Baldwin Locomotive Works in 1905. The Rahway Valley Railroad purchased it secondhand from the Lehigh & New England Railroad in 1929. It proved to be a highly reliable engine. (Courtesy of Mary E. McCoy.)

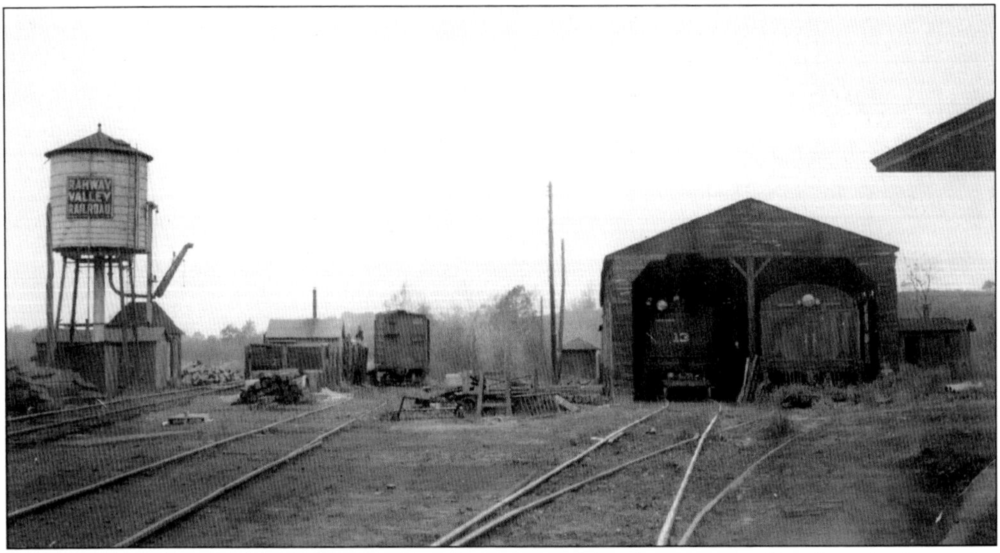

This November, 1933 view of Rahway Valley Railroad headquarters in Kenilworth shows the water tank for the railroad's steam locomotives, which were housed and serviced in a two-stall, wooden engine shed seen on the right, where Nos. 13 and 11 are being stored. The tip of the Kenilworth station roof is visible on the right. (Courtesy of Mary E. McCoy.)

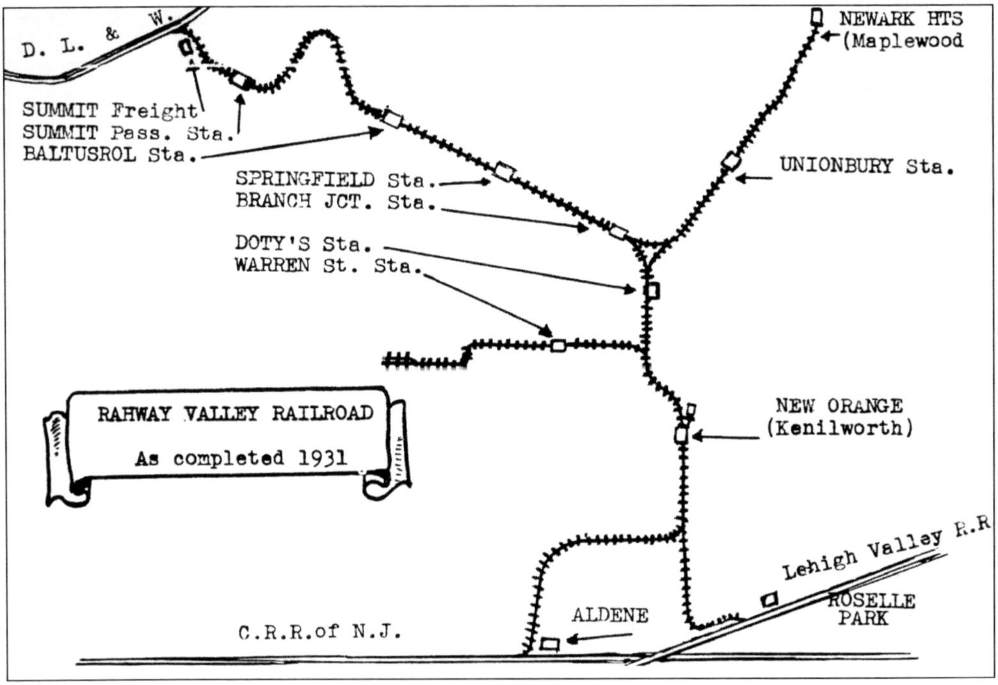

This map, drawn by John J. McCoy for *Saga of a Shortline* (his 1976 booklet on the Rahway Valley), shows the railroad as completed in 1931. This is when the long-delayed connection was made to the Delaware, Lackawanna & Western Railroad in Summit. (Collection of Donald A. Maxton.)

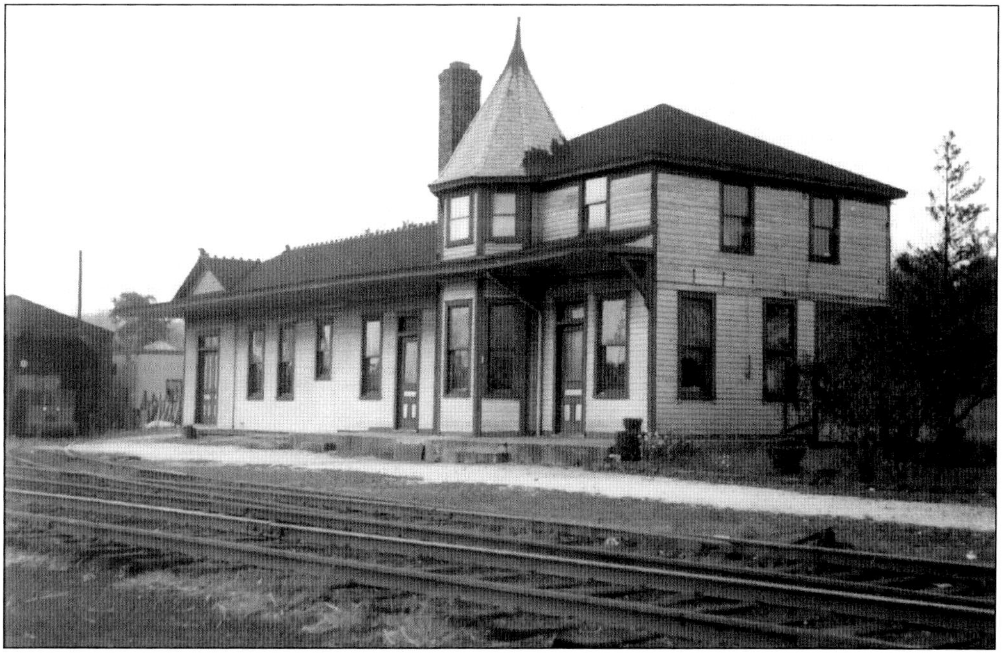

After passenger service was discontinued, the Rahway Valley Railroad's Kenilworth Station was set up as the railroad's business office and storage facility. The old wooden locomotive shed still stands on the left in this photograph, taken on October 14, 1950. Soon, it would be replaced by a more modern engine facility. (Photograph by Edward H. Weber.)

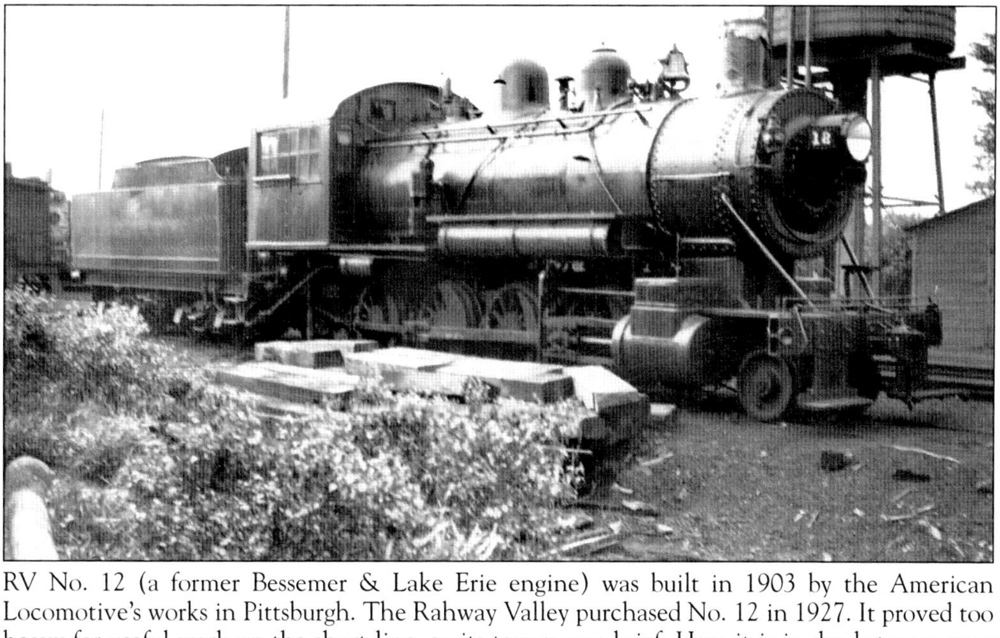

RV No. 12 (a former Bessemer & Lake Erie engine) was built in 1903 by the American Locomotive's works in Pittsburgh. The Rahway Valley purchased No. 12 in 1927. It proved too heavy for useful work on the short line, so its tenure was brief. Here it is in dead storage near the water tower at Kenilworth in June 1938. The engine was scrapped in 1943. (Courtesy of Mary E. McCoy.)

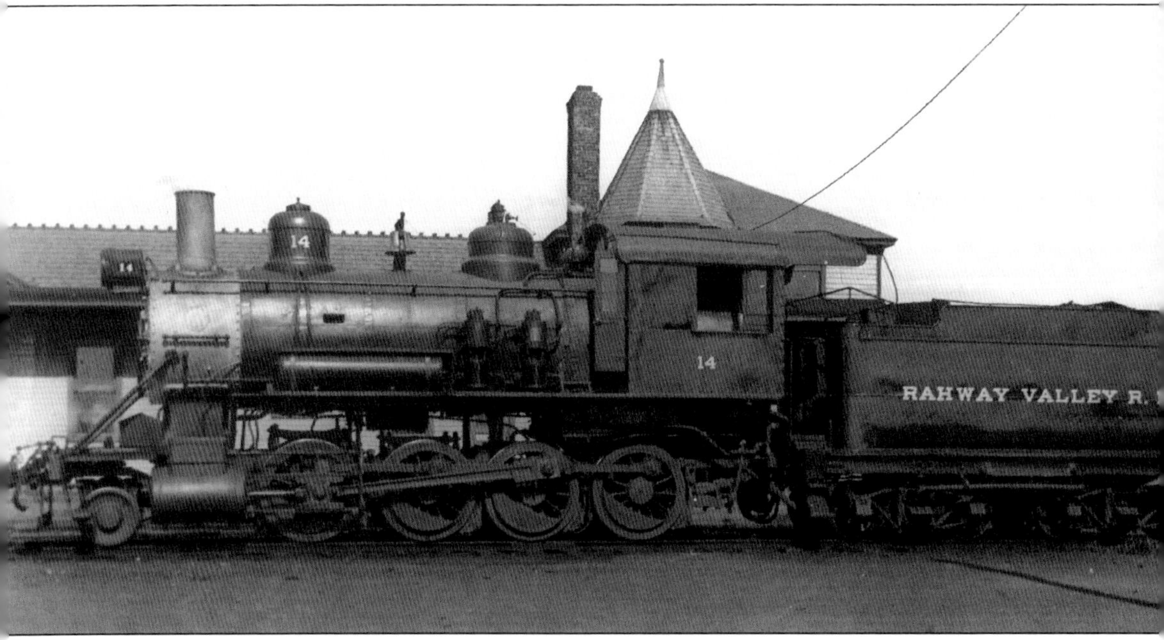

RV No. 14—another Baldwin 2-8-0 built in 1905, and a former Lehigh & New England engine—was almost identical to No. 13, and also purchased in 1929. (Photograph by Ed Francis, courtesy of Edward H. Weber.)

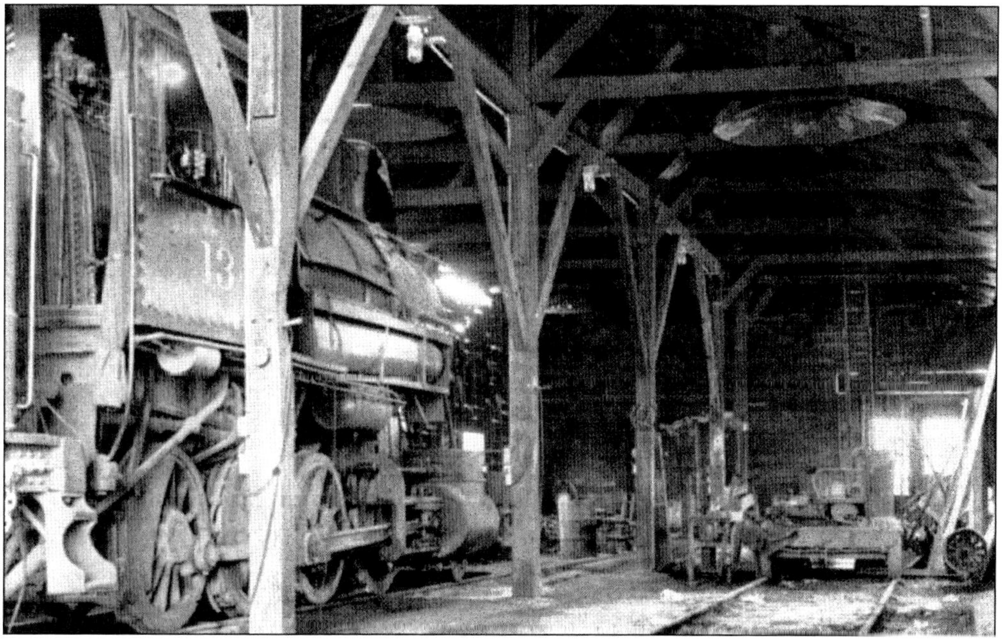

It must have been quite a challenge for mechanics to work on locomotives in this narrow old engine shed in Kenilworth, where No. 13 awaits maintenance. A maintenance-of-way vehicle rests on the other track. (Photograph by Bruce Nett.)

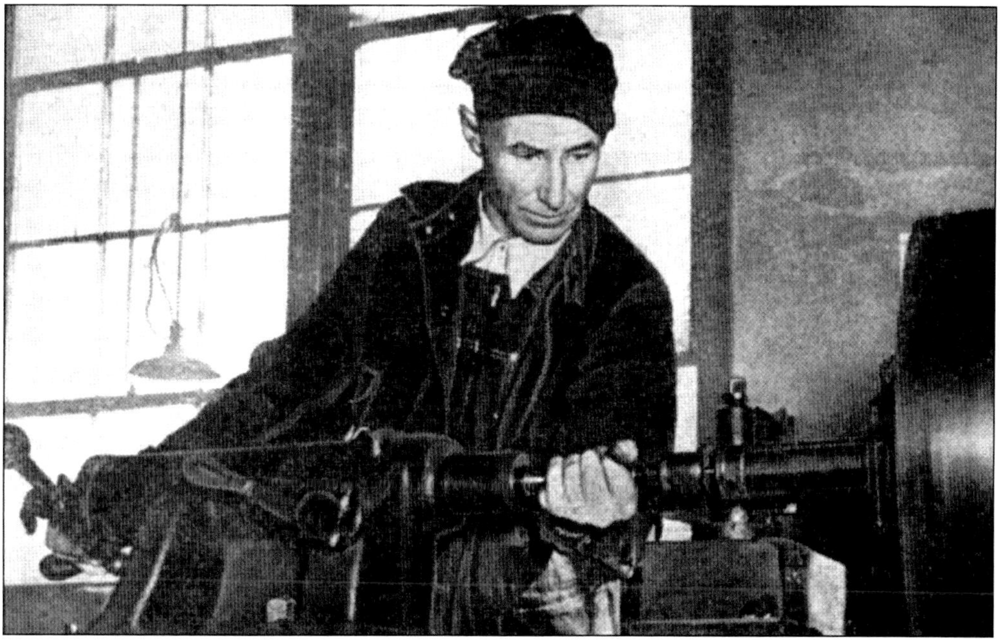

Master mechanic Carl Nees tackles a job on the lathe in the Rahway Valley's equipment shop. Nees, a native of Charlottesville, Virginia, spent many years working on the Rahway Valley, beginning as a brakeman in 1910. Following a two-year stint on the Central Railroad of New Jersey, he became a locomotive fireman on the Rahway Valley and was promoted to master mechanic several years later. (Photograph by Richard D. Fullerton, the Davart Company.)

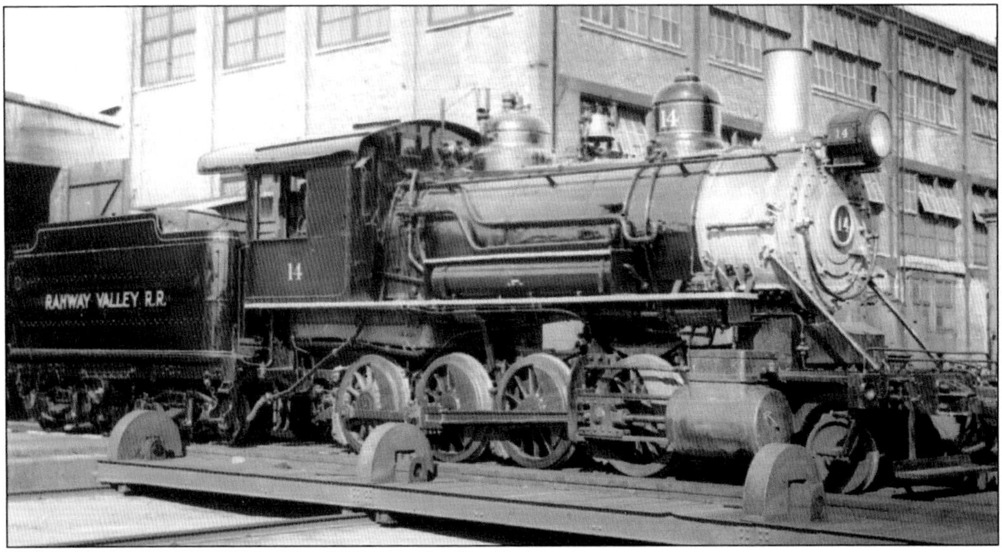

In June 1940, the Rahway Valley Railroad sent No. 14 to the Delaware, Lackawanna & Western Railroad's back shop in Kingsland for a major overhaul. Here it is on the transfer table at Kingsland. The locomotive was fitted out with new arch brick-boiler tubes. Its wedges were reset, pistons repacked, and new main rod bearings installed. The finishing touch was a fresh coat of paint. The total bill, including freight-movement charges, came to $687.50. (Courtesy of Edward H. Weber.)

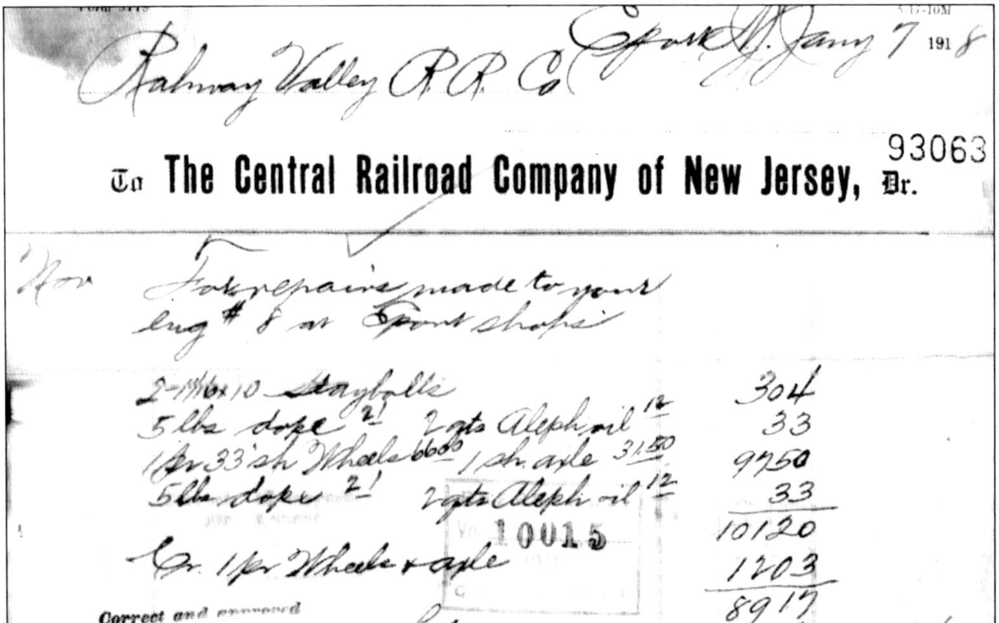

Rahway Valley R.R. Co Eport N.J. Jany 7 1918

93063

To The Central Railroad Company of New Jersey, Dr.

For repairs made to your Eng # 8 at Eport shops

2-1 1/16 x 10 staybolts	304
5 lbs dope 21 2 qts Aleph oil 12	33
1 pr 33" sh Wheels 6600 1 sh axle 3150	9750
5 lbs dope 21 2 qts Aleph oil 12	33
	10120
Cr. 1 pr Wheels + axle	1203
	8917
Labor	10352 19269

10015

Correct and approved for payment

The Rahway Valley Railroad shop was not large enough to handle all engine repairs. Here is an example. On January 7, 1918, the Jersey Central issued this bill to the Rahway Valley for repairs on No. 8, performed at the Central Railroad in Elizabethport. The bill, which totals $192.69 with labor, was approved by general manager J.S. Caldwell. (Courtesy of Mary E. McCoy.)

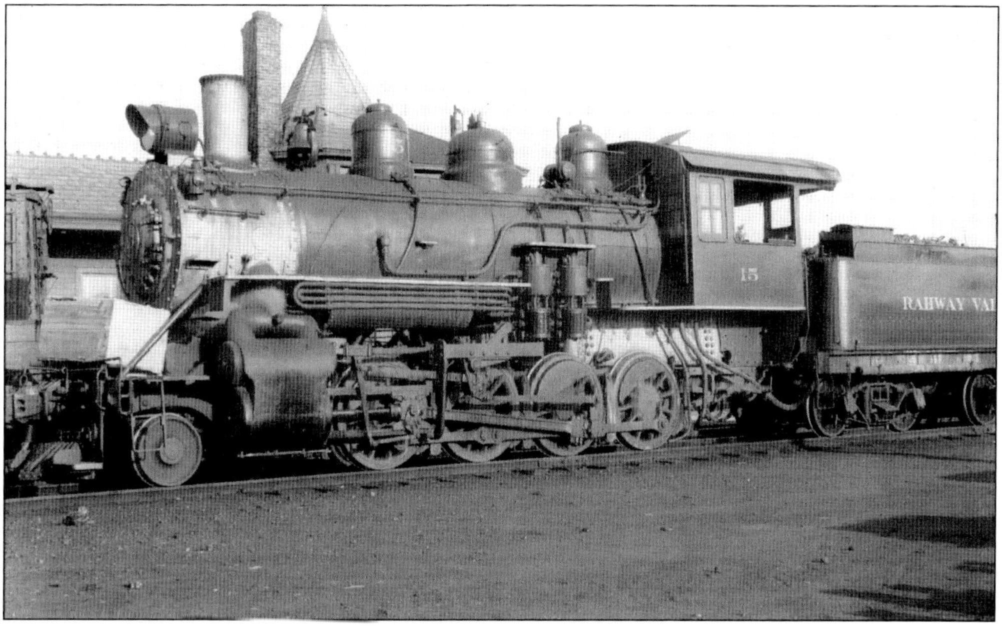

RV No. 15 rests at the Kenilworth station on April 7, 1946. Note the box of L.C.L. (less than carload) freight on the locomotive's pilot beam. No. 15 was the last of the railroad's steam engines, a 2-8-0 built by Baldwin Locomotive Works in 1916 and purchased in 1937 from the Oneida and Western Railroad. (Courtesy of Mary E. McCoy.)

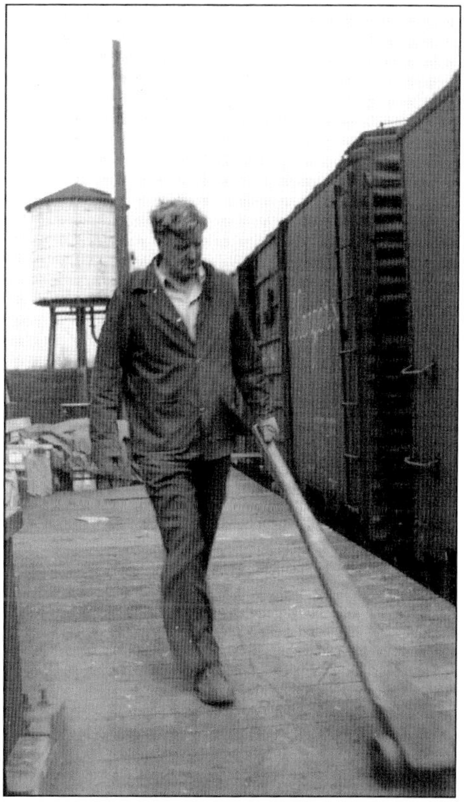

Rahway Valley president and general manager George A. Clark helps unload some freight at the Kenilworth Station on March 16, 1948. Clark's hands-on approach to running the short line was a key ingredient to its success. (Photograph by Edward H. Weber.)

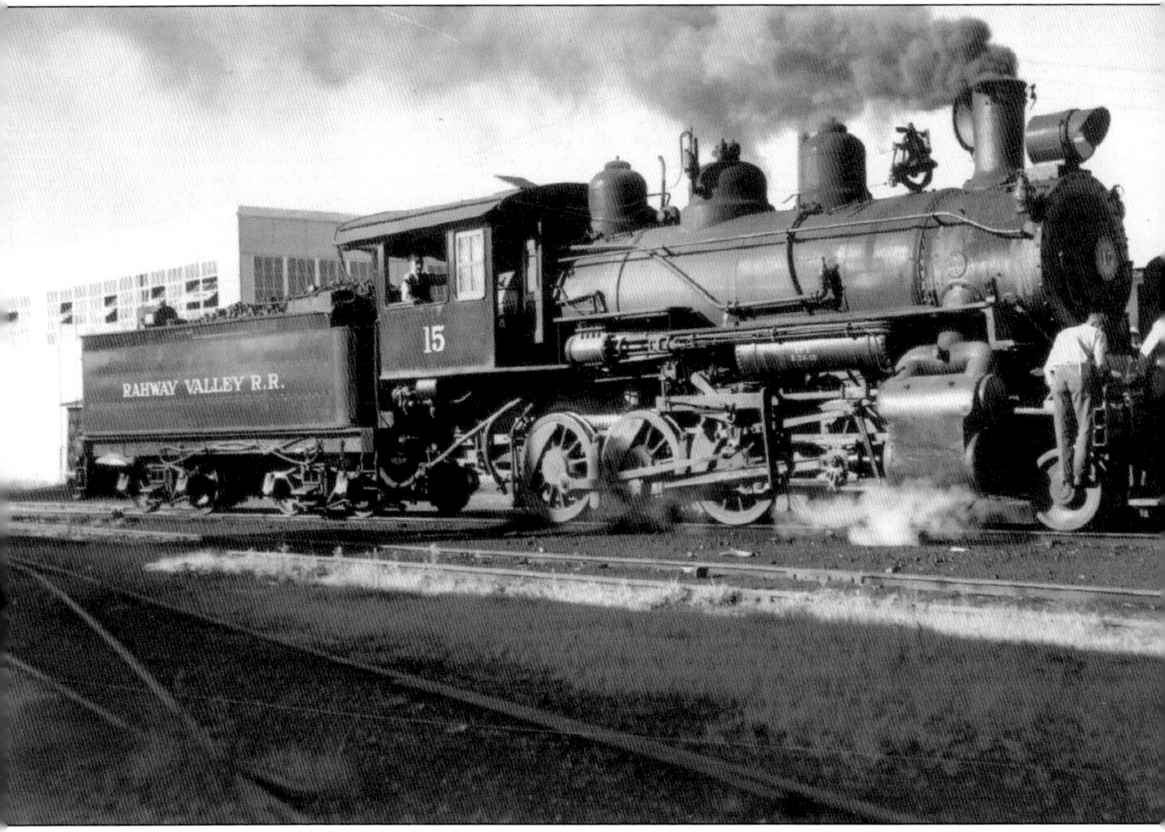

A Rahway Valley Railroad crew starts the day's work in Kenilworth with No. 15 on August 14, 1950. George A. Clark summed up his management style for *Trains* magazine in 1950: "I leave the boys alone—they know their jobs. I don't have to tell them that our only scheduled train leaves here at 8:30 on the button. I don't have to tell them we keep working until everything is finished. They know those things." The building in the background was constructed on land sold by the Rahway Valley. Real estate sales helped keep the railroad in the black during slow times and helped bring in new customers. (Collection of Edward H. Weber, courtesy of Mary E. McCoy.)

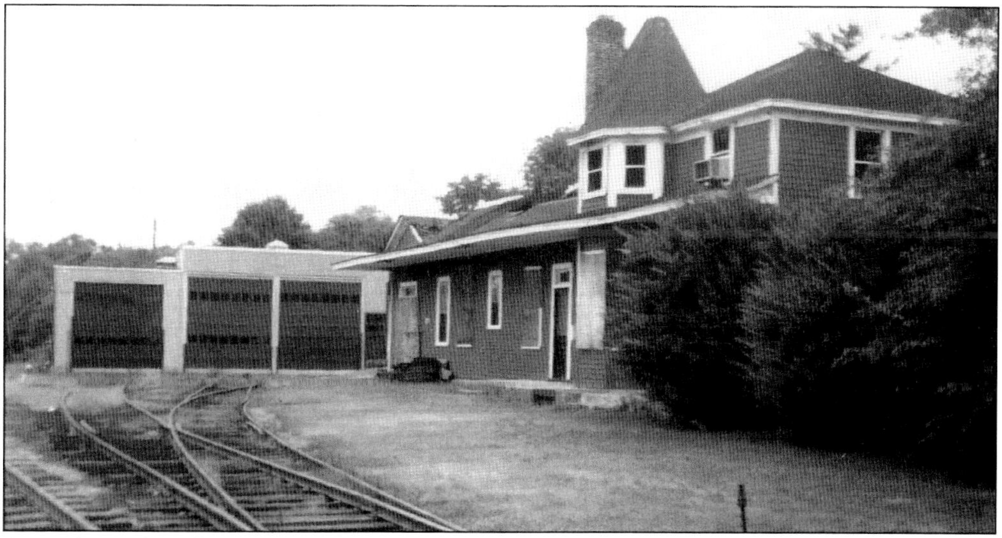

A modern, three-bay engine house was constructed in the 1950s to house and service the Rahway Valley's new diesel engines. (Courtesy of Mary E. McCoy.)

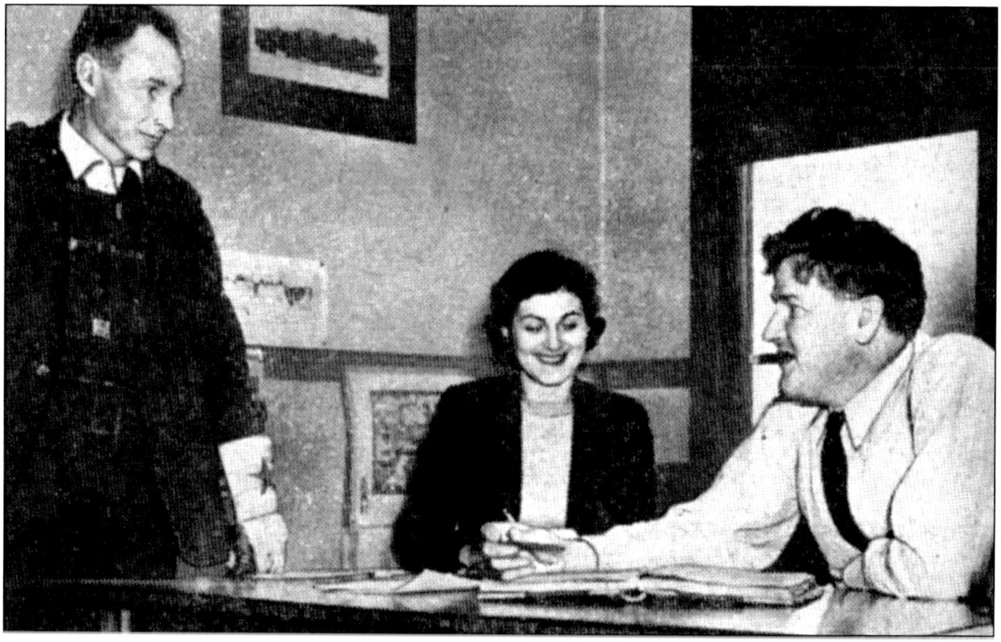

This photograph was taken at Rahway Valley headquarters in Kenilworth in 1940 for an article in *Railroad* magazine. From left to right are master mechanic Carl Nees, nicknamed "Master Maniac" and "Cadillac" for his taste in automobiles; secretary Pauline Beirach; and George A. Clark, president and general manager. Judging by the grin on Beirach's face, one of them must have just cracked a joke. Anecdotes are still told about Clark, a former lumberjack and dyed-in-the-wool railroader with an unusual sense of humor. He playfully referred to the Rahway Valley as a "Little Streak of Rust." In 1959, Clark posted this want ad in the *Elizabeth Daily Journal*: "BRAKEMAN—Steady employment in Freight Service for reliable married man, not over 42, who is not afraid of work. No Bugle Boys, Blowhards, Dreamers, Goldbrickers, Hot Shots or Wobblemouths considered." (Photograph by Richard D. Fullerton, the Davart Company.)

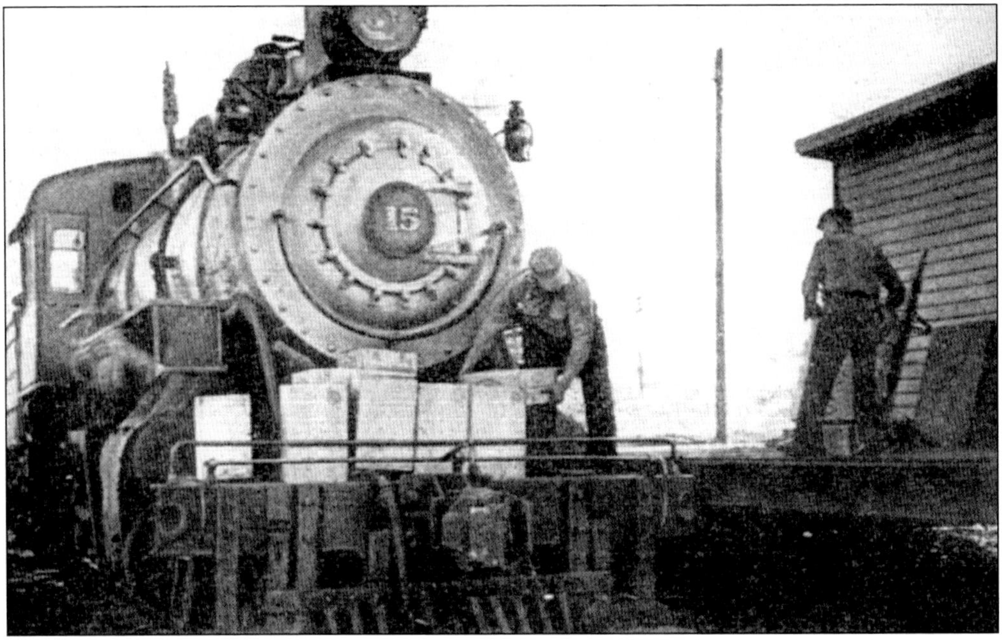

Two crewmembers handle a few boxes of L.C.L. freight in the early 1940s. The Rahway Valley Railroad often ran an engine down the line with packages on its pilot beam to save the expense of using a boxcar. It was one of the many ways this feisty short line kept expenses to a minimum in the face of increasingly heavy competition from the trucking industry. (Photograph by Richard D. Fullerton, the Davart Company.)

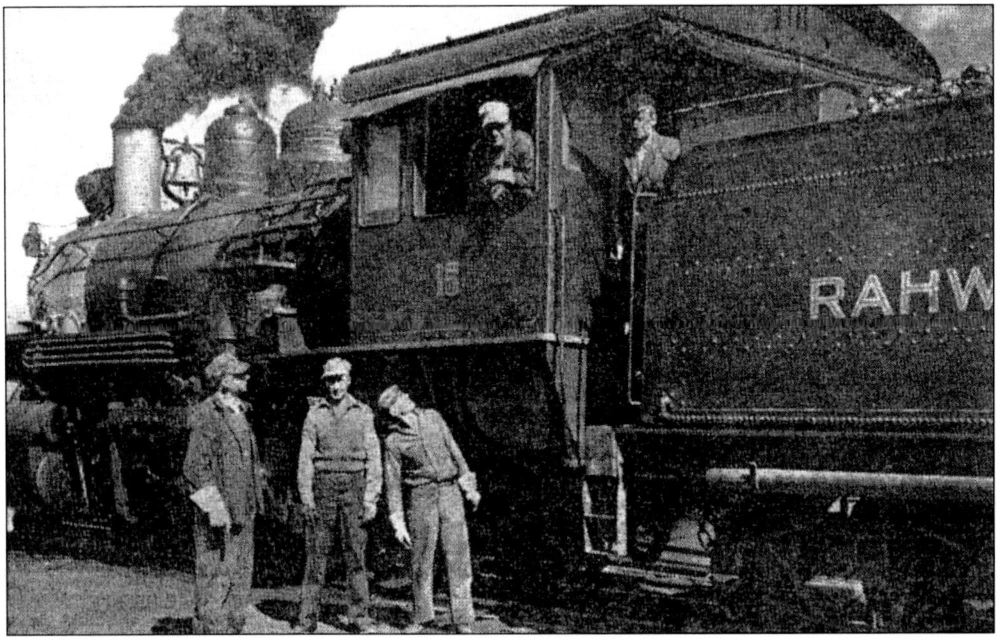

A Rahway Valley Railroad crew poses by No. 15 in this photograph taken for the April 1940 issue of *Railroad* magazine. From left to right are Carl Nees, master mechanic; George Davis, conductor; Paul Albright, brakeman; Tom Mangini, fireman; and Frank Froat, engineer. (Photograph by Richard D. Fullerton, the Davart Company.)

The head of an efficient, profitable short line railroad has to wear many hats, and that is just what George A. Clark did, serving as president, general manager, secretary, auditor, traffic manager, and titular head of just about every department. One of his tasks as auditor was the completion of an annual report to the Interstate Commerce Commission (ICC). Some of these documents survived the ravages of time and fire and are examples of Clark's painstaking, handwritten work. The ICC report for 1934 shows that the estate of Louis Keller held the majority of shares and votes. (Courtesy of Scott Schnipper.)

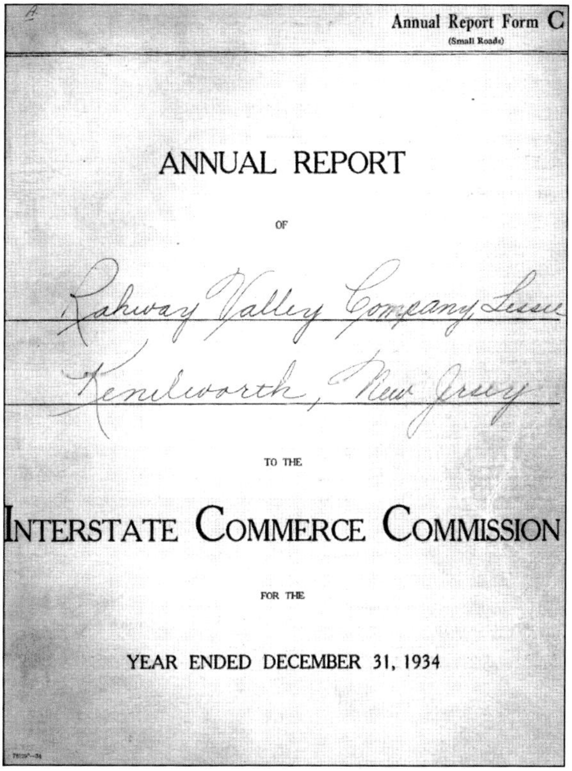

Annual Report Form C
(Small Roads)

ANNUAL REPORT

OF

Rahway Valley Company Lessee

Kenilworth, New Jersey

TO THE

INTERSTATE COMMERCE COMMISSION

FOR THE

YEAR ENDED DECEMBER 31, 1934

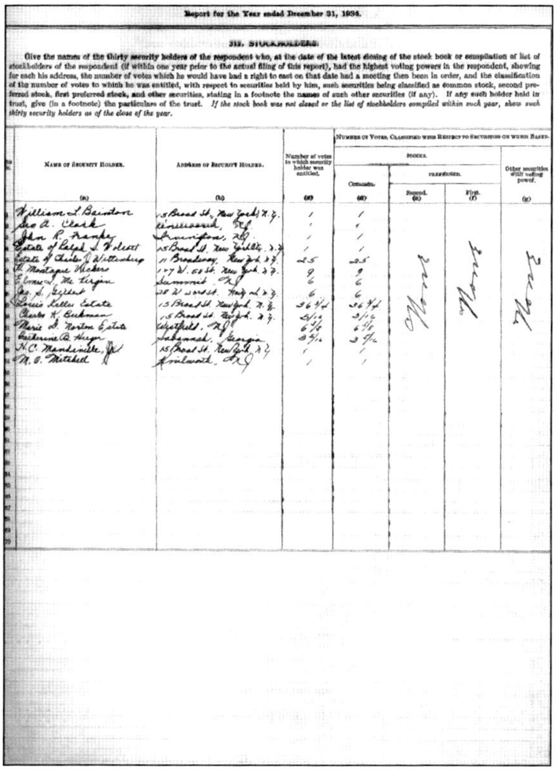

Report for the Year ended December 31, 1934.

312. STOCKHOLDERS.

Give the names of the thirty security holders of the respondent who, at the date of the latest closing of the stock book or compilation of list of stockholders of the respondent (if within one year prior to the actual filing of this report), had the highest voting powers in the respondent, showing for each his address, the number of votes which he would have had a right to cast on that date had a meeting then been in order, and the classification of the number of votes to which he was entitled, with respect to securities held by him, such securities being classified as common stock, second preferred stock, first preferred stock, and other securities, stating in a footnote the names of such other securities (if any). If any such holder held in trust, give (in a footnote) the particulars of the trust. *If the stock book was not closed or the list of stockholders compiled within such year, show such thirty security holders as of the close of the year.*

Name of Security Holder. (a)	Address of Security Holder. (b)	Number of votes to which security holder was entitled. (c)	Number of Votes, Classified with Respect to Securities on which Based. Stocks. Common. (d)	Preferred. Second. (e)	Preferred. First. (f)	Other securities with voting power. (g)
William L. Bairstow	15 Broad St., New York, N.Y.	1	1	None	None	None
Geo. A. Clark	Kenilworth, N.J.	1	1			
John R. Franke	Irvington, N.J.	1	1			
Estate of Ralph S. Wolcott	15 Broad St. New York City, N.Y.	1	1			
Estate of Charles J. Wittenberg	11 Broadway, New York, N.Y.	25	25			
H. Montague Vickers	107 W. 68 St. New York, N.Y.	9	9			
[illegible]	Summit, N.J.	6	6			
[illegible]	[illegible] New York, N.Y.	6	6			
Louis Keller Estate	15 Broad St. New York, N.Y.	36 3/4	36 3/4			
Charles K. Beekman	15 Broad St. New York, N.Y.	[illegible]	[illegible]			
Marie S. Norton Estate	Westfield, N.J.	6 5/8	6 5/8			
[illegible]	Savannah, Georgia	[illegible]	[illegible]			
H.C. Mandeville, Jr.	15 Broad St. New York, N.Y.	1	1			
[illegible]	Kenilworth, N.J.	1	1			

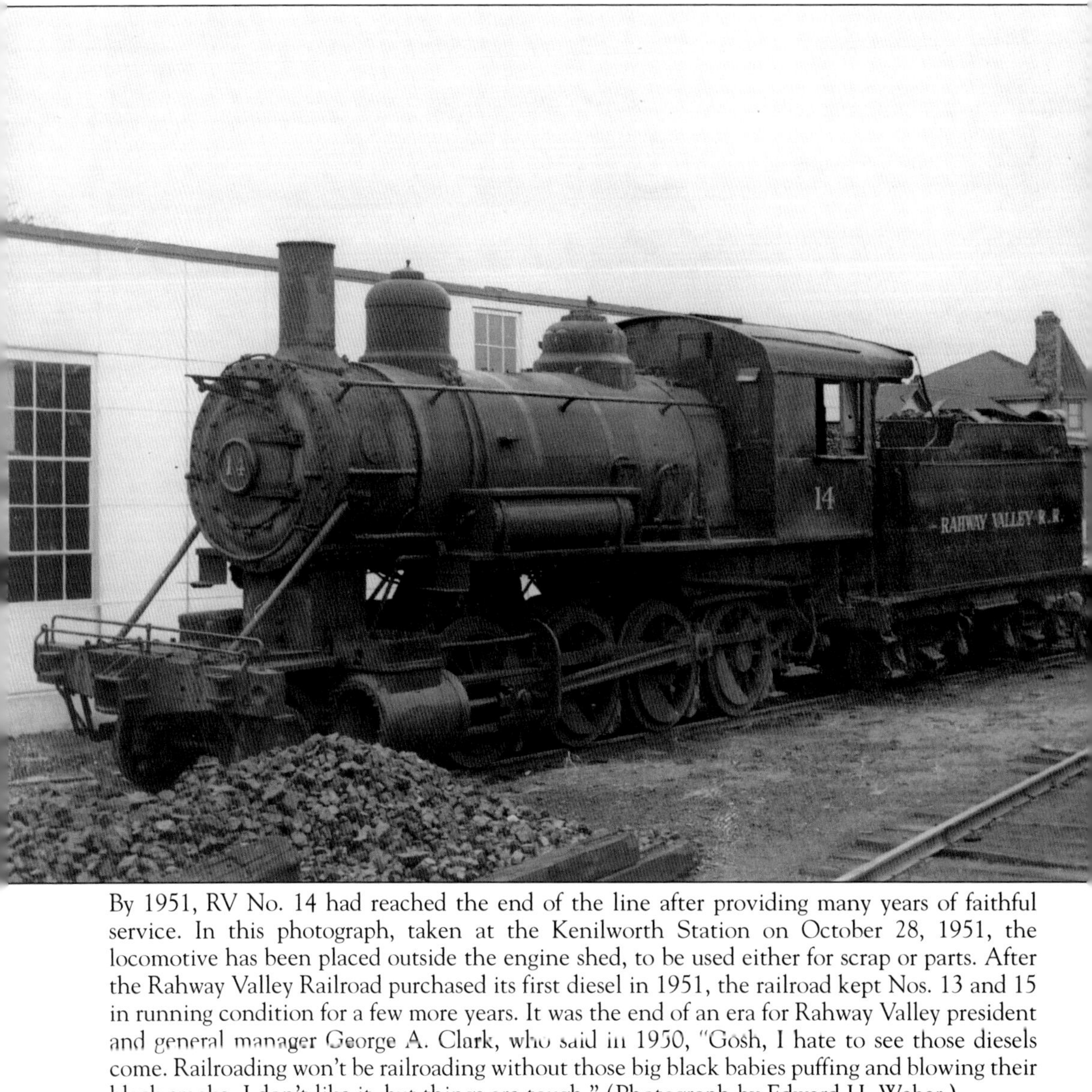

By 1951, RV No. 14 had reached the end of the line after providing many years of faithful service. In this photograph, taken at the Kenilworth Station on October 28, 1951, the locomotive has been placed outside the engine shed, to be used either for scrap or parts. After the Rahway Valley Railroad purchased its first diesel in 1951, the railroad kept Nos. 13 and 15 in running condition for a few more years. It was the end of an era for Rahway Valley president and general manager George A. Clark, who said in 1950, "Gosh, I hate to see those diesels come. Railroading won't be railroading without those big black babies puffing and blowing their black smoke. I don't like it, but things are tough." (Photograph by Edward H. Weber.)

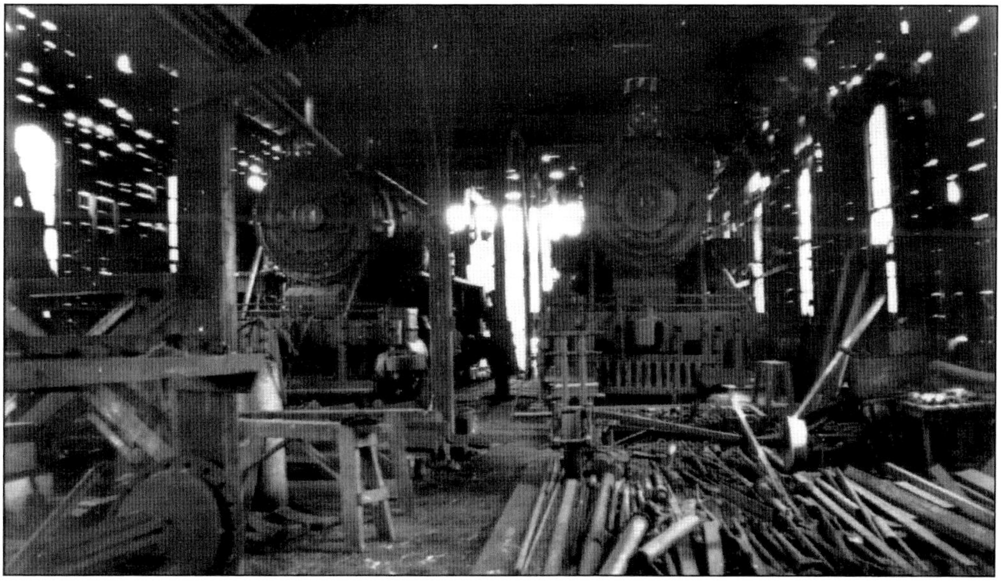

RV Nos. 14 and 15 await maintenance in the railroad's wooden engine house on March 16, 1948. (Photograph by Edward H. Weber.)

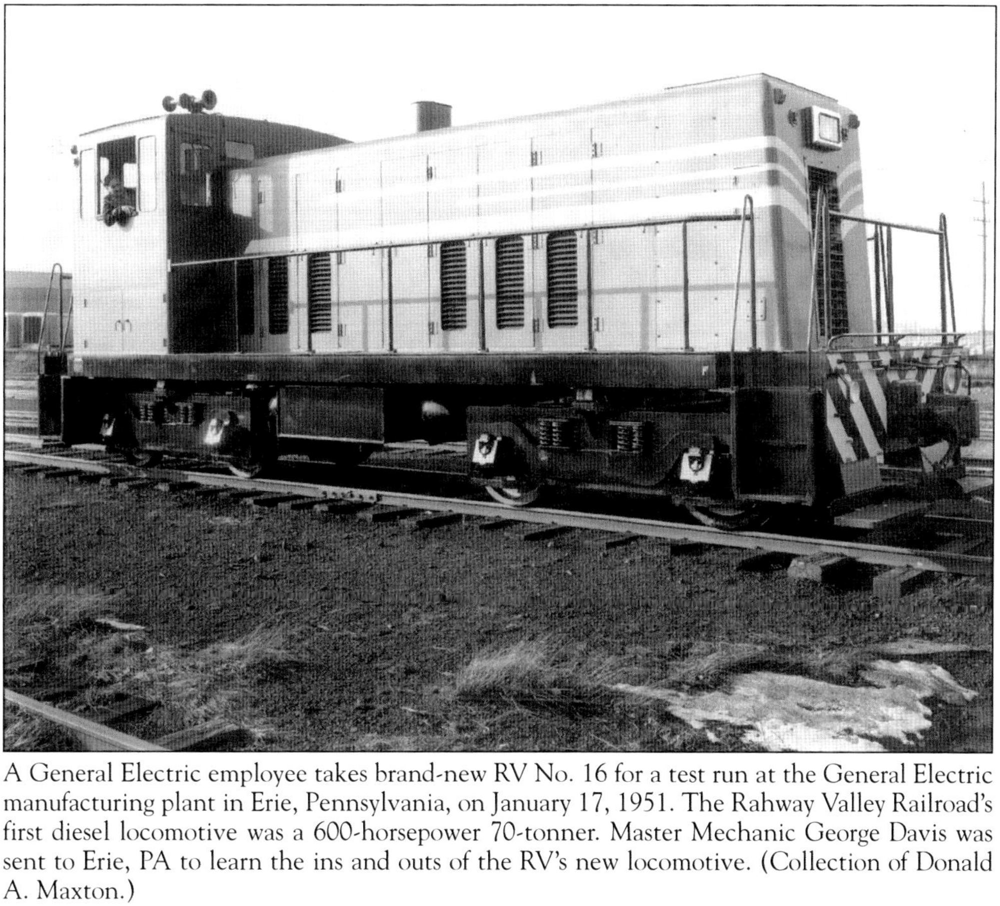

A General Electric employee takes brand-new RV No. 16 for a test run at the General Electric manufacturing plant in Erie, Pennsylvania, on January 17, 1951. The Rahway Valley Railroad's first diesel locomotive was a 600-horsepower 70-tonner. Master Mechanic George Davis was sent to Erie, PA to learn the ins and outs of the RV's new locomotive. (Collection of Donald A. Maxton.)

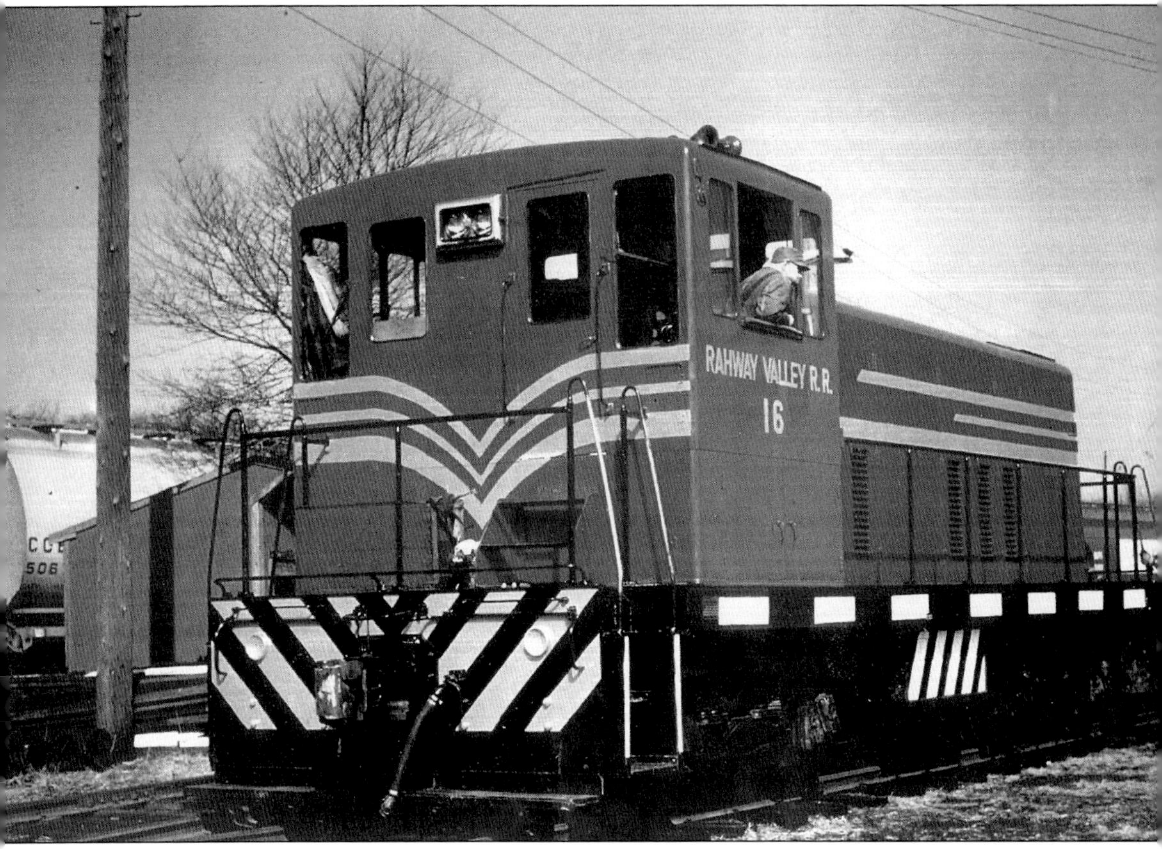

Engineer Frank Froat leans out of the cab of RV No. 16. The diesel arrived from General Electric sporting red and yellow paint in 1951. Around 1975 the engine was repainted maroon and white. (Courtesy of Bruce Trampler.)

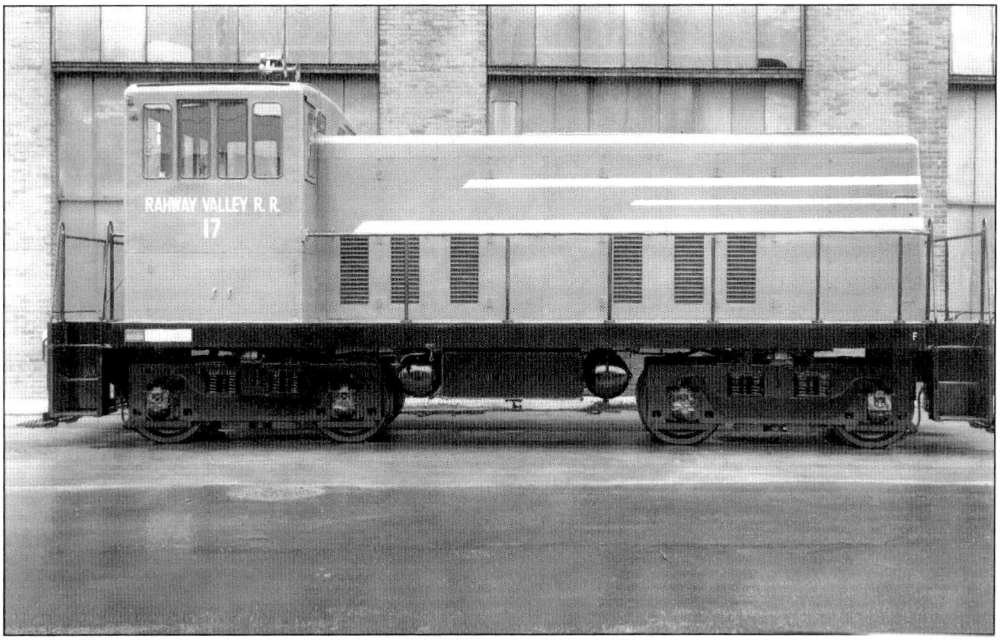

RV No. 17 is shown at the General Electric manufacturing plant in Erie, Pennsylvania, on January 26, 1954. No. 17 arrived in a green and yellow paint scheme, and like No. 16, was repainted maroon and white around 1975. The delivery of this second diesel marked the end of steam power on the Rahway Valley. (Collection of Donald A. Maxton.)

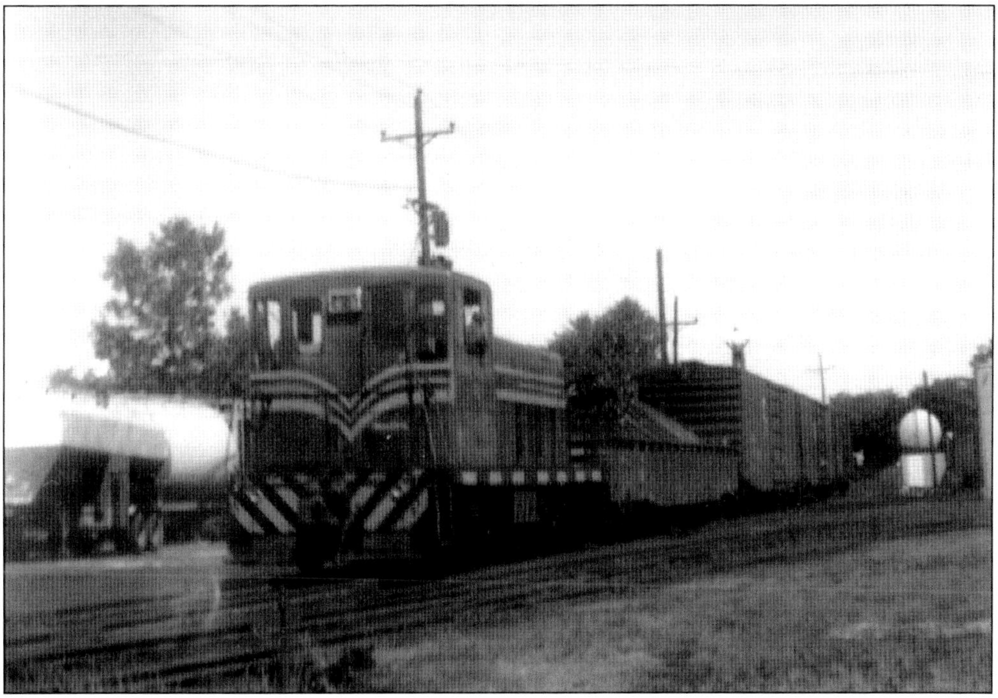

RV No. 16 pushes a flatcar and two boxcars into the Kenilworth Station in 1963. Note the crewman (on top of one of the boxcars) and the brakeman (just visible at the front of the train). (Photograph by Bruce Trampler.)

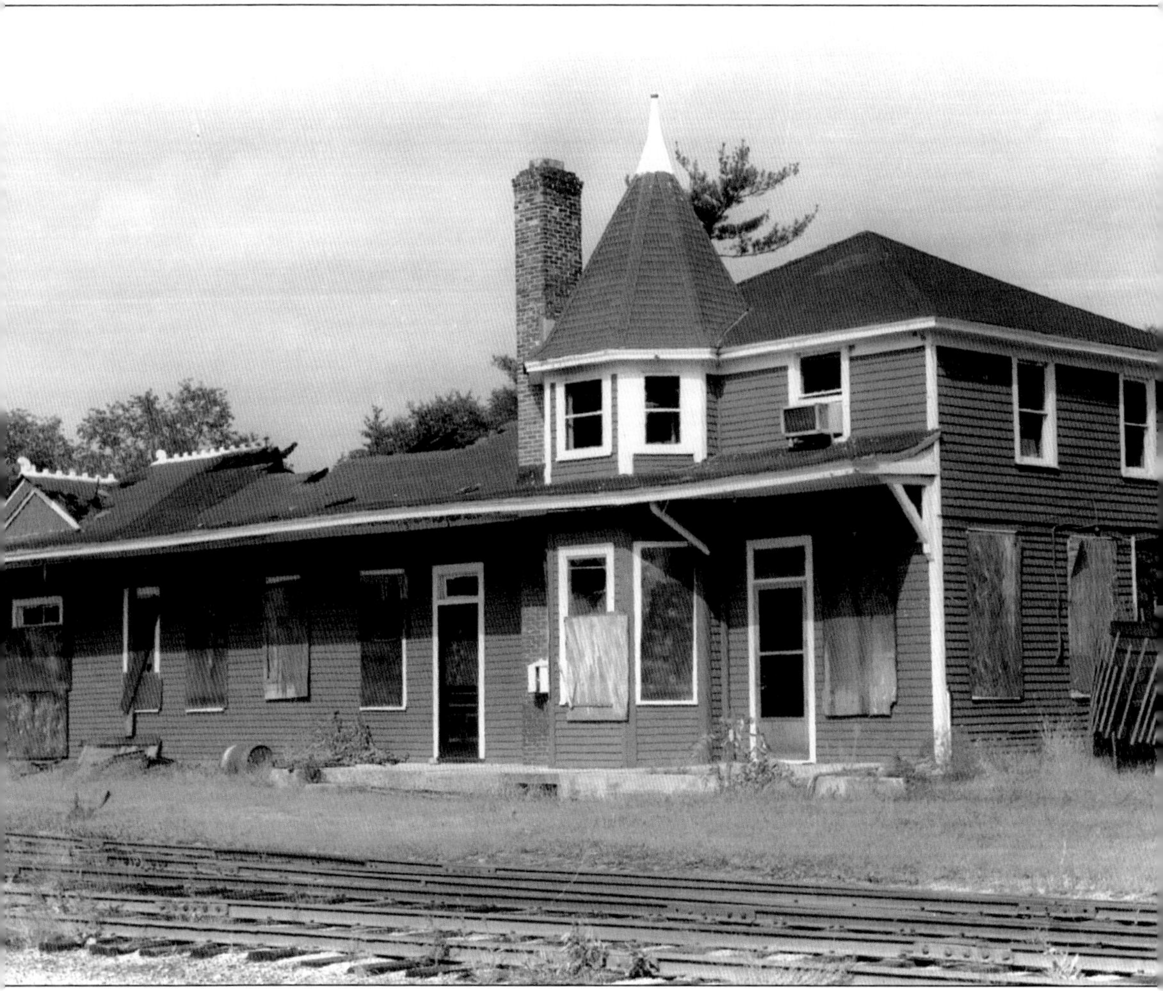

When this picture was taken on September 20, 1978, the old Kenilworth Station designed by J. Wallace Higgins was still standing, although it had sustained a great deal of damage from a fire on August 20, 1974. The damage is especially noticeable in the roof. Many valuable records were lost in the fire (caused by an attempt to destroy some insect infestation), but some were salvaged before the station was demolished in 1979. The Kenilworth Historical Society made an effort to have the building moved and restored as a public museum. Unfortunately, sufficient funds and property were not available to accomplish this worthy goal. The original structure was so sturdy that even the Rahway Valley's locomotives had difficulty pulling it down. (Photograph by D.T. Walker.)

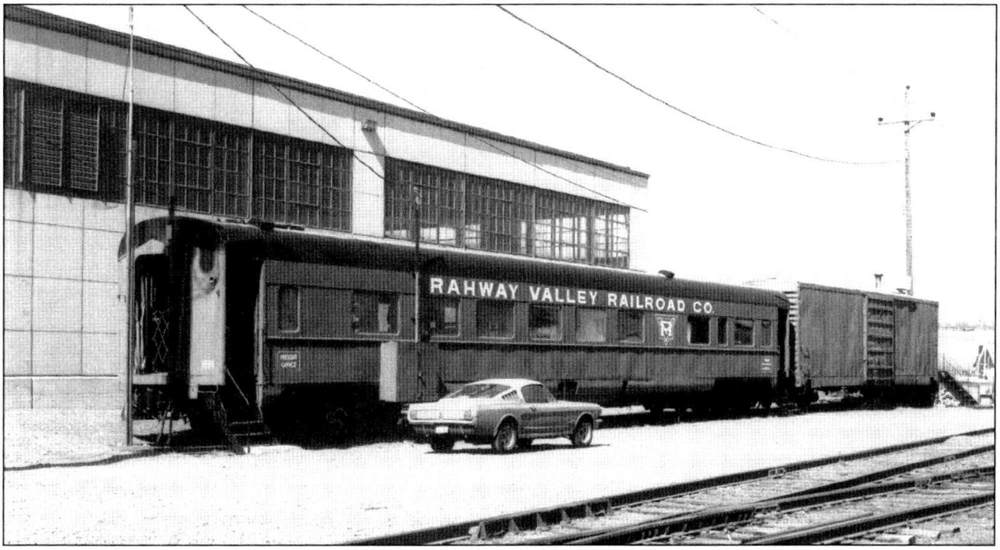

Following the death of Robert G. Clark in 1975, Bernard J. Cahill, a 30-year railroad veteran, assumed the position of Rahway Valley Railroad president and general manager. The old Kenilworth station was in poor condition, so he purchased a former Lehigh Valley Railroad "Black Diamond" club car for $3,500. He fitted it out to serve as the Rahway Valley's headquarters, with three 30-foot-long, air-conditioned offices. The Delaware Otsego Corporation eventually moved the car to its headquarters in Cooperstown, New York, where it still stands. (Photograph by Jon Franz.)

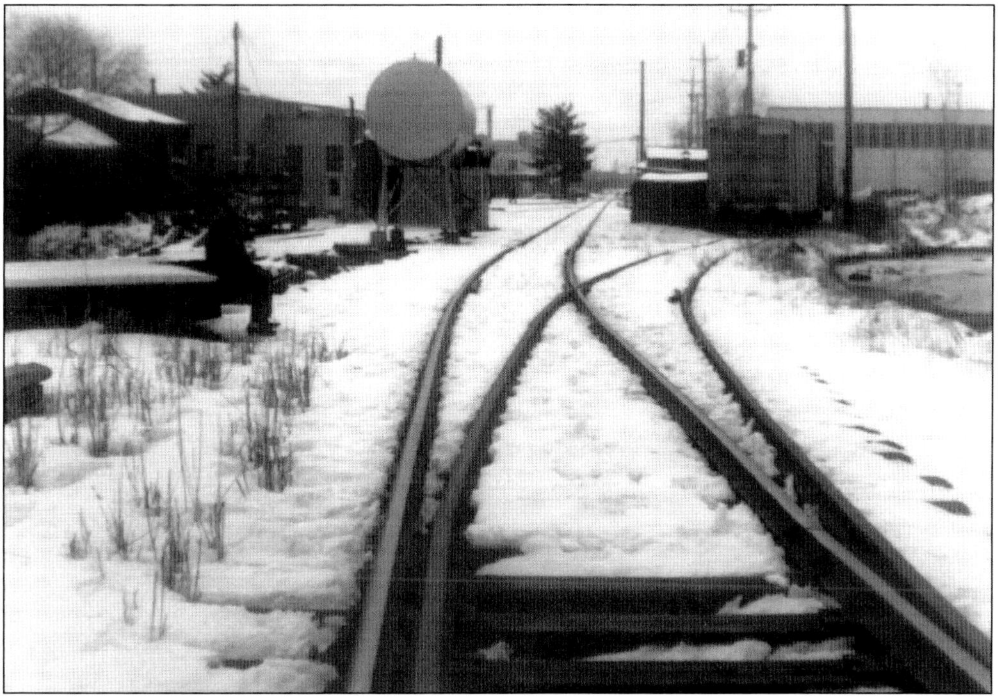

A winter view of Rahway Valley headquarters, facing south toward Roselle Park, reveals the back of the engine house, a diesel fuel tank, and a boxcar on the siding. The old water tower was demolished in the 1950s. (Photograph by Bruce Trampler.)

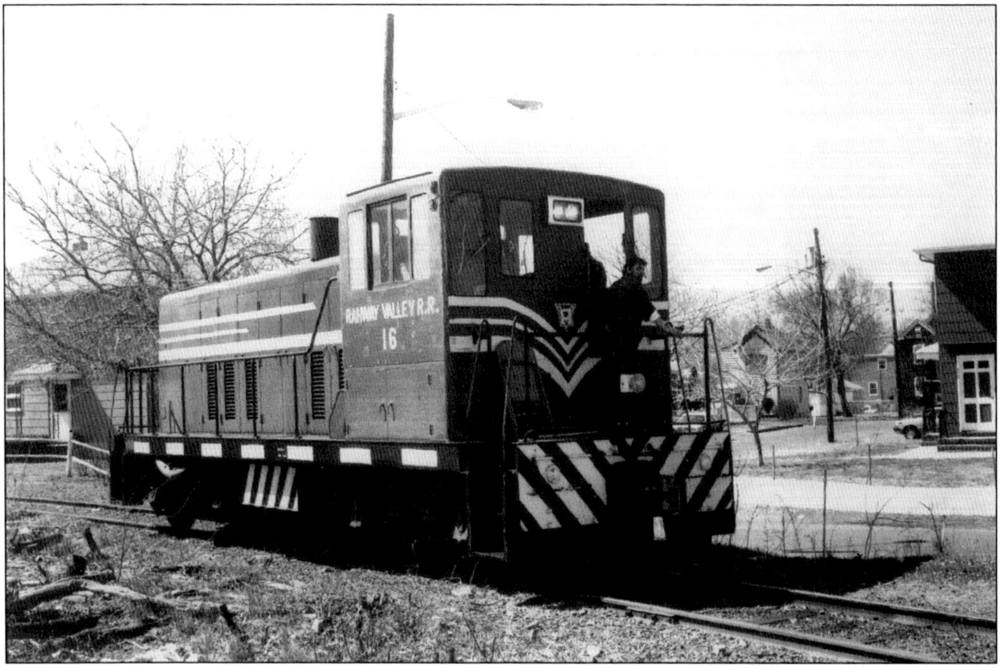

A Rahway Valley crew works the Monsanto Branch in Kenilworth on March 28, 1986, just nine days after the railroad lost its liability insurance and operations were assumed by the Delaware Otsego Corporation. The Monsanto Chemical Company, a manufacturer of plastic products, was one of the railroad's most lucrative accounts until the plant closed in 1990. The tracks on this section—formerly called the Can Branch for the American Can Company, a former customer—were torn up soon after Monsanto shut down operations in Kenilworth. (Photograph by Jon Franz.)

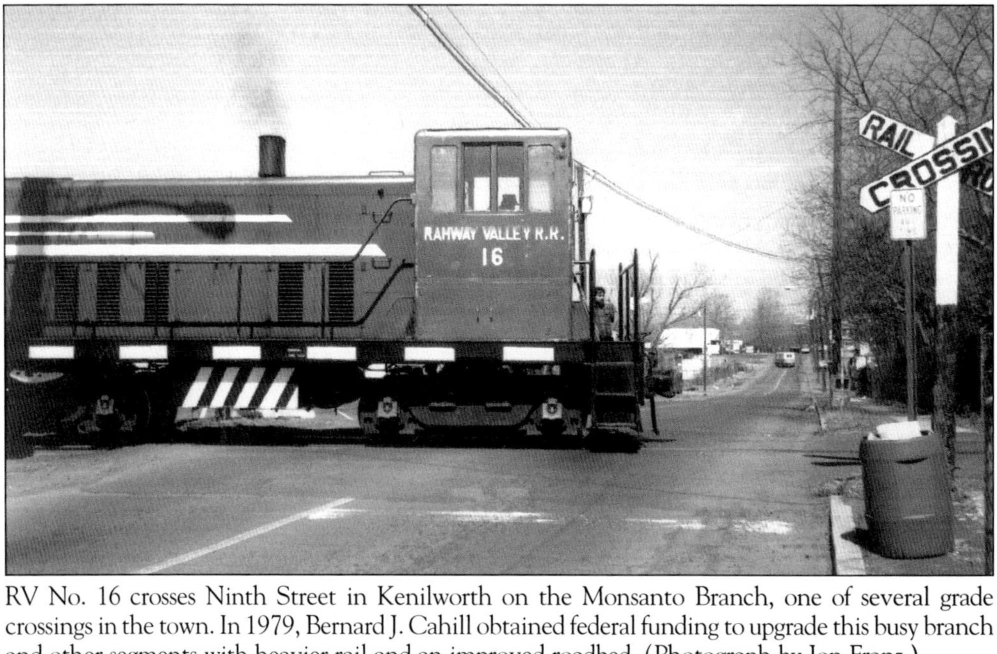

RV No. 16 crosses Ninth Street in Kenilworth on the Monsanto Branch, one of several grade crossings in the town. In 1979, Bernard J. Cahill obtained federal funding to upgrade this busy branch and other segments with heavier rail and an improved roadbed. (Photograph by Jon Franz.)

An advertisement placed by the Monsanto Chemical Company for a booklet celebrating Kenilworth's 75th anniversary features an aerial view of the Kenilworth plant. (Collection of Donald A. Maxton.)

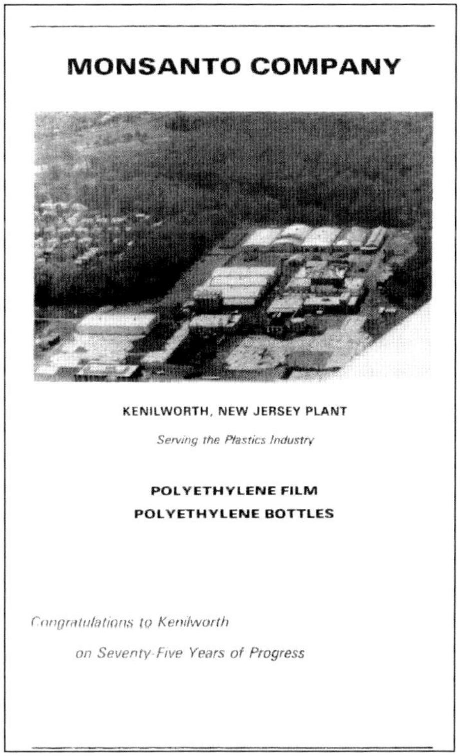

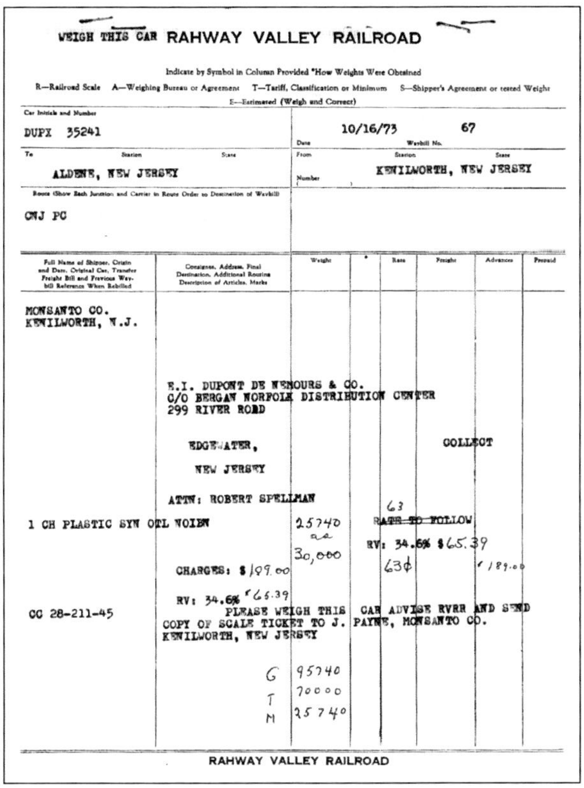

WEIGH THIS CAR RAHWAY VALLEY RAILROAD

Indicate by Symbol in Column Provided *How Weights Were Obtained

R—Railroad Scale A—Weighing Bureau or Agreement T—Tariff, Classification or Minimum S—Shipper's Agreement or tested Weight E—Estimated (Weigh and Correct)

Car Initials and Number: DUPX 35241
Date: 10/16/73 Waybill No.: 67

To Station State: ALDENE, NEW JERSEY
From Station State: KENILWORTH, NEW JERSEY
Number ( )

Route (Show Each Junction and Carrier in Route Order to Destination of Waybill): CNJ PC

Full Name of Shipper, Origin and Date, Original Car, Transfer Freight Bill and Previous Waybill Reference When Rebilled	Consignee, Address, Final Destination, Additional Routing Description of Articles, Marks	Weight	*	Rate	Freight	Advances	Prepaid
MONSANTO CO. KENILWORTH, N.J.	E.I. DUPONT DE NEMOURS & CO. C/O BERGAN NORFOLK DISTRIBUTION CENTER 299 RIVER ROAD EDGEWATER, NEW JERSEY ATTN: ROBERT SPELLMAN				COLLECT		
1 CH PLASTIC SYN OIL NOIBN		25740 as 30,000		~~RATE TO FOLLOW~~ 63 RV: 34.6% $65.39 63¢		$189.00	
CC 28-211-45	CHARGES: $189.00 RV: 34.6% $65.39 PLEASE WEIGH THIS CAR ADVISE RVRR AND SEND COPY OF SCALE TICKET TO J. PAYNE, MONSANTO CO. KENILWORTH, NEW JERSEY						
	G T M	95740 70000 25740					

RAHWAY VALLEY RAILROAD

On this 1973 Rahway Valley Railroad waybill for the Monsanto Chemical Company, Monsanto requests the E.I. DuPont Company in Edgewater, New Jersey, to weigh a covered hopper and report the weight to both Monsanto and the Rahway Valley. (Courtesy of Mary E. McCoy.)

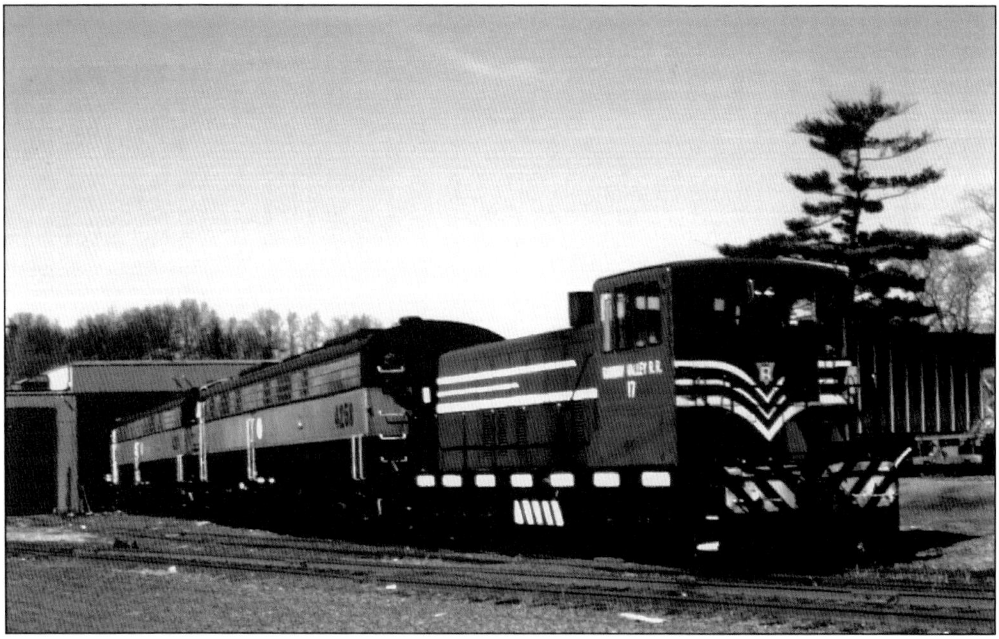

RV No. 17 couples onto two vintage E8 diesels—formerly New Jersey Transit Nos. 4324 and 4258—on March 31, 1988. A rail company leased space at the Rahway Valley shops in Kenilworth to restore these diesels for a private owner. (Photograph by Carl G. Perelman.)

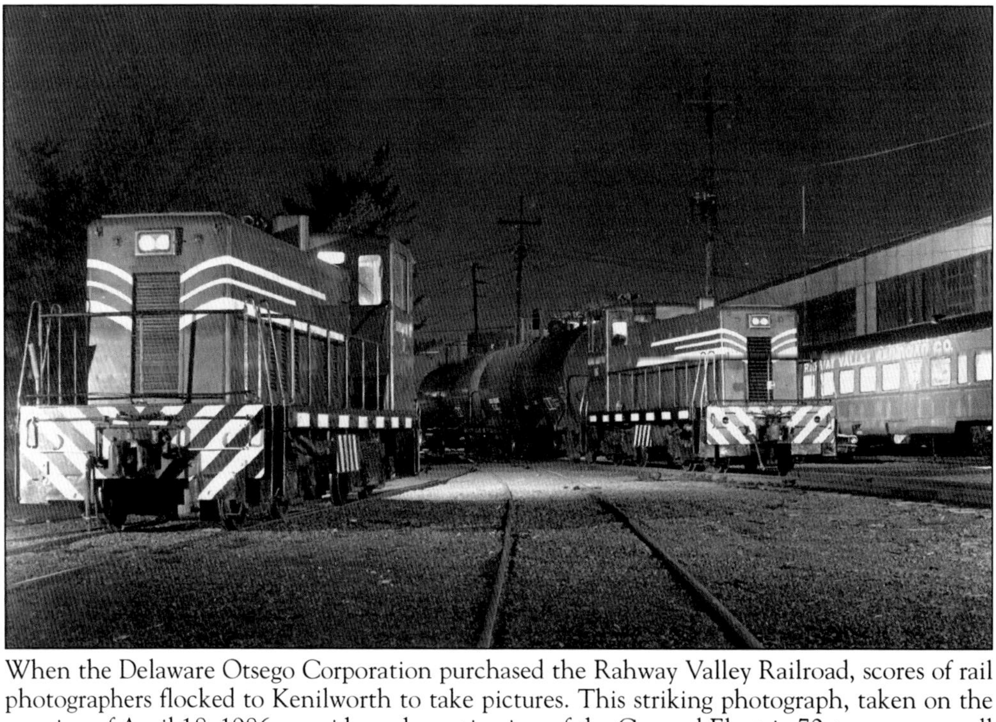

When the Delaware Otsego Corporation purchased the Rahway Valley Railroad, scores of rail photographers flocked to Kenilworth to take pictures. This striking photograph, taken on the evening of April 18, 1986, provides a dramatic view of the General Electric 70-tonners, as well as the coach car that served as the Rahway Valley Railroad offices. (Photograph by Denis E. Connell, courtesy of Ronald F. Pietranowicz.)

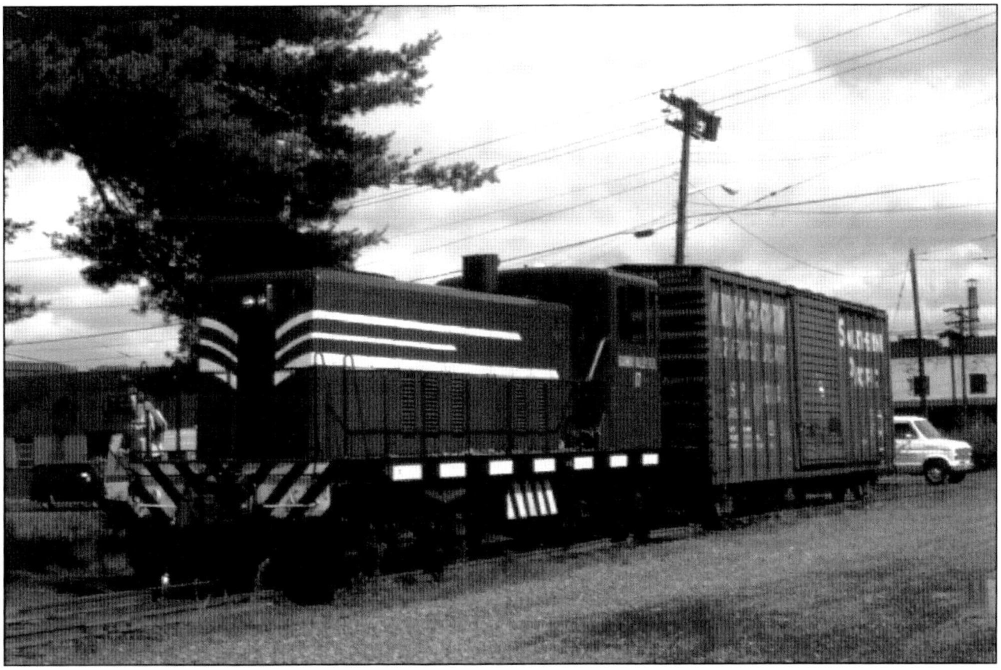

RV No. 17 hauls a boxcar through Kenilworth on July 2, 1986. Most of the improvements instituted by Bernard J. Cahill were on 2.4 miles of the line in Kenilworth and Roselle Park. (Photograph by Carl G. Perelman.)

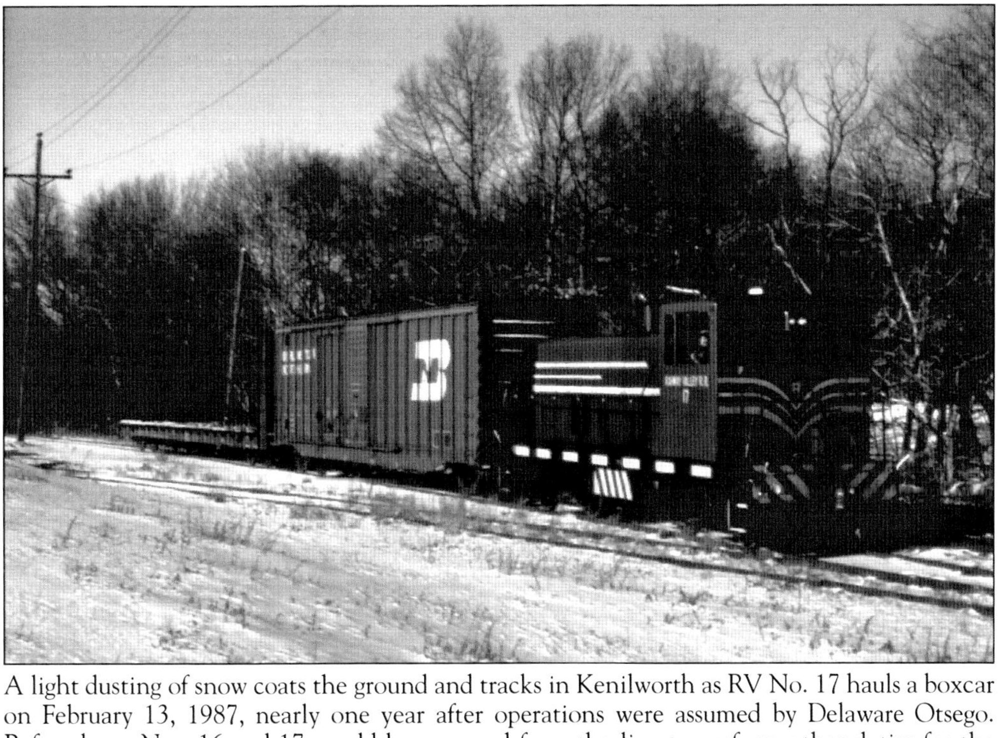

A light dusting of snow coats the ground and tracks in Kenilworth as RV No. 17 hauls a boxcar on February 13, 1987, nearly one year after operations were assumed by Delaware Otsego. Before long, Nos. 16 and 17 would be removed from the line to perform other duties for the New York, Susquehanna & Western Railroad (NYSW). (Photograph by Carl G. Perelman.)

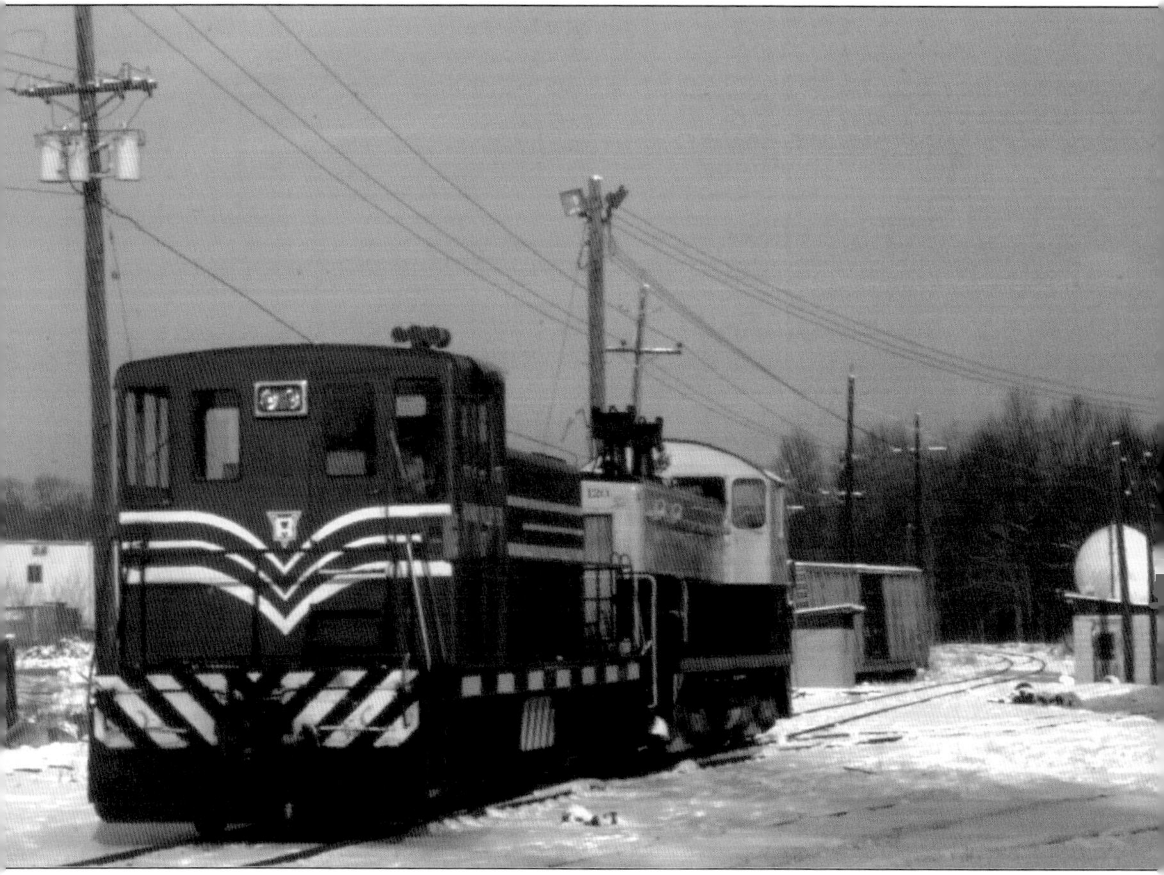

When Delaware Otsego assumed Rahway Valley operations, NYSW SW9 120 frequently operated the line, sometimes working in tandem with a Rahway Valley diesel. This engine, photographed in Kenilworth on January 28, 1988, with RV No. 17, gradually assumed most of the work on the short line. (Photograph by Carl G. Perelman.)

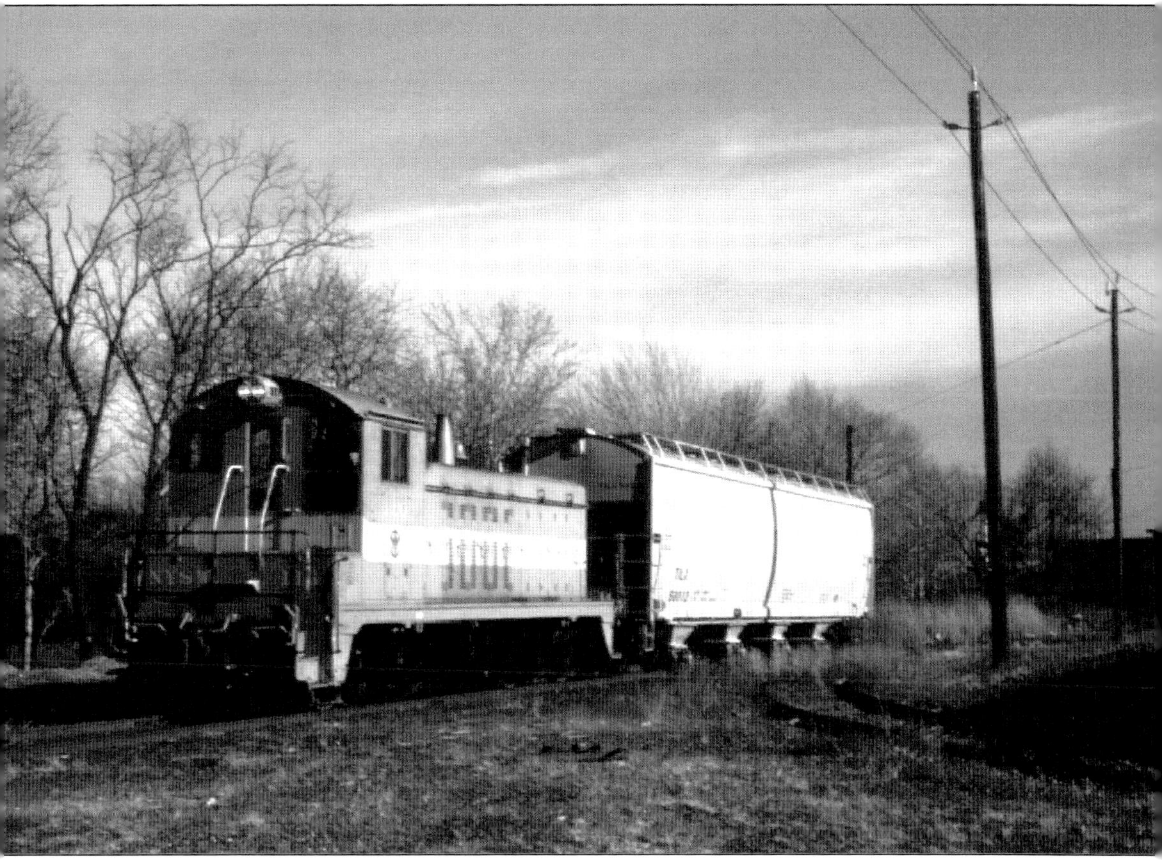

During Delaware Otsego's operation of the Rahway Valley Railroad, another colorful diesel sometimes worked the line—former New York Ontario & Western NW2 116, owned by one of Delaware Otsego's directors. Here, it handles a covered hopper in Kenilworth on March 2, 1989. (Photograph by Carl G. Perelman.)

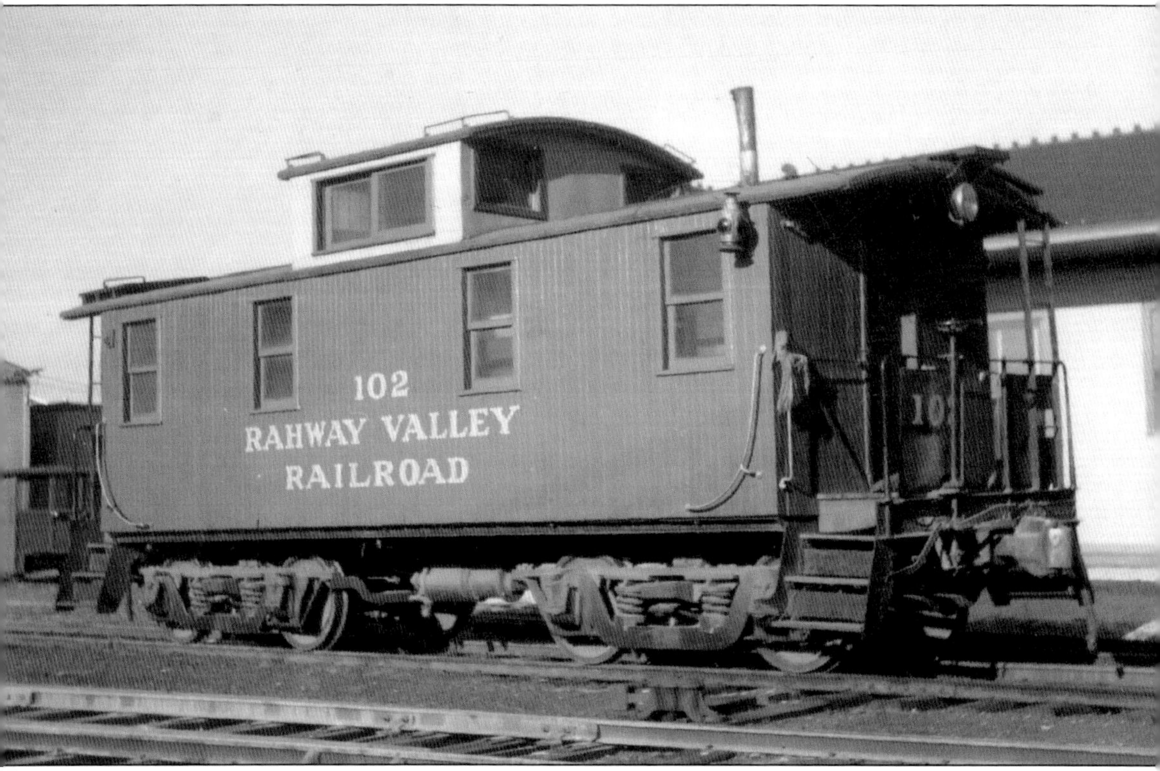

RV Caboose No. 102—purchased secondhand from the Delaware, Lackawanna & Western Railroad between 1932 and 1934—was a favorite sight along the Rahway Valley. Here it is in Kenilworth on October 14, 1951. (Courtesy of Mary E. McCoy.)

Two

KENILWORTH TO SUMMIT: YEARS OF GROWTH

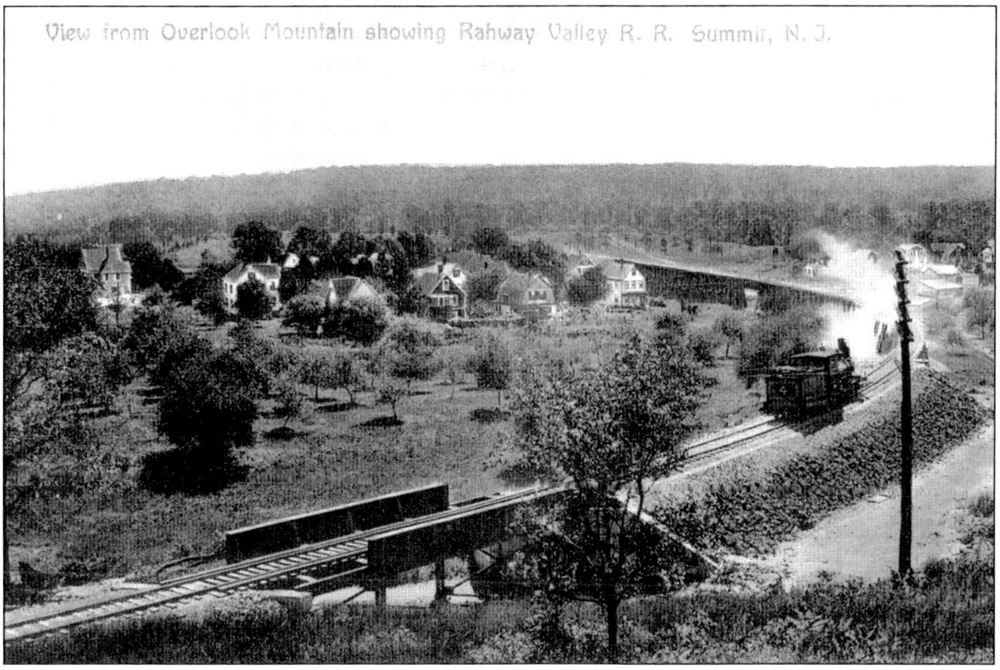

This postcard view from Overlook Mountain shows the Rahway Valley Railroad during a busy period of construction in the early 1900s. The locomotive, No. 4, backs towards the Morris Avenue Bridge, seen in the foreground. Farther down the tracks, around a sharp curve, the opening of the Ashwood Avenue Bridge is visible. (Courtesy of Scott Schnipper.)

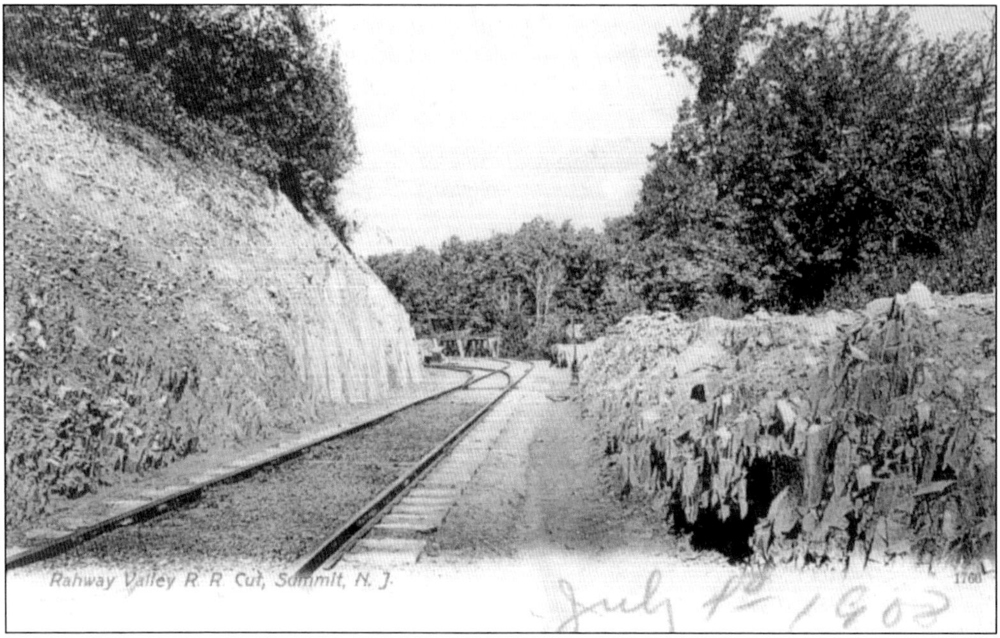

This rare postcard shows the Rahway Valley cut through Overlook Mountain in Summit, looking toward the Broad Street Bridge and the tracks of the Delaware, Lackawanna & Western Railroad. The switch, seen just up ahead, leads to the RV's Summit Station. (Courtesy of Bruce Trampler.)

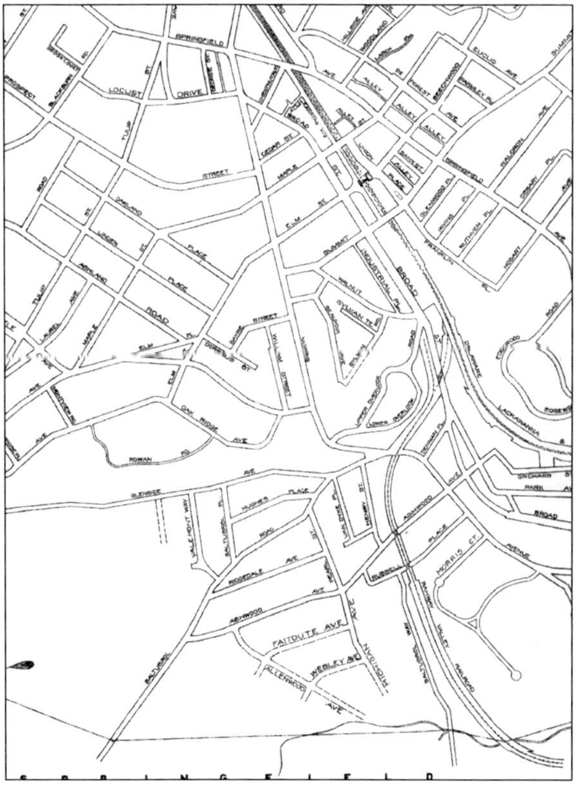

This map of Summit from 1953 traces the route of the Rahway Valley Railroad through town, from its border with Springfield to its connection with the Delaware, Lackawanna & Western Railroad near Broad Street. (Collection of Donald A. Maxton.)

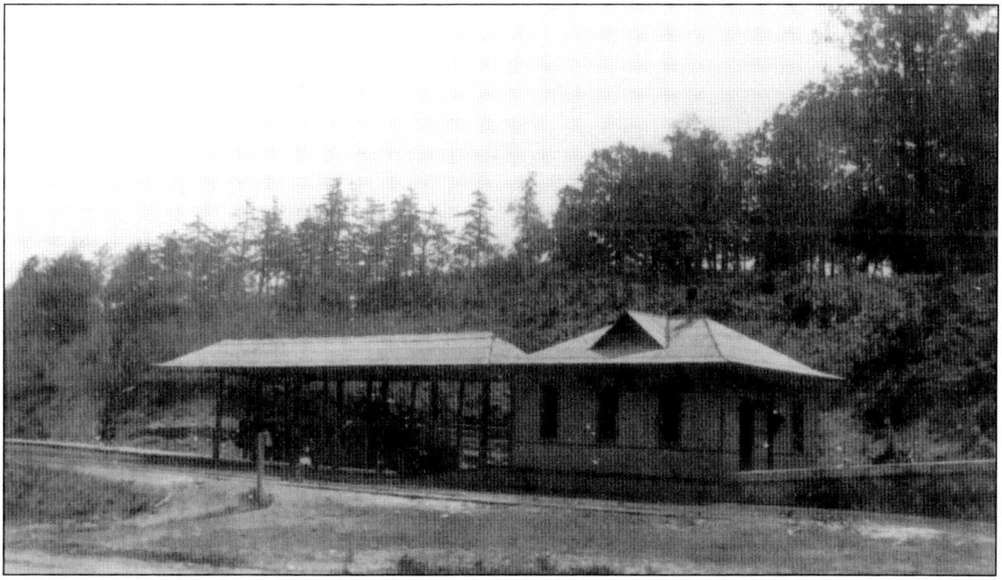

Summit Station, constructed in 1906, was one of the busiest spots on the Rahway Valley Railroad. During the passenger service era, there were seven scheduled trains a day from here. Passengers included families traveling to Asbury Park and other points along the New Jersey shore via the Central Railroad of New Jersey and members of the Baptist and Methodist churches, which sponsored numerous excursions. (Courtesy of the Summit Historical Society.)

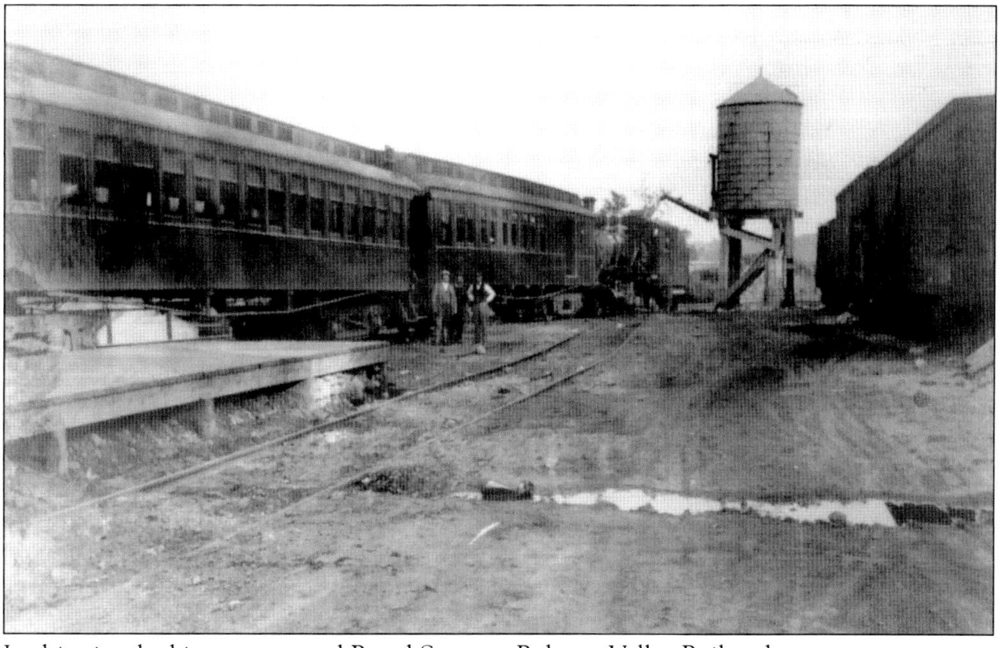

In this view looking east toward Broad Street, a Rahway Valley Railroad passenger crew poses while their locomotive No. 7 takes on water from the tower at Summit Station in 1915. The passenger depot, not visible in this photograph, stood to the left of this train. (Photograph by Warren Crater, courtesy of the Summit Historical Society.)

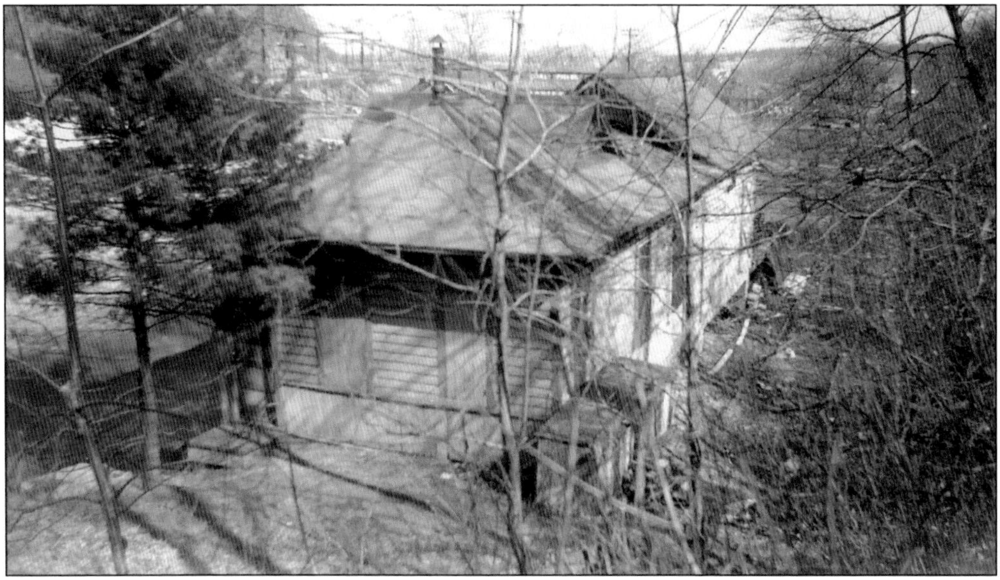

This photograph of Summit Station was taken on April 9, 1950, from the slopes of Overlook Mountain. An apartment building for nurses at nearby Overlook Hospital now stands on the site. (Photograph by Edward H. Weber.)

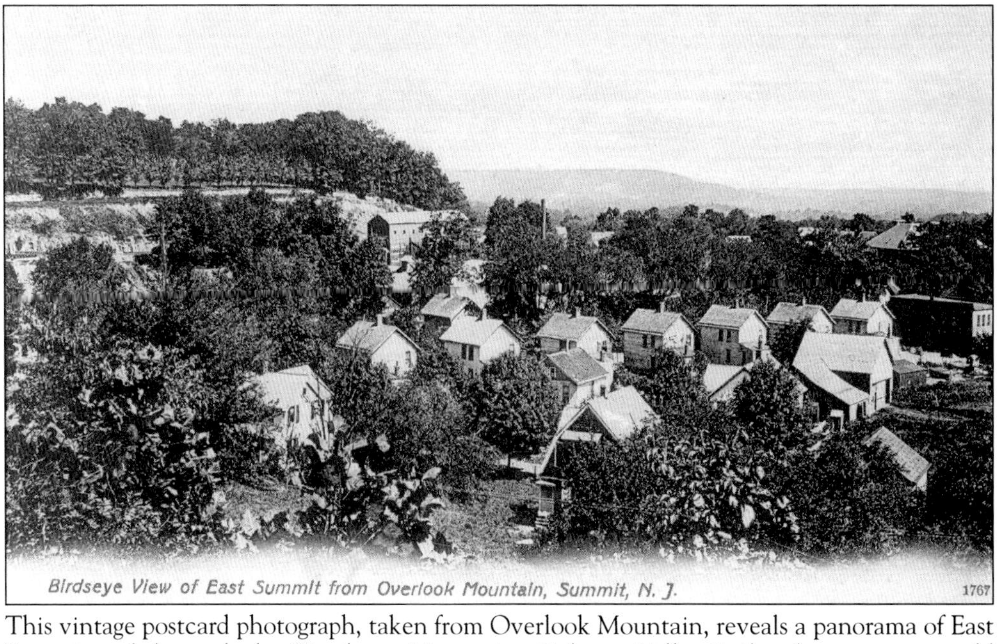

This vintage postcard photograph, taken from Overlook Mountain, reveals a panorama of East Summit and, beyond, the Watchung Mountains. Rahway Valley Railroad passengers would have caught a glimpse of this view as they began their journey from Summit Station. (Courtesy of Scott Schnipper.)

Over the years, a succession of steam locomotives operated over the Rahway Valley Railroad. As steam engines broke down and became too expensive to repair, railroads commonly purchased used engines from manufacturers or from other lines. Pictured is an advertisement for an overhauled locomotive sent to the Rahway Valley in 1905 by the Baldwin Equipment & Supply Company in Chicago. The price was $5,000, and the Rahway Valley Railroad did not make this particular purchase. (Courtesy of Mary E. McCoy.)

FOR SALE.

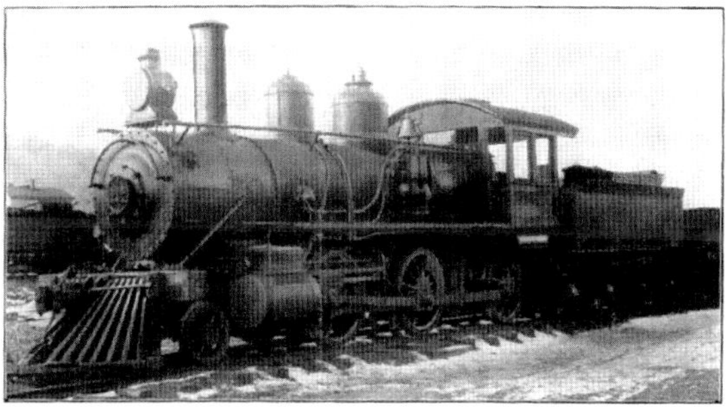

One ~~Two~~ Baldwin 50-ton Mogul Locomotives.

Cylinders, 19x24 inches.
Drivers, 6 46-inch diameter.
Tires, 2½ inches thick.
Truck, 2-wheel front, 26-in. diam.
Weight, total, 100,000 lbs.
" on drivers, 85,000 lbs.
Wheel-base, of engine, 23 ft. 4½ in.
" rigid, 15 ft. 3½ in.
Boiler, square, wagon top, 60-in. dia.
" pressure, 160, tested 180 lbs.
Fire-box, 72 long, 33 wide, 65 high.
" condition, first-class.

Flues, 220 2-inch, 12 ft. long.
Injectors, two No. 9 Monitor.
Oil feed, triple sight feed.
Brakes, Westinghouse air on drivers tender and train.
Couplers, Janney.
TENDER: Wheels, 8 33-in.
Frame, wood.
Brakes, air.
Tank capacity, 3200 gals.

~~Both~~ offered thoroughly overhauled in every part, and at reasonable price. Address, BALDWIN EQUIPMENT & SUPPLY CO.

B-10738

November 16th, 1936

Mr. E. J. Lanneck, Purchasing Agent,
Pennsylvania Railroad Company,
Broad Street Station,
Philadelphia, Pennsylvania.

Dear Sir:

I wish to thank you for your letter of November 12th, File No. 68, dealing with class B8 locomotive which you have for sale.

This specific type of locomotive might possibly be of some interest to us but as we have some mighty heavy grades we would really like a locomotive with more tractive effort and smaller driving wheels.

Due to our heavy grades and light bridge construction, coupled with fairly heavy traffic it is necessary for us to operate light power with a maximum of tractive effort.

I would be very pleased to have you advise where this power could be inspected and if you have anything that might more closely meet our requirements we would be very pleased to hear from you.

Yours very truly,

GAC:PL

Pres. & Gen'l Mgr.

In this 1936 letter from Rahway Valley Railroad president and general manager George A. Clark to the purchasing agent of the Pennsylvania Railroad, Clark discusses what he is looking for in a locomotive: "This specific type of locomotive might possibly be of some interest to us but as we have some mighty heavy grades we would really like a locomotive with more tractive effort and smaller driving wheels. Due to our heavy grades and light bridge construction, it is necessary for us to operate light power with a maximum of tractive effort." (Courtesy of Mary E. McCoy.)

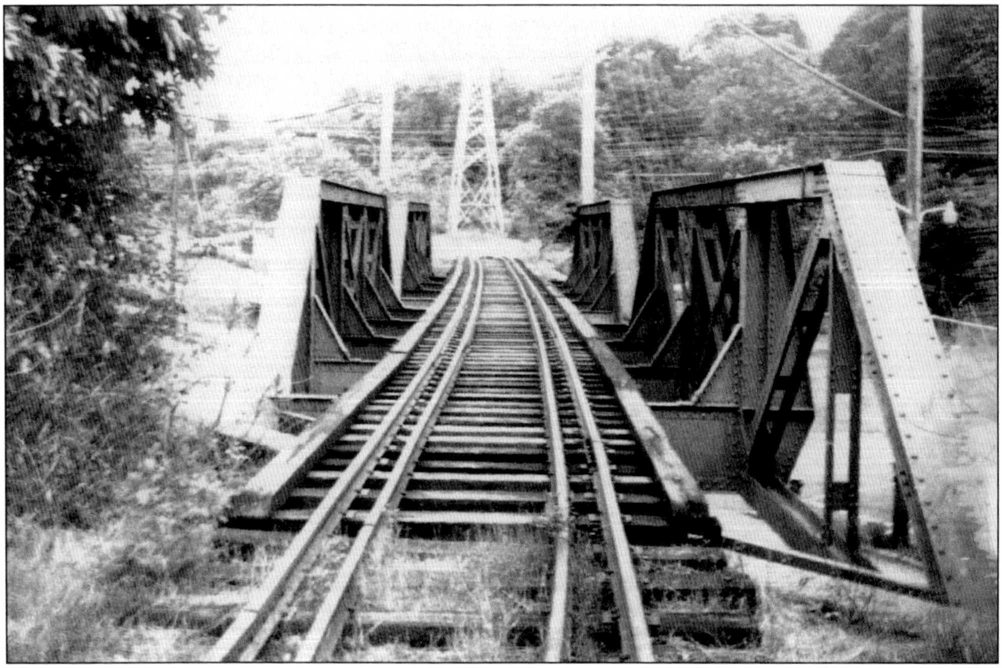

The Rahway Valley's bridge over Broad Street, Summit, overlooked the short line's connection with the Delaware, Lackawanna & Western Railroad. Although the Rahway Valley Railroad was completed to Summit in 1906, the Delaware, Lackawanna & Western did not permit the short line to make this connection until 1931. (Courtesy of Mary E. McCoy.)

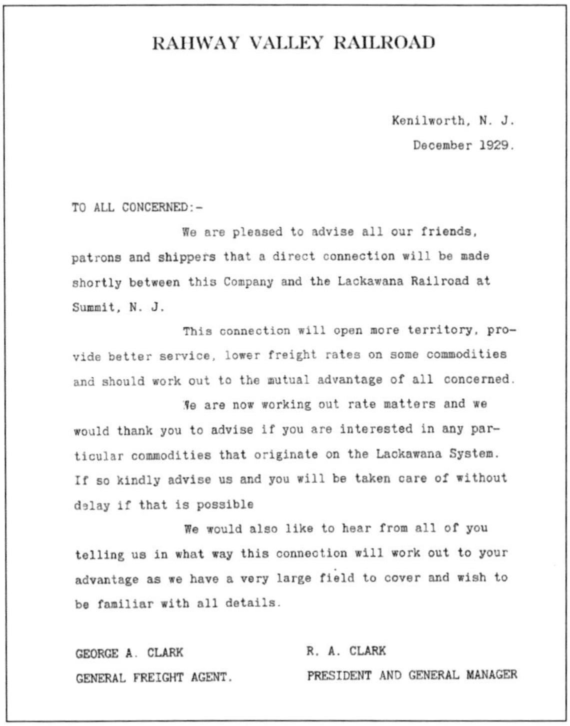

RAHWAY VALLEY RAILROAD

Kenilworth, N. J.
December 1929.

TO ALL CONCERNED:-

We are pleased to advise all our friends, patrons and shippers that a direct connection will be made shortly between this Company and the Lackawana Railroad at Summit, N. J.

This connection will open more territory, provide better service, lower freight rates on some commodities and should work out to the mutual advantage of all concerned.

We are now working out rate matters and we would thank you to advise if you are interested in any particular commodities that originate on the Lackawana System. If so kindly advise us and you will be taken care of without delay if that is possible

We would also like to hear from all of you telling us in what way this connection will work out to your advantage as we have a very large field to cover and wish to be familiar with all details.

GEORGE A. CLARK
GENERAL FREIGHT AGENT.

R. A. CLARK
PRESIDENT AND GENERAL MANAGER

This December 1929 letter from Rahway Valley president Roger Clark and his son, general freight agent George A. Clark, announced to the railroad's customers that they would not have to wait much longer for interchange service with the Delaware, Lackawanna & Western Railroad. This connection would open up major markets to shippers along the Rahway Valley Railroad and prove essential to the line's survival. The connection enabled the short line to operate in the black, even during the years of the Great Depression. (Courtesy of Mary E. McCoy.)

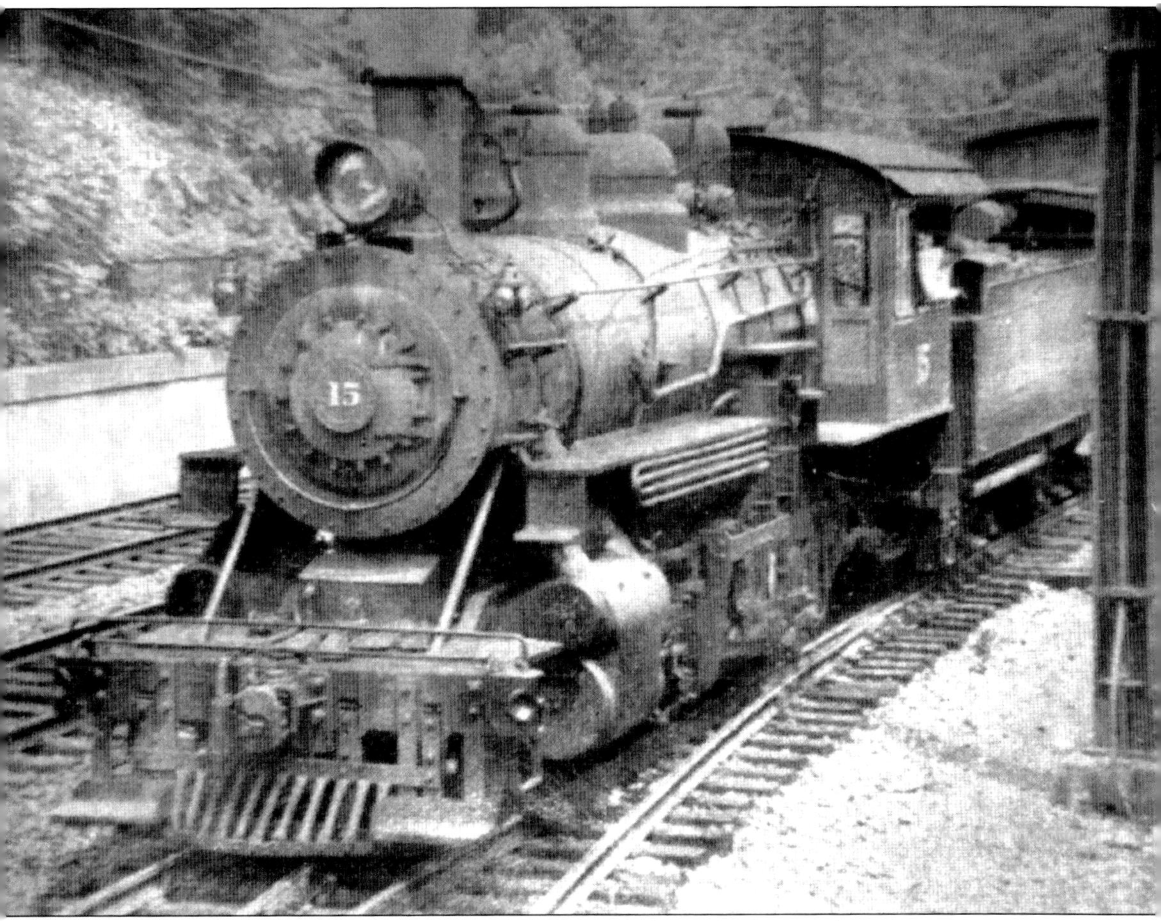

In 1950, RV No. 15 backs onto the electrified tracks of the Delaware, Lackawanna & Western Railroad on the interchange in Summit. (Photograph by Bruce Nett.)

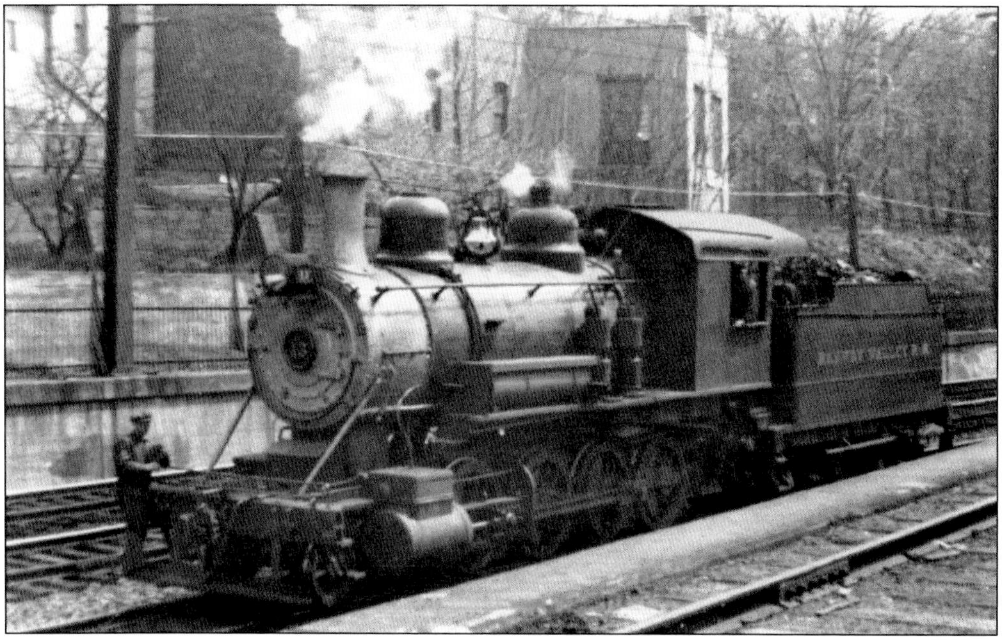

A Rahway Valley crew works with No. 13 at the Delaware, Lackawanna & Western interchange in Summit. Beginning in 1931, when this important connection was made, Rahway Valley locomotives were a familiar sight to commuters traveling on the Delaware, Lackawanna & Western passenger trains. (Photograph by Homer Hill.)

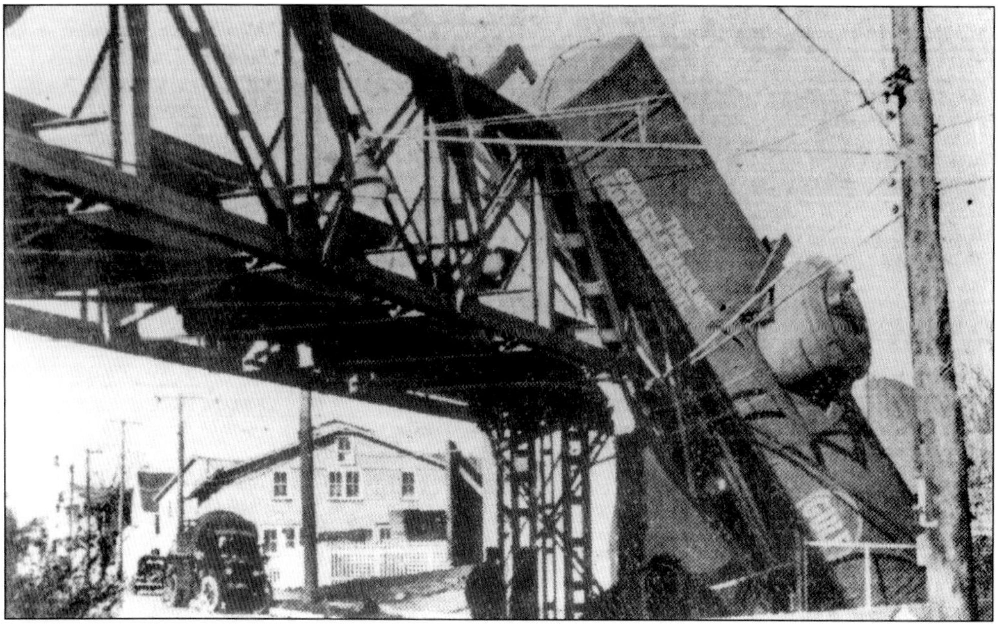

Like most railroads, the Rahway Valley occasionally experienced a mishap. In early December 1935, a Gulf tank car broke loose from a train and hung precariously from the Broad Street Bridge in Summit. The *Newark News* reported that a Delaware, Lackawanna & Western crew rectified the situation after only a half hour's work, while a large crowd gathered to watch. The tank car sustained some slight damage. (Courtesy of the Summit Historical Society.)

Cigar-loving, six-foot three-inch George A. Clark, in his pine-paneled office at Rahway Valley headquarters in Kenilworth, works on monthly business statements—just one of the many jobs he handled efficiently for almost 40 years as president and general manager.

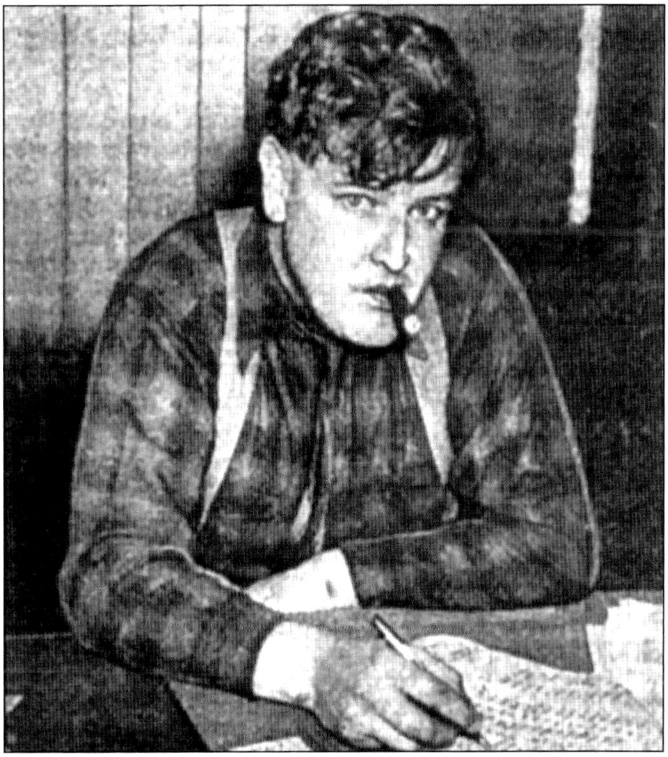

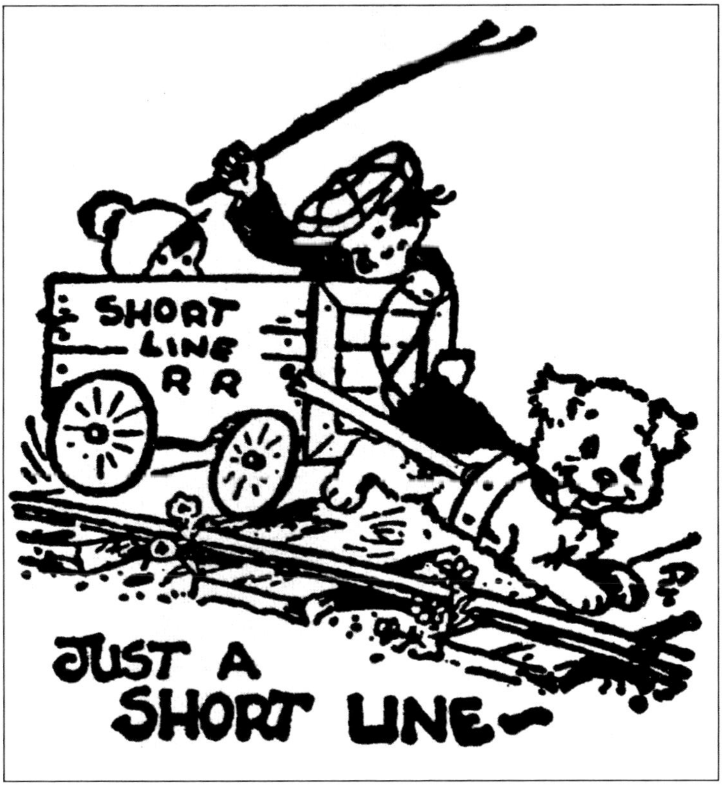

George A. Clark, a former lumberjack, has been described as "rough and tough," but he had a humorous side as well. His letterhead was inspired by Gene Byrnes's "Reg'lar Fellers" comic strip. Clark was proud to manage "Just a Short Line."

RAHWAY VALLEY RAILROAD
RAHWAY VALLEY COMPANY, LESSEE
OFFICE OF
PRESIDENT AND GENERAL MANAGER

JUST A SHORT LINE

GEO. A. CLARK
PRESIDENT AND GENERAL MANAGER

REFER TO FILE No. B-17498

KENILWORTH, N. J., March 26th, 1947.

Master Edward Weber,
8 Garden Avenue,
Chatham, New Jersey.

Dear Eddie:

In response to yours dated March 24th, please permit me to inform you that we only operate freight service and due to the element of risk involved we do not permit any riders on any equipment engaged in such operations except our own employees.

Suppose you be a real good boy and rake up the yard and do a dozen or so little odd jobs around the house for "Mother" and then when you have "Dad" in a very good mood don't you think you could induce him to write a letter to me relieving the Rahway Valley Company, Lessee and/or Rahway Valley Railroad Company and/or Rahway Valley Line from all liability. If you can accomplish this I shall see to it that you have a ride in our caboose from Kenilworth to Summit, on some Saturday. We require your parents signature because you are a minor.

Go to work on this Eddie and in this connection I wish you all the luck in the world.

Sincerely yours,

Geo. A. Clark

President & General Manager.

GAC:mee

P.S.: Tell "Dad" that no risk of accident really exists just as long as you behave yourself and if you don't behave---- well we still believe in the old fashioned backside fanning.

This charming pair of letters from Rahway Valley Railroad president and general manager George A. Clark to the Weber family of Chatham conveys a friendly, informal tone that endeared the little railroad to many residents throughout Union and Essex Counties. In the first letter, Clark advises 12-year-old Edward H. Weber—who had written to Clark, requesting a

RAHWAY VALLEY RAILROAD
RAHWAY VALLEY COMPANY, LESSEE

OFFICE OF

PRESIDENT AND GENERAL MANAGER

GEO. A. CLARK
PRESIDENT AND GENERAL MANAGER

REFER TO FILE No. B-17498

KENILWORTH, N. J., April 8th, 1947.

Mr. Edward H. Weber, Sr.,
8 Garden Avenue,
Chatham, New Jersey.

Dear Mr. Weber:

Many thanks for your letter dated April 1st. If your Son, Edward, will report to this office in old clothes on some Saturday I shall see to it that he has his ride.

For your information our engine and crew reports out of Kenilworth, N. J. right on the dot at 8:30 A.M. on Saturdays. This engine and crew takes care of all industrial switching at Kenilworth, N. J. after which they pick up cars from the Central Railroad Company of New Jersey at Aldene, N. J. and the Lehigh Valley Railroad at Roselle Park, New Jersey and report back into Kenilworth, N. J. around 11:00 A.M. After water pick up at Kenilworth, N. J. this train will work its way into Summit, N. J. about two hours later which is generally between 1:00 P. M. and 2:00 P.M.

If Edward wishes to cover our whole Main Line operation he should be here by 8:30 A.M., but if he will be satisfied with a ride from Kenilworth to Summit, N. J., 11:00 A.M. will do the trick.

He will find the office of this little streak of rust right on the Boulevard at Kenilworth, N. J. His route I should think would be down Morris Turnpike through Springfield, N. J. to Union, N. J. Turn right at Union Center and at the Five Points in Union(directly in front of Tretolas Restaurant) turn right again from Chestnut Street to the Kenilworth Boulevard and we will be found less than a mile beyond.

Do not worry at all about Edward as he will be in good hands.

Very truly yours,

Geo A. Clark.

President & General Manager.

GAC:mee.

ride on the railroad—to "be a real good boy and rake up the yard and do a dozen or so little odd jobs around the house for 'Mother'" in order to secure "Dad's" permission and letter of release from liability. Young Edward H. Weber took Clark's advice to heart and enjoyed a daylong ride in RV Caboose No. 102 one month later. (Courtesy of Edward H. Weber.)

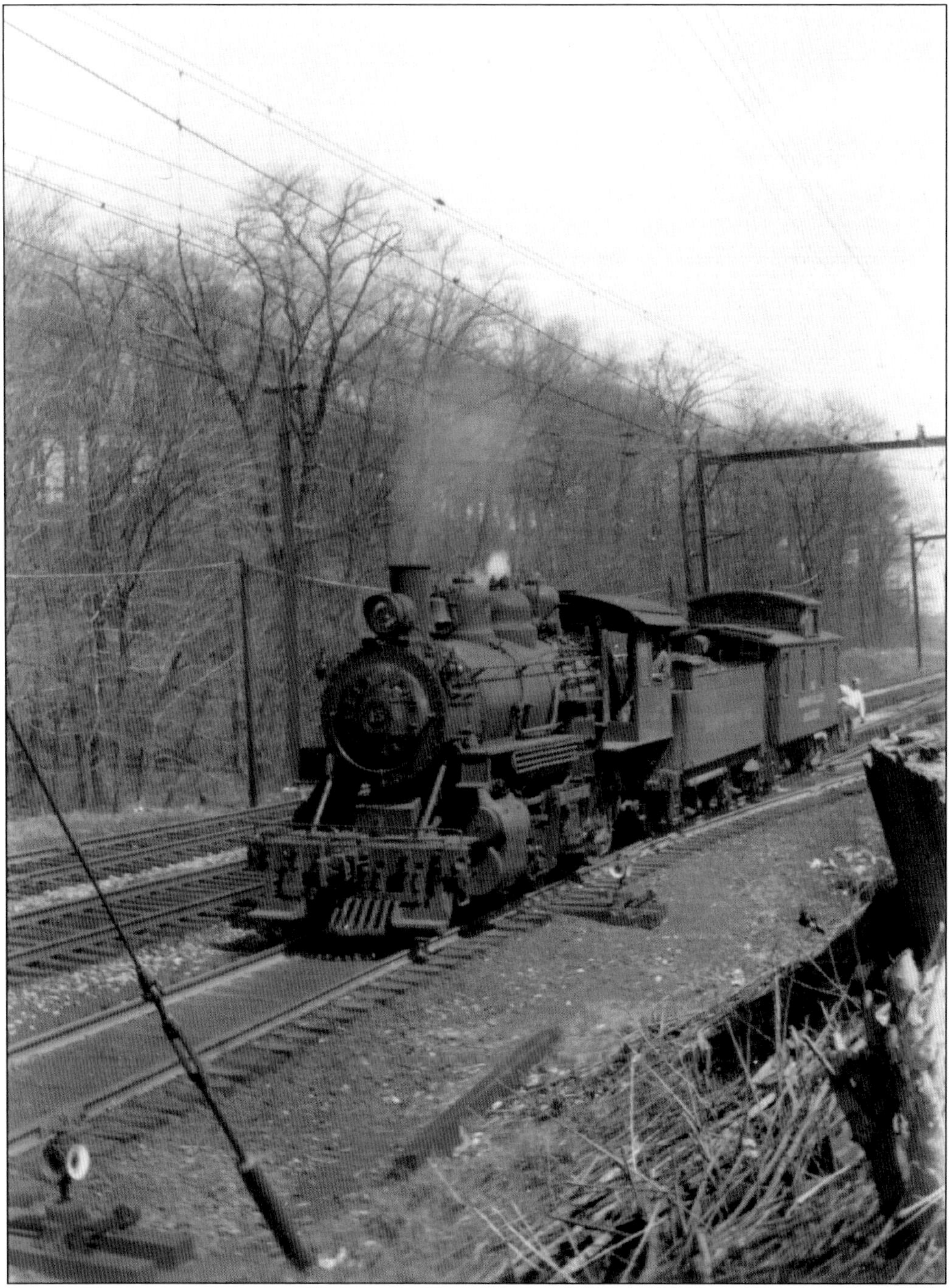

RV No. 15 and Caboose No. 102 are seen here on the Delaware, Lackawanna & Western interchange in Summit in April 1947. Edward J. Weber snapped this photograph after enjoying a daylong ride in the caboose from Kenilworth to Aldene and Summit.

This 1963 view of the Broad Street Bridge in Summit looks toward Overlook Mountain. (Photograph by Bruce Trampler.)

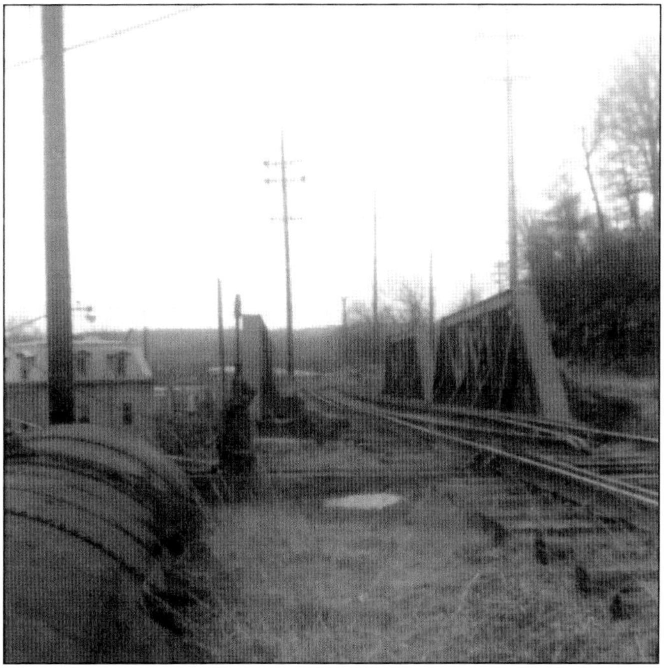

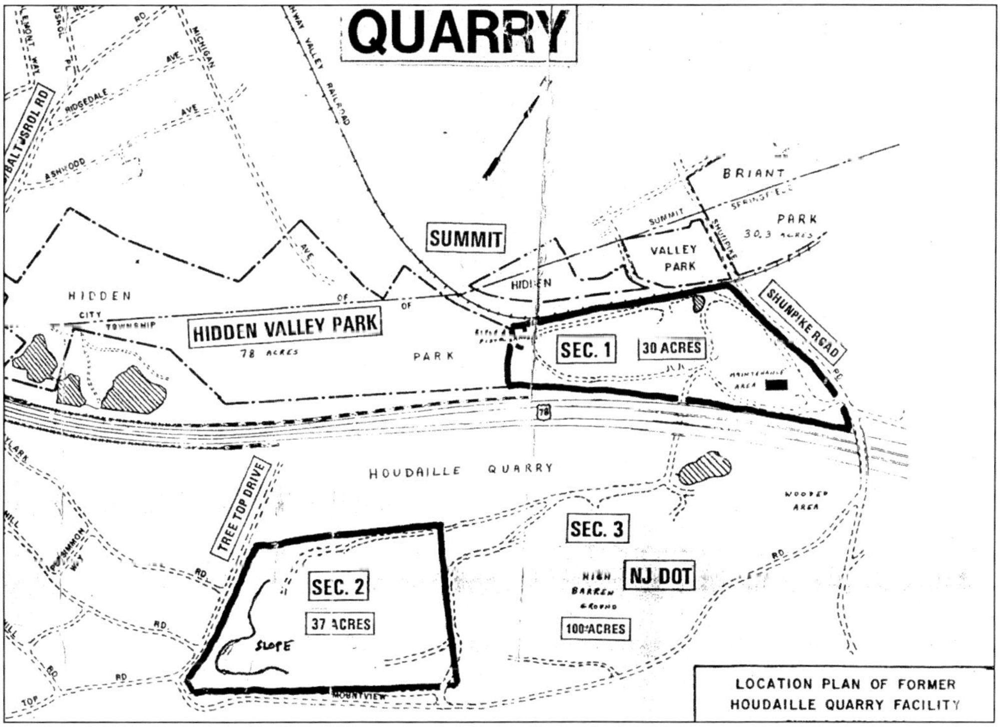

The Houdaille Quarry, which spanned the towns of Springfield and Summit, was one of the Rahway Valley Railroad's major customers for many years, shipping thousands of carloads of crushed stone along the line. This map shows the Rahway Valley Railroad right of way. Hidden Valley Park now borders the quarry, which is no longer in operation. (Courtesy of the Summit Historical Society.)

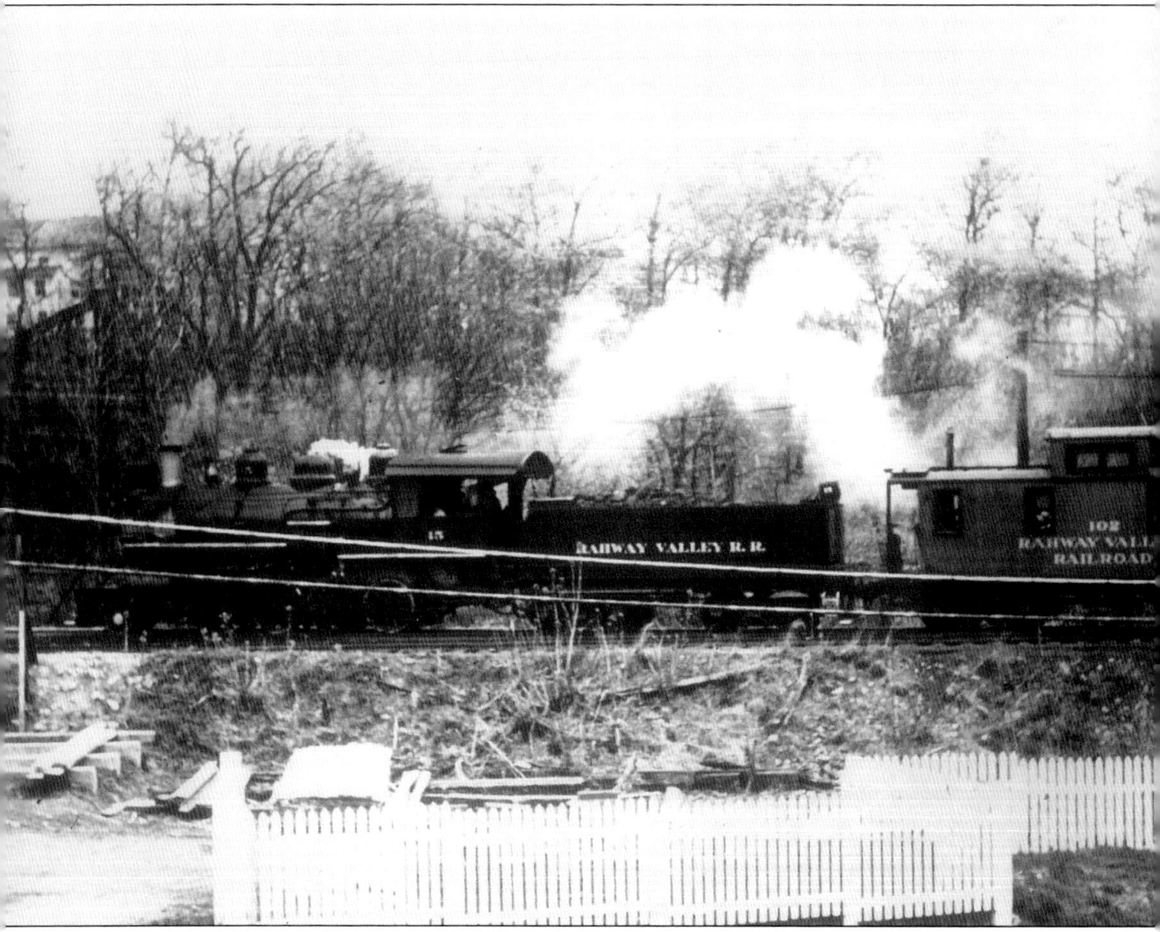

RV No. 15 and Caboose 102 have just crossed over the Broad Street Bridge in Summit, approaching the Delaware, Lackawanna, and Western Railroad. (Courtesy of the Summit Historical Society.)

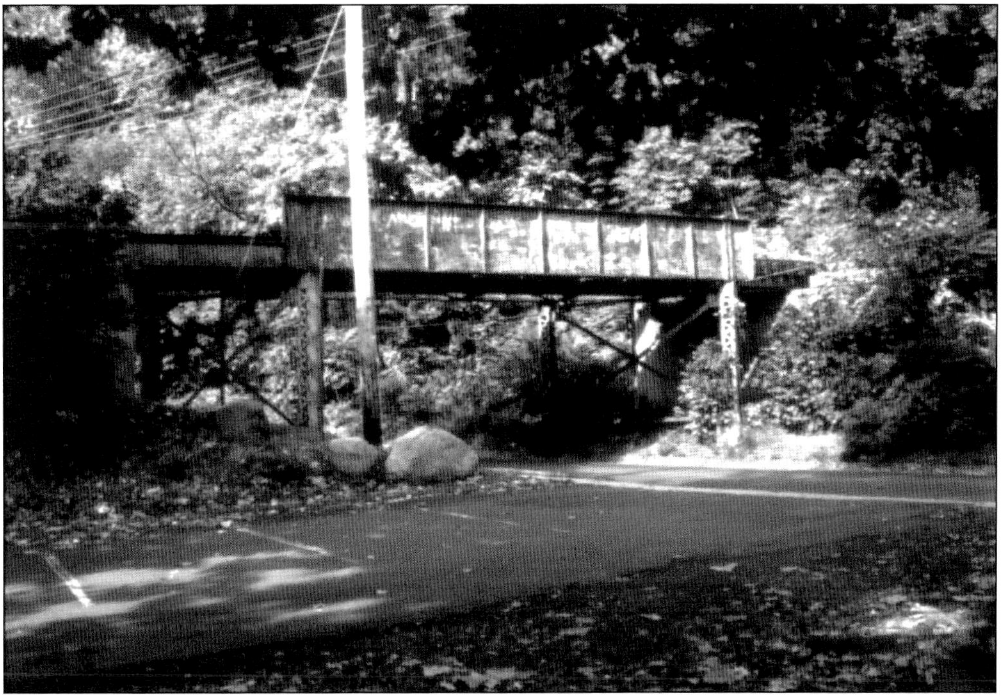

Here are street-level views of two Rahway Valley Railroad bridges spanning Morris Avenue (above) and Broad Street (below) in Summit. They were photographed in October 1991, shortly before the Rahway Valley was formally abandoned. The bridges were demolished several years later. (Photographs by John Sheppard.)

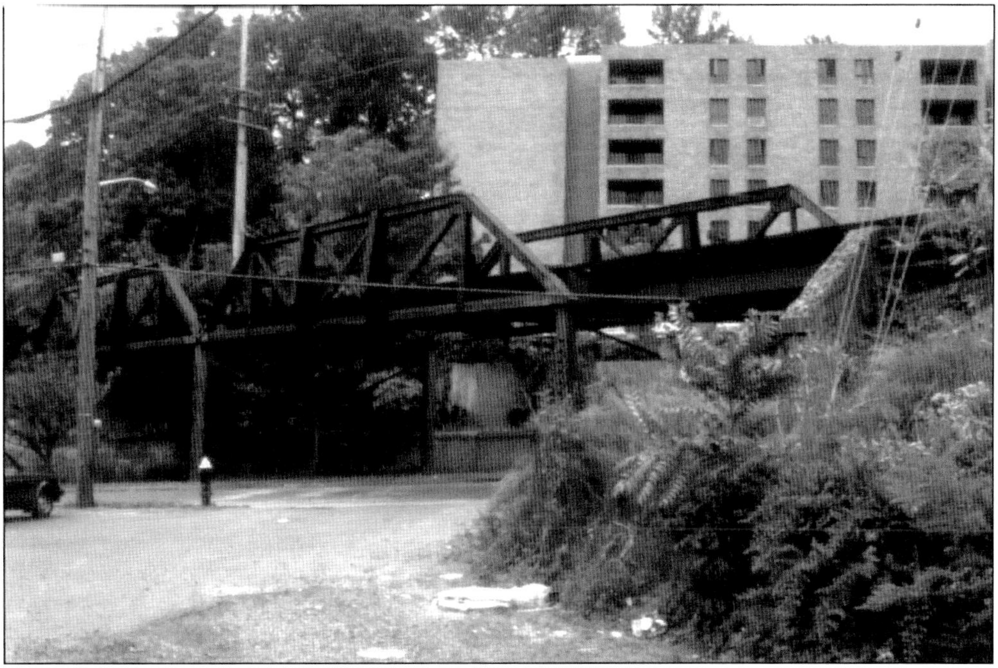

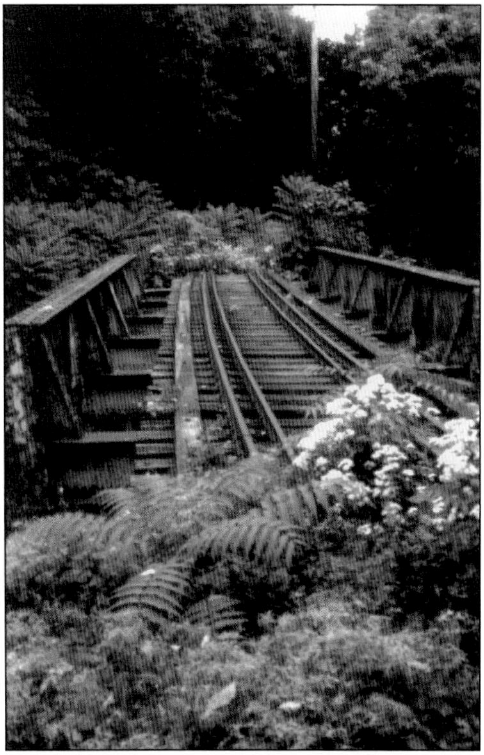

By October 1991, the Rahway Valley right of way in the Summit area was overgrown with thick vegetation, as shown in this view taken on the bridge over Morris Avenue. (Photograph by John Sheppard.)

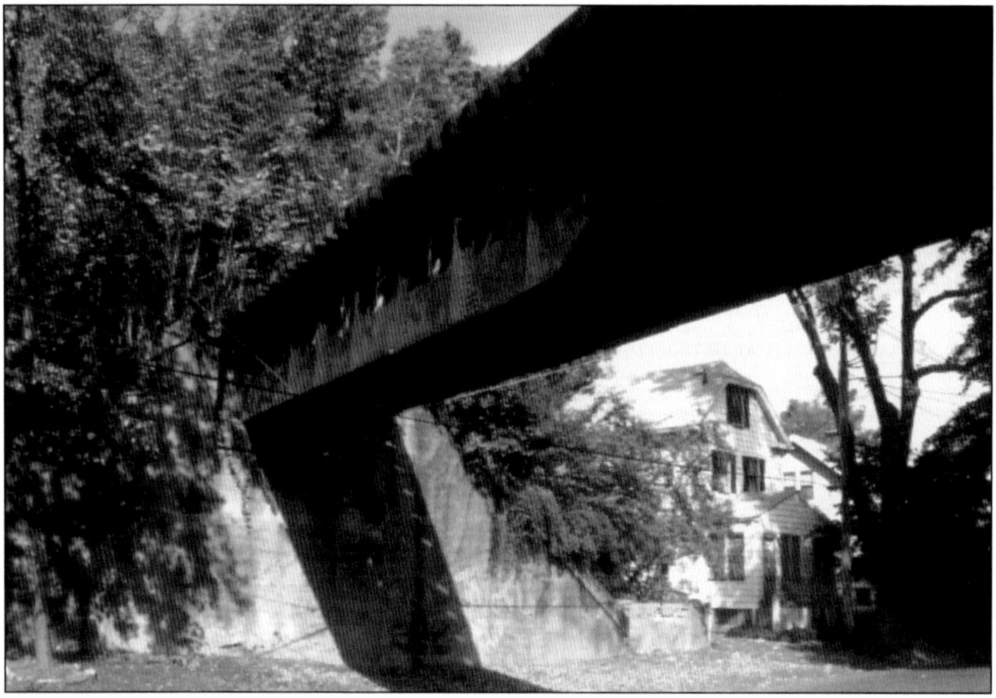

This high, narrow bridge spanning Ashwood Avenue in Summit is one of only two surviving Rahway Valley bridges left in town. The last Rahway Valley train to Summit ran in 1976. (Photograph by John Sheppard.)

Three

SPRINGFIELD: GOLF CLUBS AND RIVER CROSSINGS

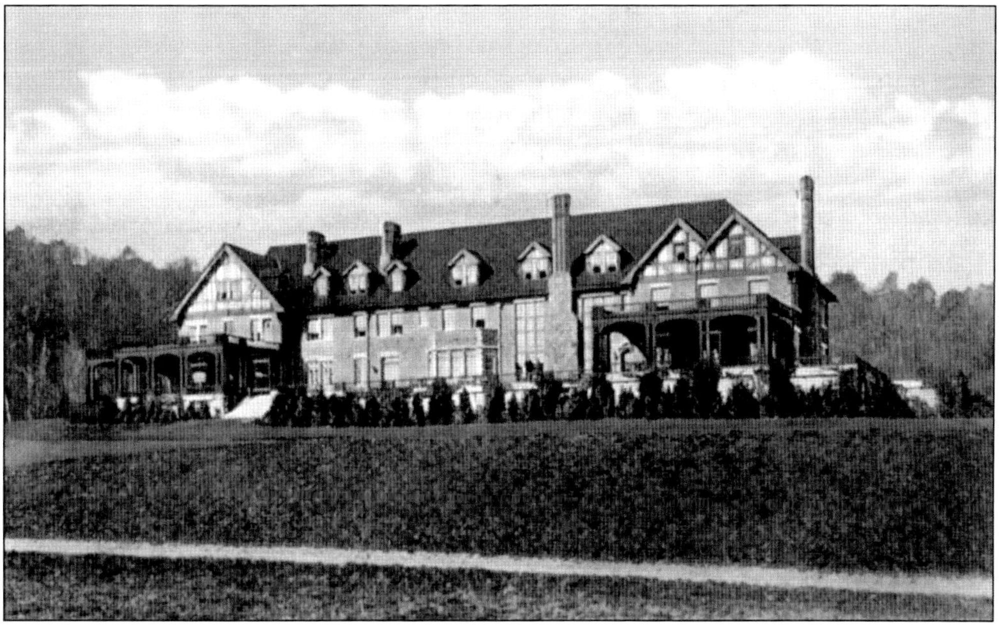

Louis Keller, who organized the Baltusrol Golf Club in Springfield in the mid-1890s, chartered the Rahway Valley Railroad in 1904. After consolidating with the New Orange Four Junction Railroad in 1905, he extended the railroad through Springfield into Summit, constructing a passenger station near the club. Baltusrol Station provided golfers convenient access from New York City via the Rahway Valley Railroad's connection with the Central Railroad of New Jersey at Aldene. (Collection of Donald A. Maxton.)

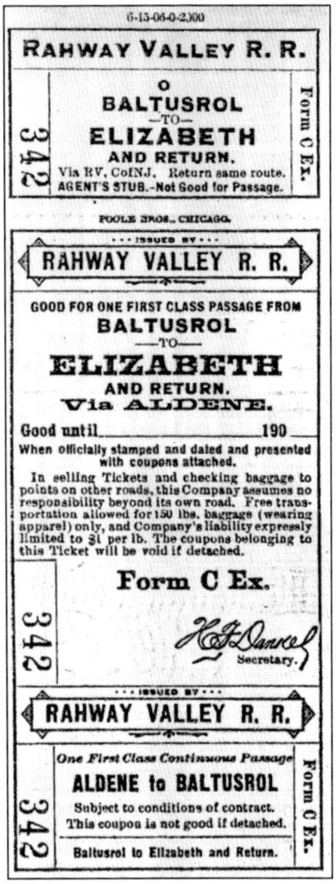

6-15-06-0-2,500

RAHWAY VALLEY R. R.

O
BALTUSROL
—TO—
ELIZABETH
AND RETURN.
Via RV, CofNJ. Return same route.
AGENT'S STUB.-Not Good for Passage.

342 Form C Ex.

POOLE BROS., CHICAGO.

··· ISSUED BY ···
RAHWAY VALLEY R. R.

GOOD FOR ONE FIRST CLASS PASSAGE FROM
BALTUSROL
—TO—
ELIZABETH
AND RETURN.
Via ALDENE.

Good until__________190___
When officially stamped and dated and presented with coupons attached.
In selling Tickets and checking baggage to points on other roads, this Company assumes no responsibility beyond its own road. Free transportation allowed for 150 lbs. baggage (wearing apparel) only, and Company's liability expressly limited to $1 per lb. The coupons belonging to this Ticket will be void if detached.

Form C Ex.

342

H. F. Dansel
Secretary.

··· ISSUED BY ···
RAHWAY VALLEY R. R.

One First Class Continuous Passage
ALDENE to BALTUSROL
Subject to conditions of contract.
This coupon is not good if detached.
Baltusrol to Elizabeth and Return.

342 Form C Ex.

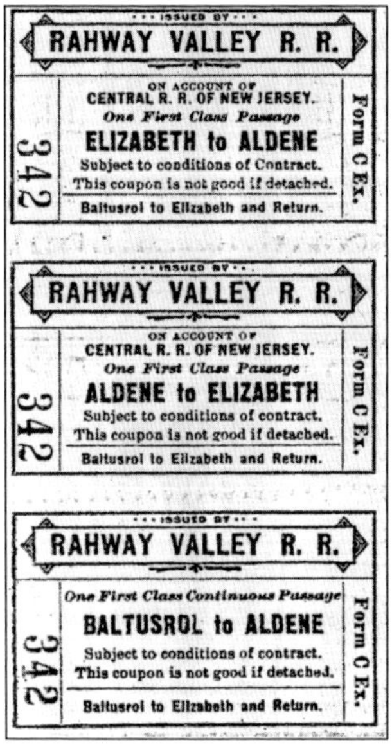

··· ISSUED BY ···
RAHWAY VALLEY R. R.

ON ACCOUNT OF
CENTRAL R. R. OF NEW JERSEY.
One First Class Passage
ELIZABETH to ALDENE
Subject to conditions of Contract.
This coupon is not good if detached.
Baltusrol to Elizabeth and Return.

342 Form C Ex.

··· ISSUED BY ···
RAHWAY VALLEY R. R.

ON ACCOUNT OF
CENTRAL R. R. OF NEW JERSEY.
One First Class Passage
ALDENE to ELIZABETH
Subject to conditions of contract.
This coupon is not good if detached.
Baltusrol to Elizabeth and Return.

342 Form C Ex.

··· ISSUED BY ···
RAHWAY VALLEY R. R.

One First Class Continuous Passage
BALTUSROL to ALDENE
Subject to conditions of contract.
This coupon is not good if detached.
Baltusrol to Elizabeth and Return.

342 Form C Ex.

Golfers heading for the greens at Baltusrol Golf Club in Springfield carried Rahway Valley passenger tickets like this one. The tickets were good for a round trip between Elizabeth and Baltusrol Station. (Collection of Donald A. Maxton.)

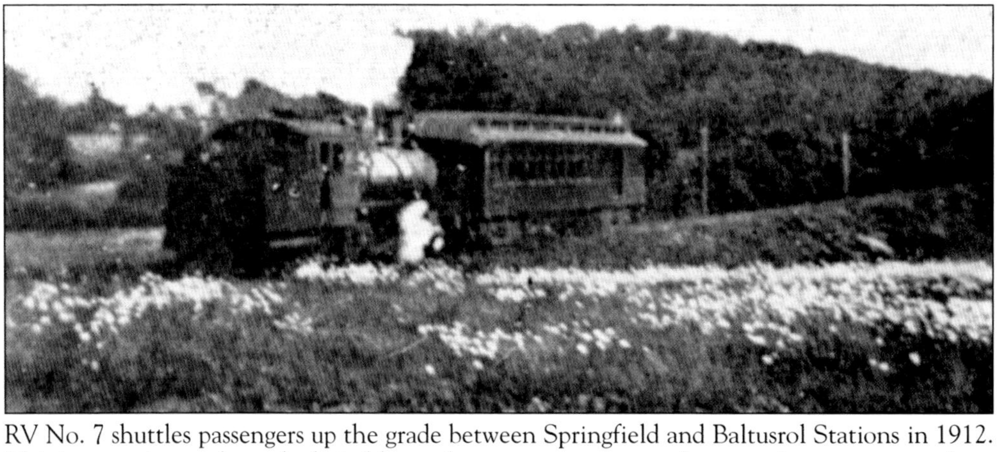

RV No. 7 shuttles passengers up the grade between Springfield and Baltusrol Stations in 1912. This locomotive performed admirably on the passenger runs up the steep four percent grade to Summit. Before the Rahway Valley Railroad acquired this engine, crews often had to cut long trains in Springfield, making two trips up and down the hill to complete the run. (Photograph by George B. Whitfield.)

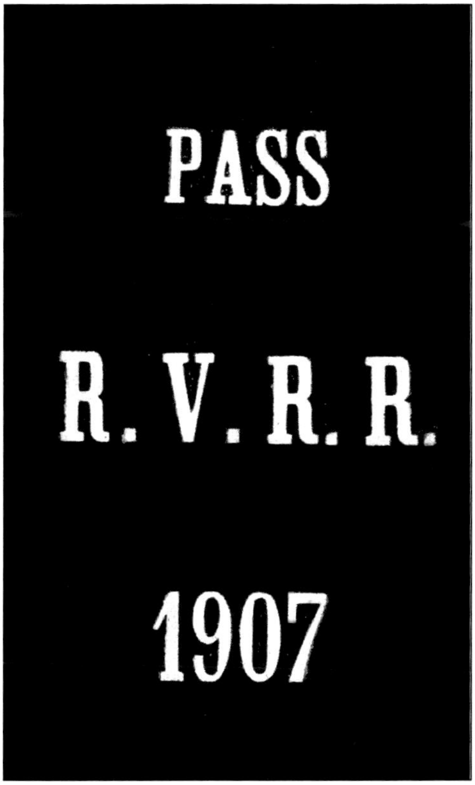

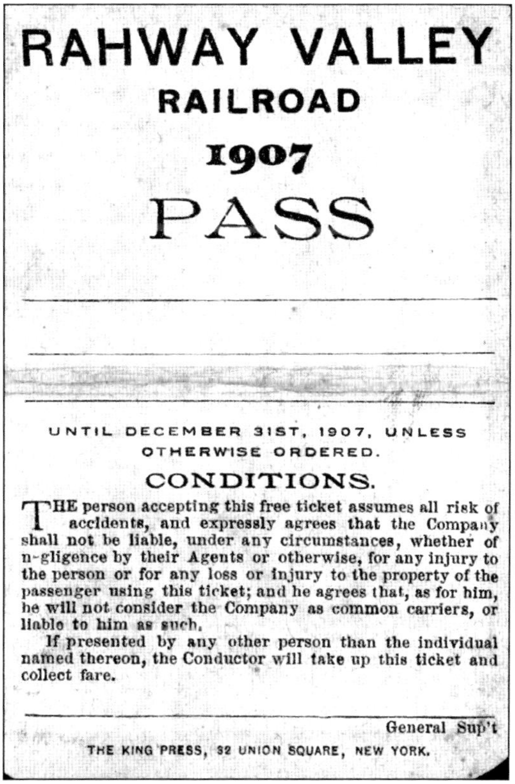

RAHWAY VALLEY
RAILROAD
1907
PASS

UNTIL DECEMBER 31ST, 1907, UNLESS OTHERWISE ORDERED.

CONDITIONS.

THE person accepting this free ticket assumes all risk of accidents, and expressly agrees that the Company shall not be liable, under any circumstances, whether of n-gligence by their Agents or otherwise, for any injury to the person or for any loss or injury to the property of the passenger using this ticket; and he agrees that, as for him, he will not consider the Company as common carriers, or liable to him as such.

If presented by any other person than the individual named thereon, the Conductor will take up this ticket and collect fare.

General Sup't

THE KING PRESS, 92 UNION SQUARE, NEW YORK.

Louis Keller's friends and business associates probably carried train passes like these, signed by the general manager of the Rahway Valley Railroad and entitling them to a year's worth of rides. One pass is mounted in a handsome gold-stamped, leather pocket case. (Courtesy of Scott Schnipper.)

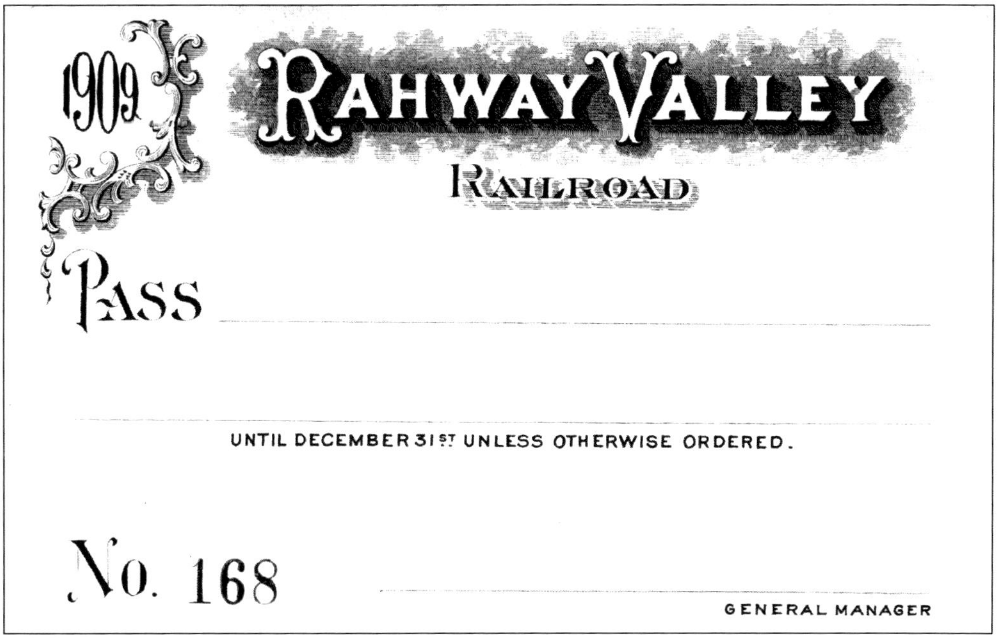

1909

RAHWAY VALLEY
RAILROAD

PASS

UNTIL DECEMBER 31ST UNLESS OTHERWISE ORDERED.

No. 168

GENERAL MANAGER

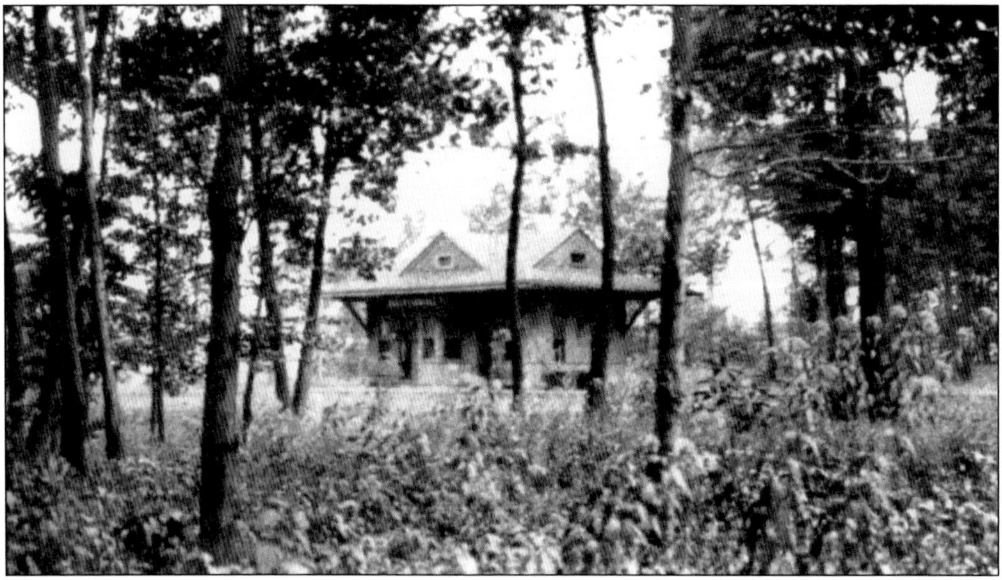

The Rahway Valley Railroad's picturesque "Golfer's Station" was located near the Baltusrol Golf Club. After the end of passenger service, the structure was served a variety of purposes including a stint as the Baltusrol Post Office, before suffering a substantial fire. The station was subsequently demolished. (Collection of Donald A. Maxton.)

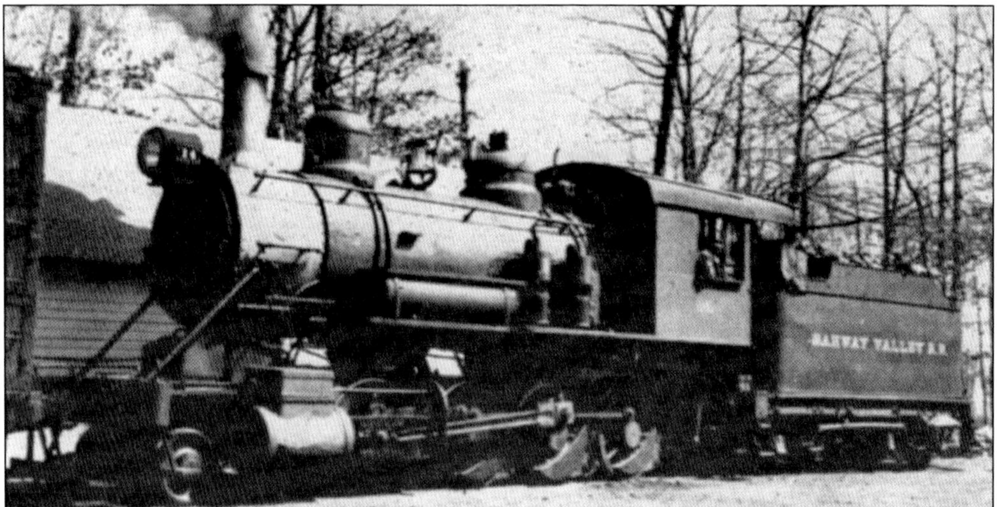

RV No. 14 waits on a siding at Baltusrol Station on March 19, 1934. (Photograph by Howard E. Johnston.)

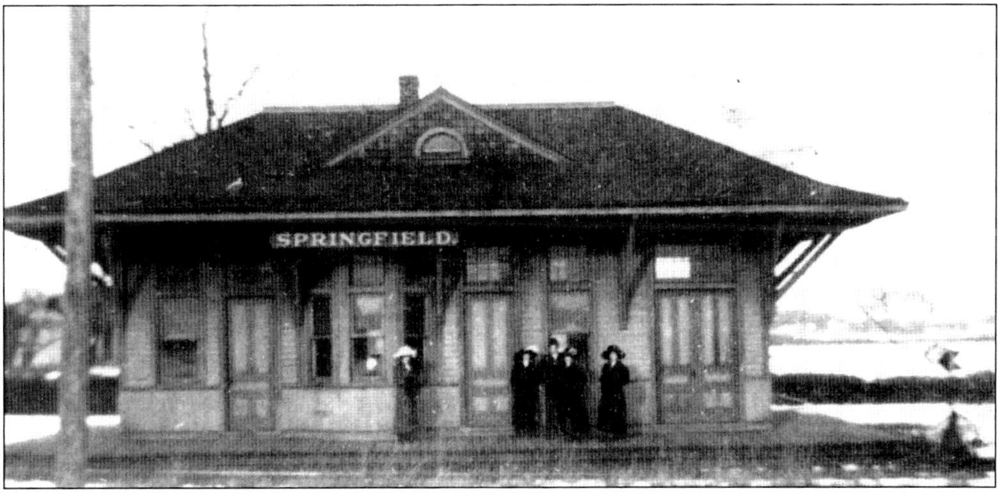

Several passengers pose in the earliest-known photograph of the Rahway Valley Railroad station in Springfield. This sturdy structure, constructed in the Stick style of architecture, is still standing. It is well cared for and currently houses a chiropractor. (Courtesy of Mary E. McCoy.)

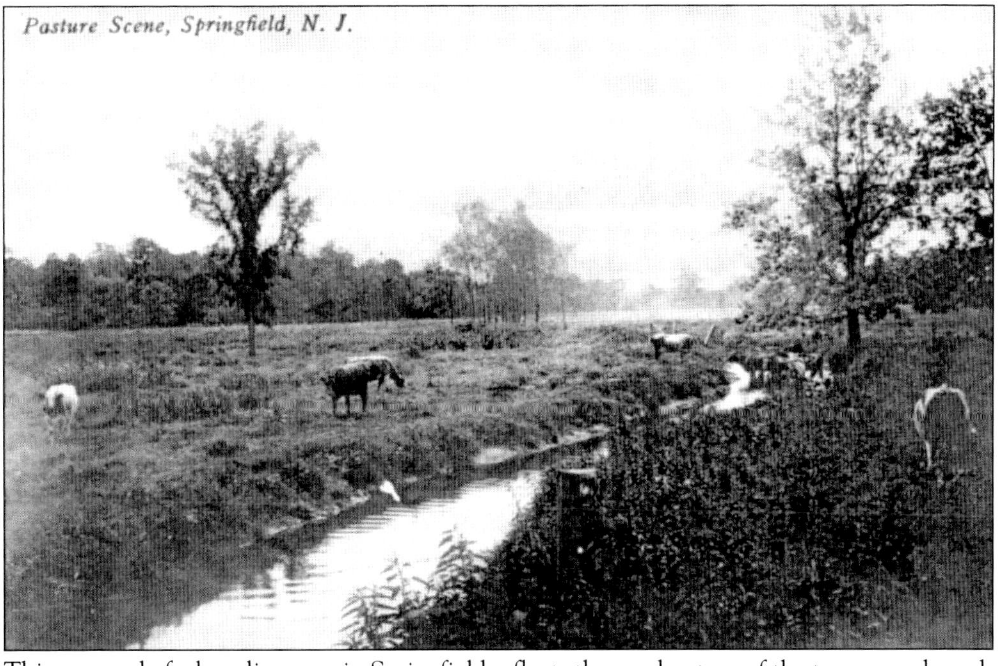

This postcard of a bucolic scene in Springfield reflects the rural nature of the town—and much of Union County—in the early years of the 20th century. (Collection of Donald A. Maxton.)

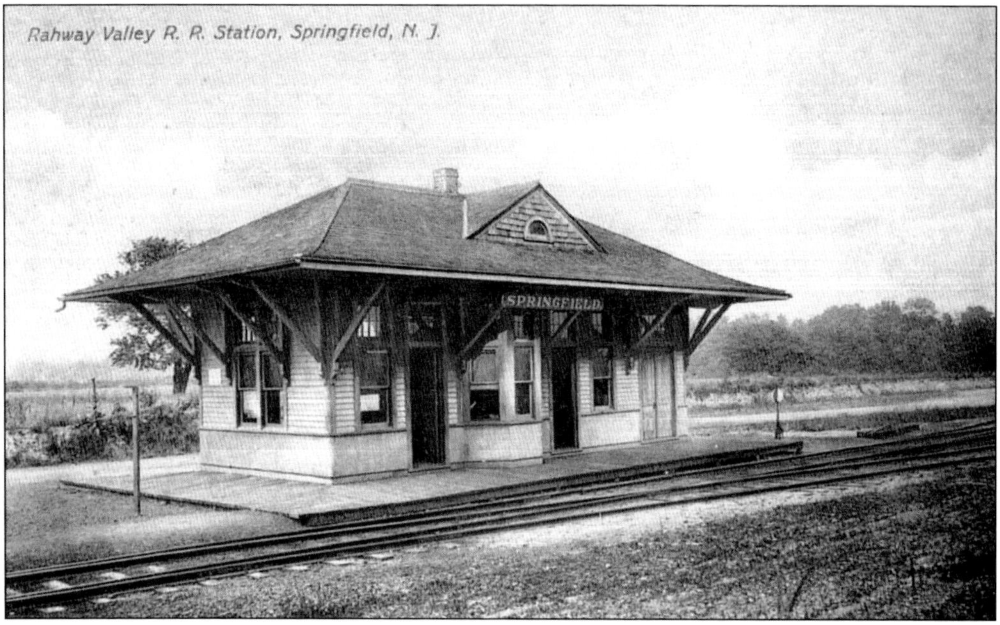

An early-20th-century postcard view of the Rahway Valley's Springfield Station shows that the surrounding countryside was still quite rural in character. The station is one of the few surviving structures on the railroad. (Collection of Donald A. Maxton.)

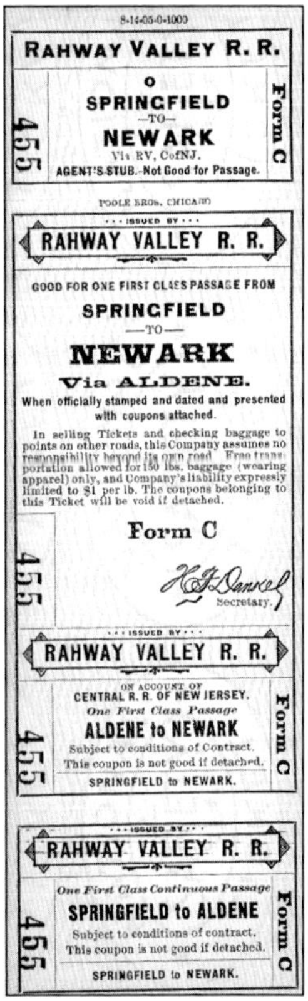

8-14-05-0-1000

RAHWAY VALLEY R. R.

O

SPRINGFIELD

—TO—

NEWARK

Via RV, CofNJ.

AGENT'S STUB.-Not Good for Passage.

Form C

455

POOLE BROS., CHICAGO

· · · ISSUED BY · · ·

RAHWAY VALLEY R. R.

GOOD FOR ONE FIRST CLASS PASSAGE FROM

SPRINGFIELD

—TO—

NEWARK

Via ALDENE.

When officially stamped and dated and presented with coupons attached.

In selling Tickets and checking baggage to points on other roads, this Company assumes no responsibility beyond its own road. Free transportation allowed for 150 lbs. baggage (wearing apparel) only, and Company's liability expressly limited to $1 per lb. The coupons belonging to this Ticket will be void if detached.

Form C

455

H. F. Dansel
Secretary.

· · · ISSUED BY · · ·

RAHWAY VALLEY R. R.

ON ACCOUNT OF
CENTRAL R. R. OF NEW JERSEY.

One First Class Passage

ALDENE to NEWARK

Subject to conditions of Contract.
This coupon is not good if detached.

SPRINGFIELD to NEWARK.

Form C

455

· · · ISSUED BY · · ·

RAHWAY VALLEY R. R.

One First Class Continuous Passage

SPRINGFIELD to ALDENE

Subject to conditions of contract.
This coupon is not good if detached.

SPRINGFIELD to NEWARK.

Form C

455

This round-trip ticket provided service between Springfield and Newark, with a transfer at the Aldene Station in Roselle. (Collection of Donald A. Maxton.)

Here is the Rahway Valley's sturdy truss bridge spanning the Rahway River in Springfield, in a view looking toward the Meisel Avenue grade crossing. When the railroad was being extended from Kenilworth to Summit, the construction of this bridge posed quite a problem, due to the marshy ground in the area. This watershed area experienced chronic flooding for many years. The bridge remains in place, although it is nearly impossible to see because of vegetation. (Photograph by Bruce Trampler.)

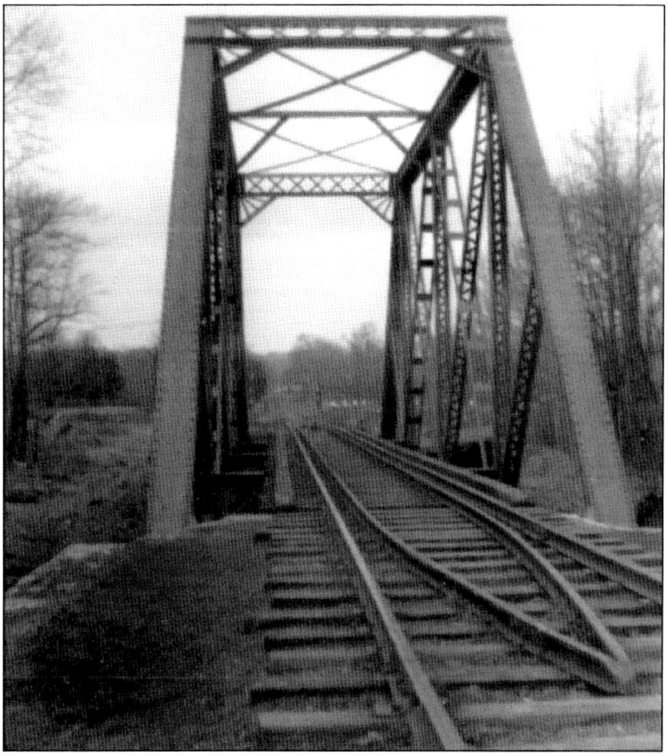

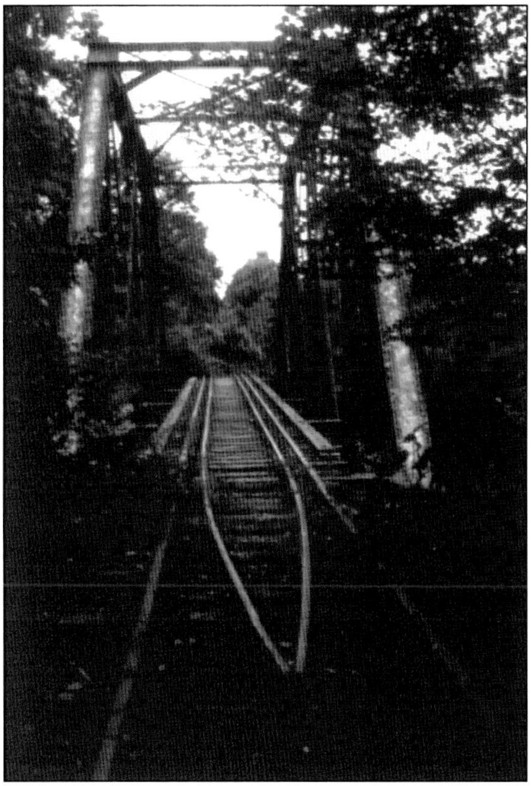

This view of the Rahway River Bridge in October 1991 shows that dense vegetation has covered the tracks on the far side. (Photograph by John Sheppard.)

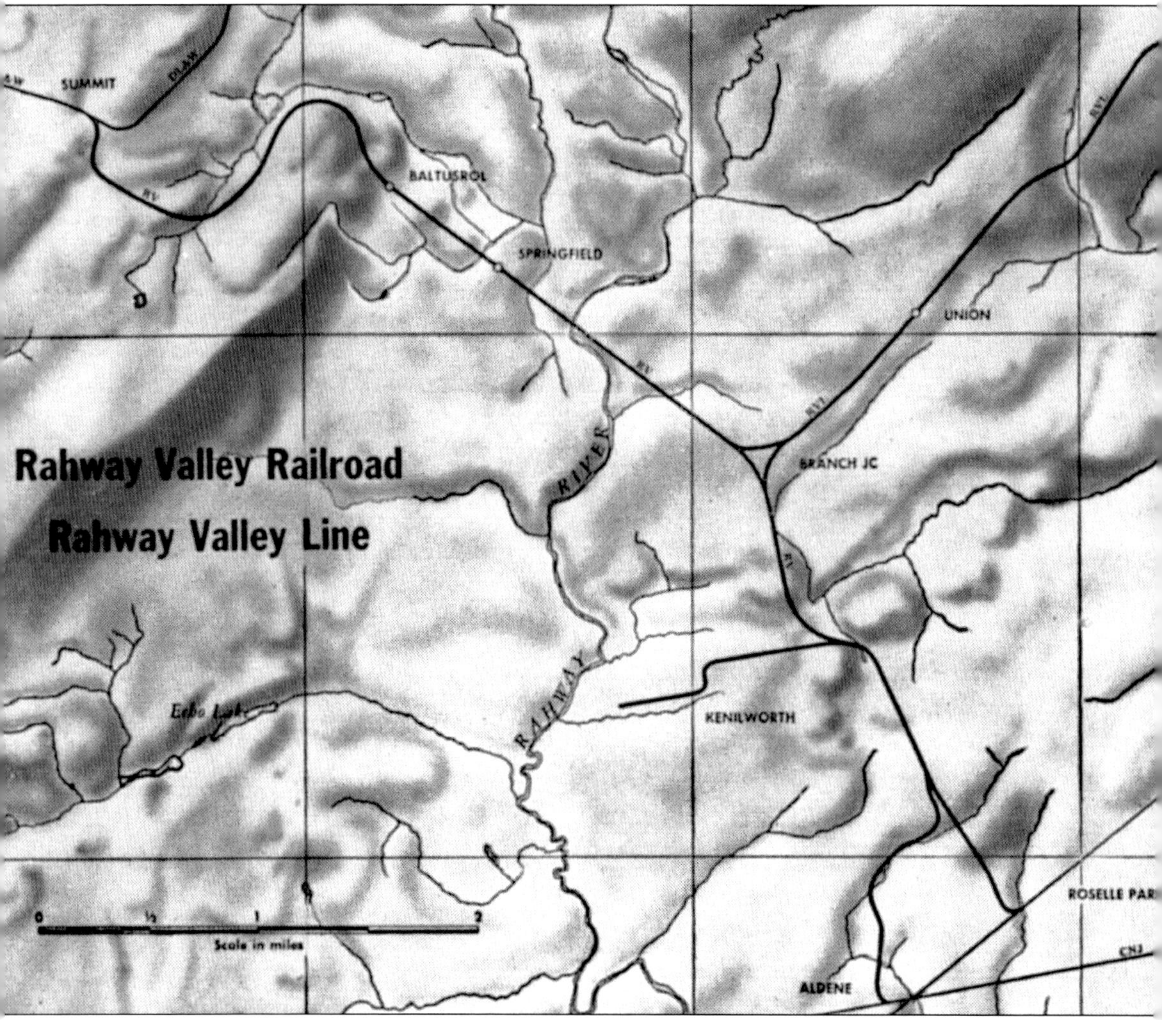

This map shows that the Rahway Valley Railroad crossed the Rahway River and several creeks on its way through Springfield and Summit. (Courtesy of *Trains* magazine.)

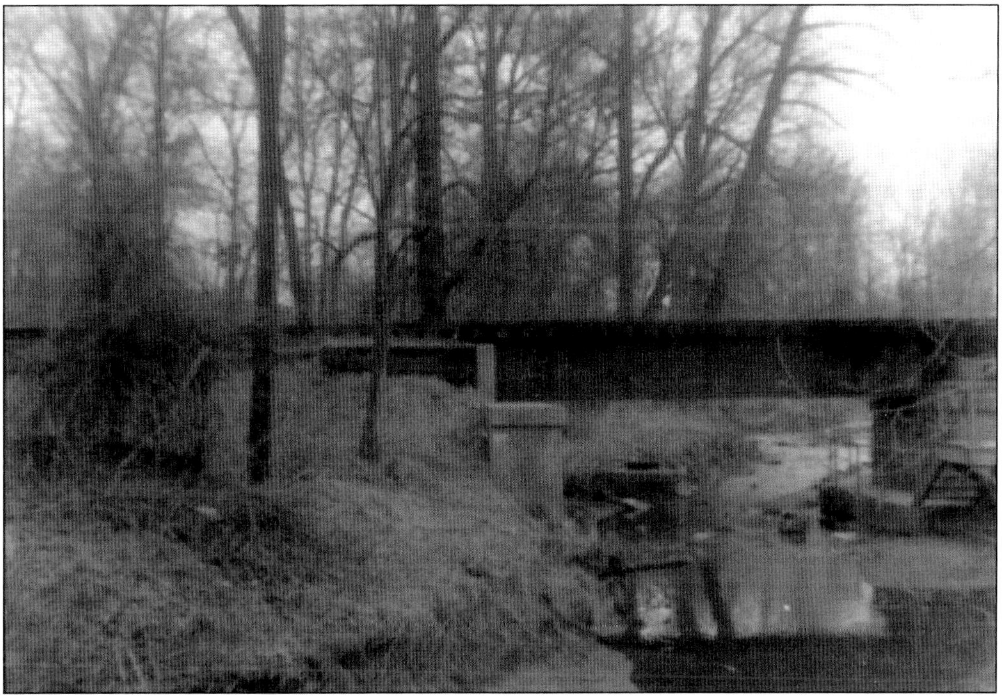

Here is a tranquil view of the rarely seen Rahway Valley bridge over Van Winkle's Creek, near the Springfield Station. (Photograph by Bruce Trampler.)

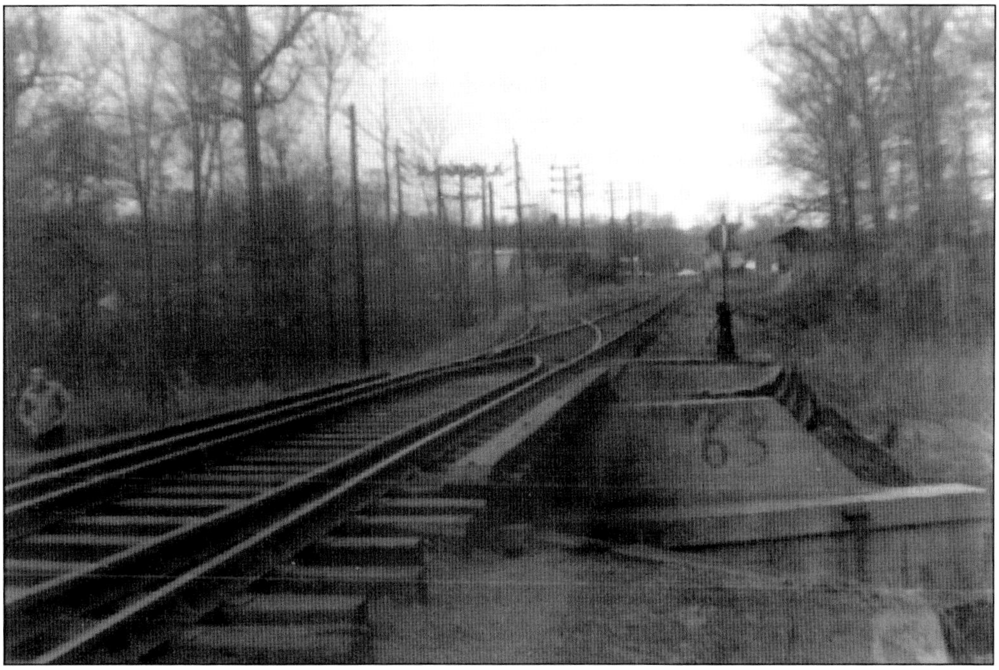

Another view of the Van Winkle's Creek Bridge shows a hand switch and freight siding. The Springfield Station and busy Mountain Avenue are just ahead. These photographs were taken in the early 1960s, when the Rahway Valley conducted a busy freight service in the area. (Photograph by Bruce Trampler.)

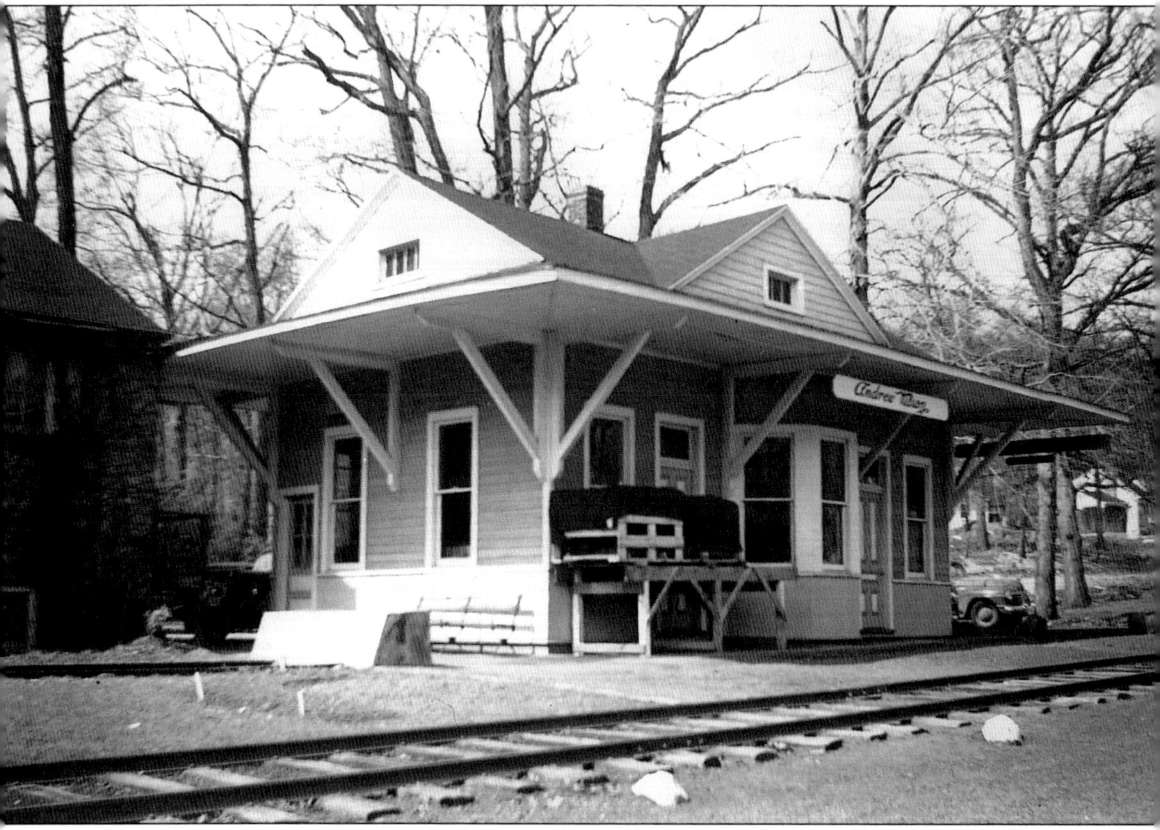

When passenger service was discontinued on the Rahway Valley Railroad, the Baltusrol Station in Springfield was leased out for a variety of purposes; it even served as a post office. On April 8, 1950, when this photograph was taken, it was the office of Andrew Wilson, a company specializing in DDT products, such as disinfectants, fertilizer, and agricultural chemicals. (Photograph by Edward H. Weber.)

This August 1963 view looks north toward Baltusrol Station, which is just visible on the left behind the boxcar. (Photograph by Bruce Trampler.)

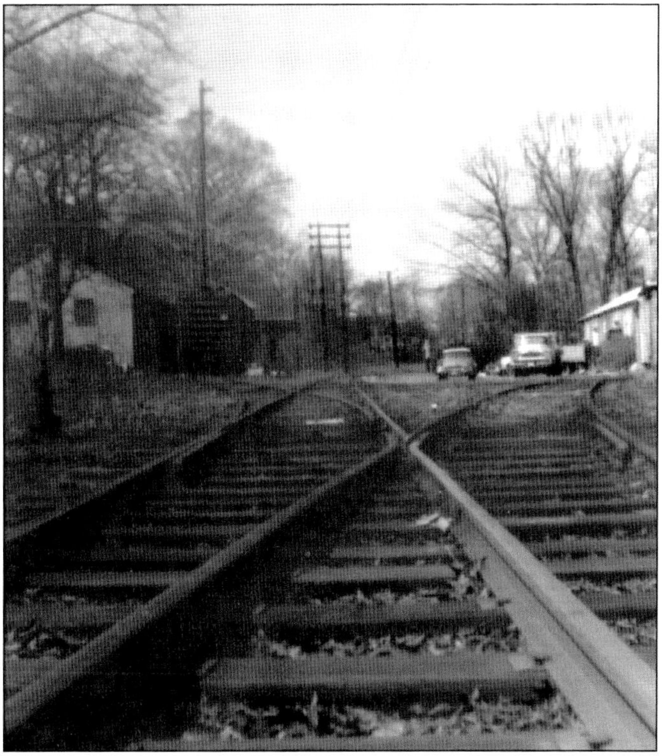

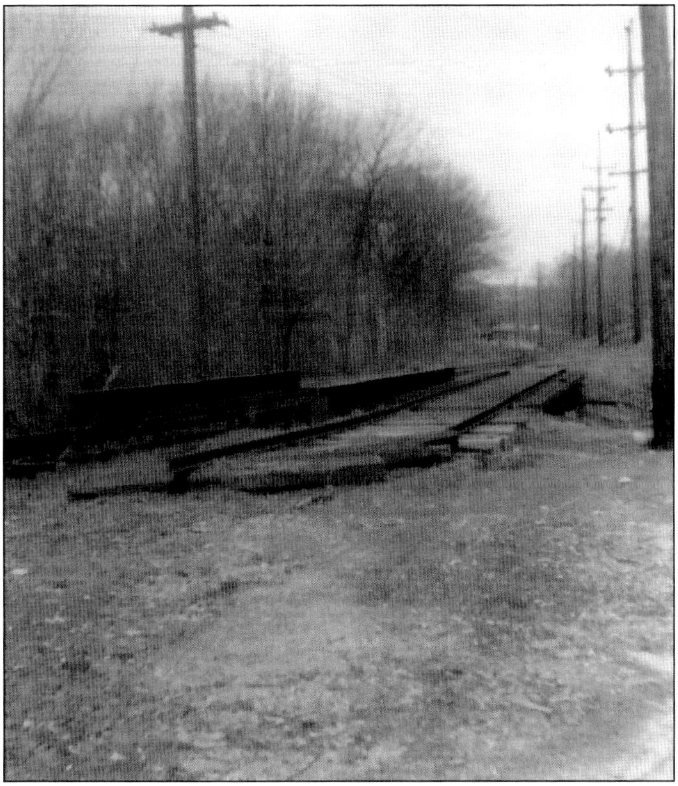

This 1963 view shows Rahway Valley's twin bridges over Orchard Street (now Shunpike Road) in Springfield, near the border of Summit. The bridge on the left carried the mainline while the one on the right carried a siding built to serve the Houdaille Stone Quarry. (Photograph by Bruce Trampler.)

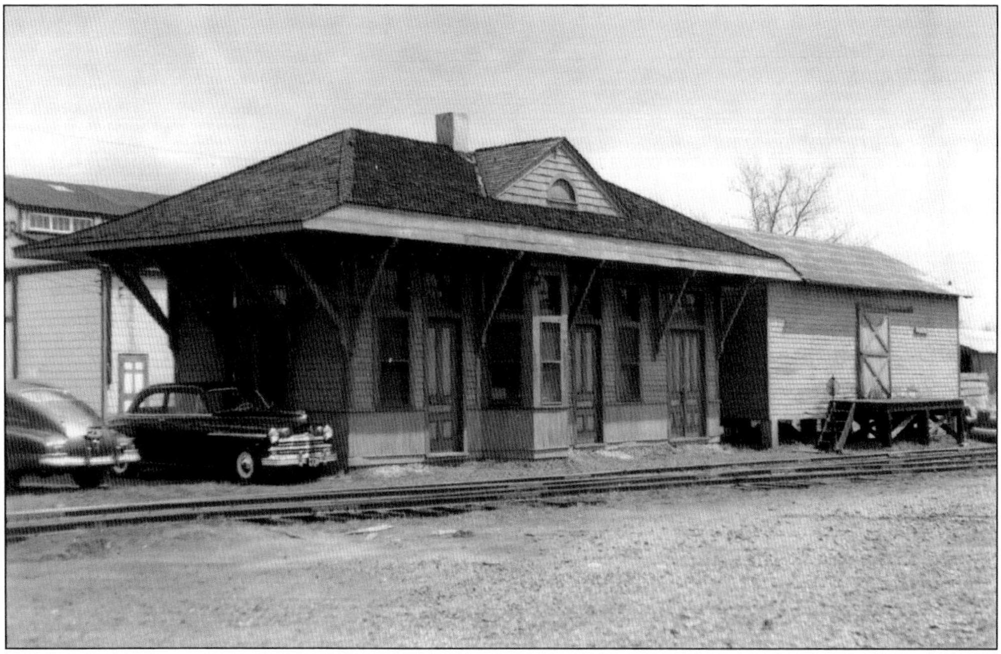

This 1951 photograph shows the Rahway Valley Railroad's Springfield Station. Compare this photo to the one on page 69; notice the brim of the station's roof was cut off. This was done to accommodate wider freight cars without having to move the entire structure. (Photograph by Edward H. Weber.)

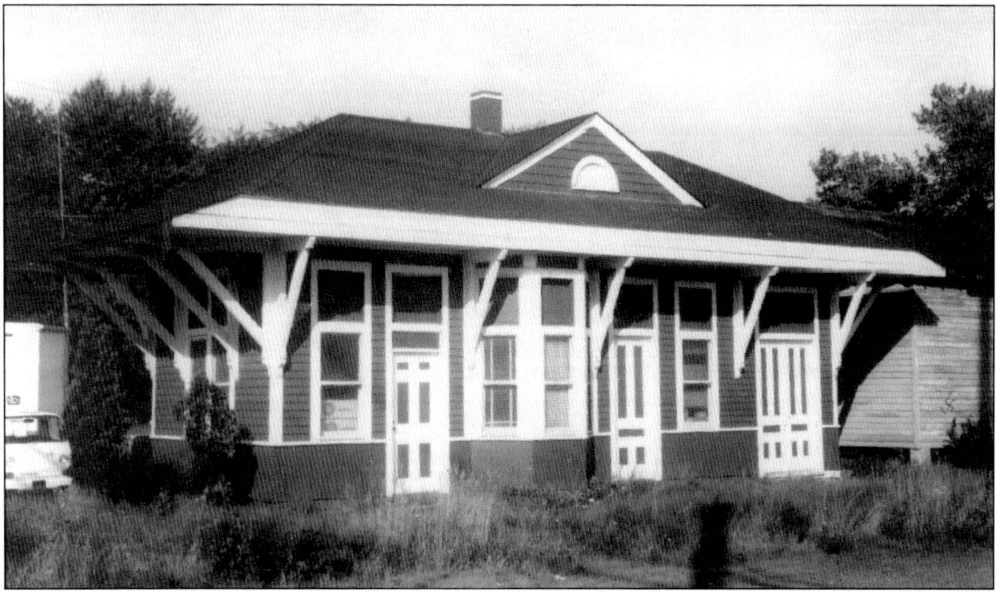

This view of the Springfield Station shows a small structure adjacent to the depot that was used to store freight in this 1970 photograph. The station building looks much the same today, as it did when the U.S. Open passed by it in June 1980, but the freight building has been demolished. (Courtesy of Scott Schnipper.)

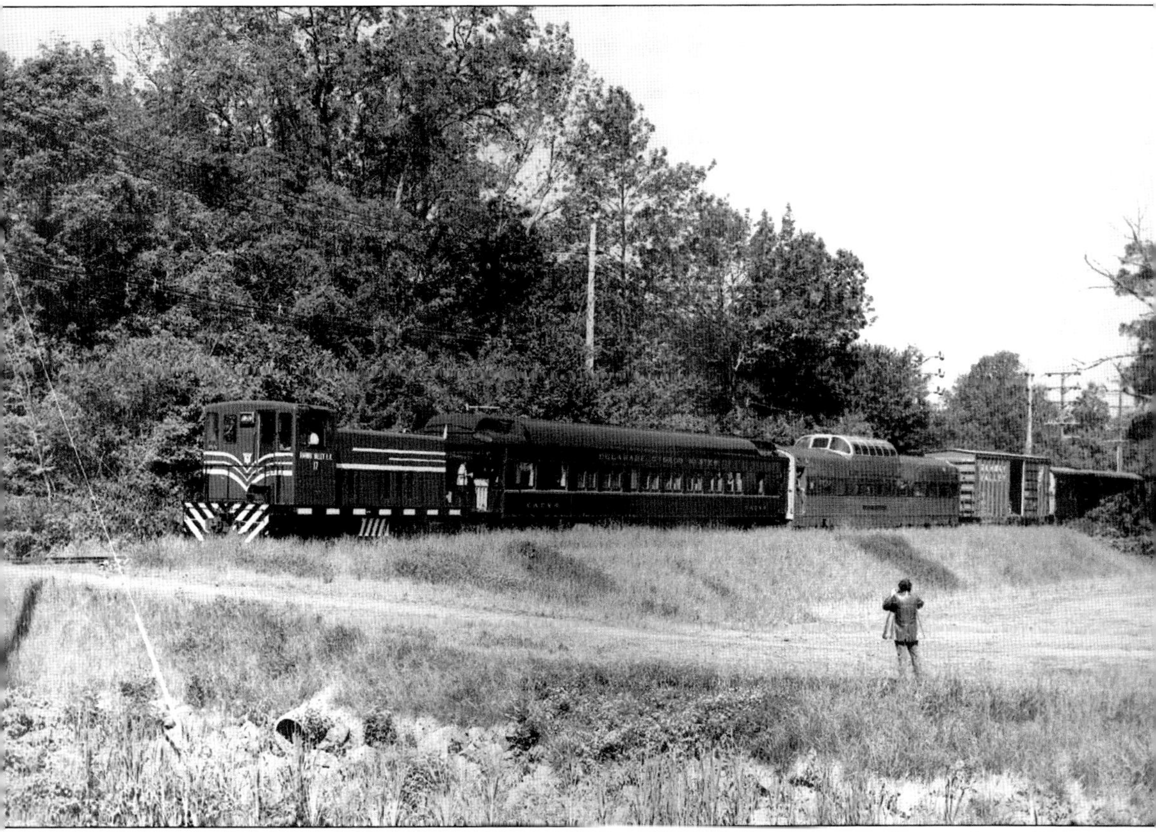

Passenger service on the Rahway Valley Railroad officially ended in 1919, and more than 60 years would pass before another passenger run took place on the line. During the 1980 U.S. Open at Baltusrol Golf Club in Springfield, the Rahway Valley Railroad, in conjunction with the United Counties Trust Company (UCTC), sponsored the *UCTC Limited*, a passenger excursion train from Kenilworth to Baltusrol. The special ran from June 9, 1980, to June 15, 1980, turning back the clock and providing a wonderful treat to golfing fans and rail photographers. (Photograph by Bob Pennisi, Railroad Avenue Enterprises.)

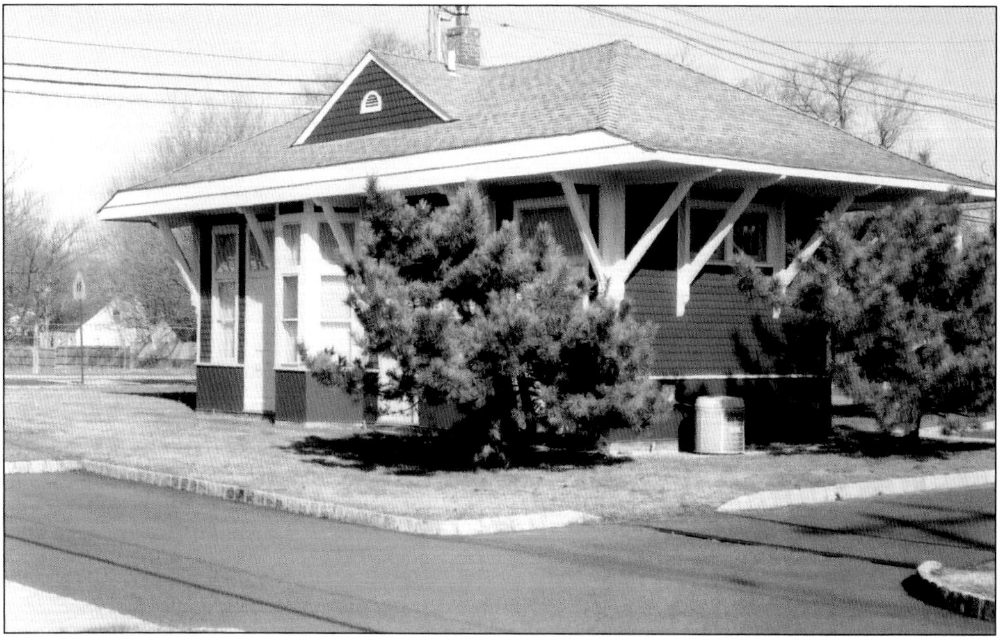

The Springfield passenger station has maintained its looks over the years, thanks to regular upkeep and preservation of its architectural detail. It is considered to be one of Union County's significant old structures. Today, the freight building is gone and most of the tracks are covered by grass and macadam, but it is easy to picture a train approaching if you spend a few moments in front of the station, as so many travelers did in the past. (Photograph by Donald A. Maxton.)

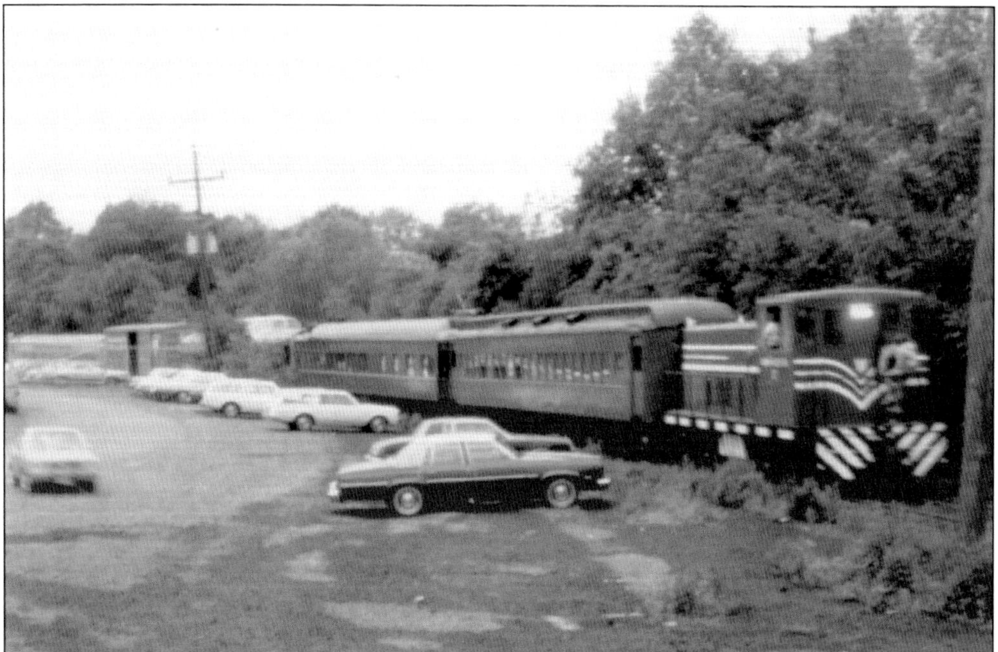

The *UCTC Limited* slowly runs down the Rahway Valley's rails toward the Kenilworth Station. (Photograph by Doug Chieff.)

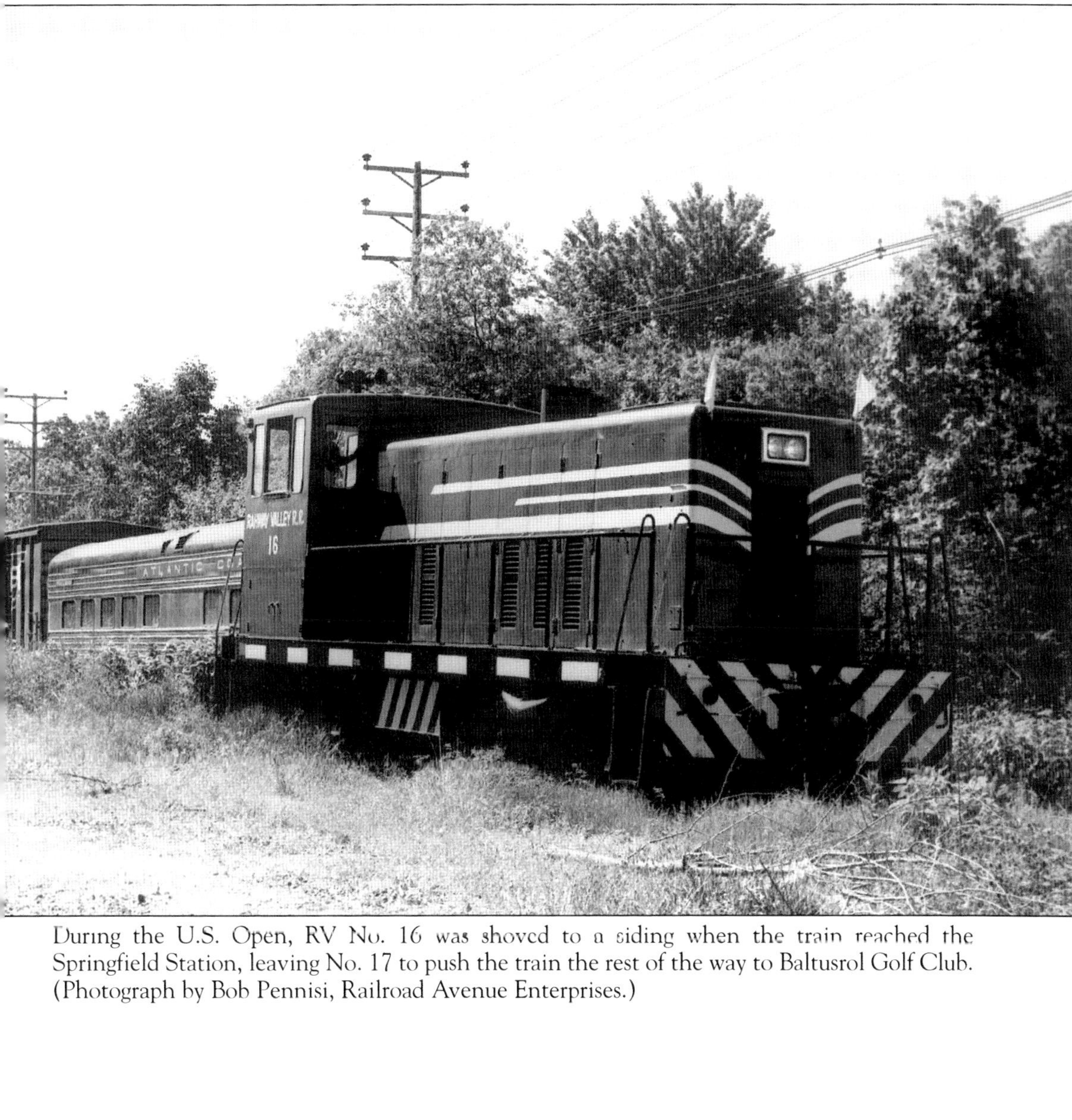

During the U.S. Open, RV No. 16 was shoved to a siding when the train reached the Springfield Station, leaving No. 17 to push the train the rest of the way to Baltusrol Golf Club. (Photograph by Bob Pennisi, Railroad Avenue Enterprises.)

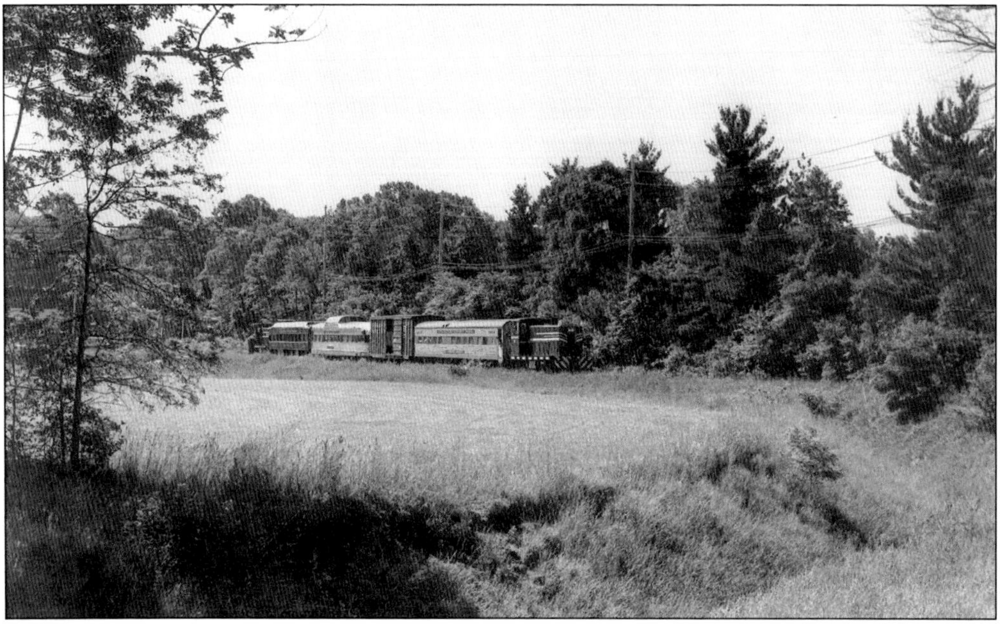

RV Nos. 16 and 17 operated the *UCTC Limited* in a push-pull arrangement. The train consisted of the two General Electric 70-tonners and several luxurious passenger cars, powered by a generator in a Rahway Valley boxcar. Passengers were treated to meals and musical entertainment. (Photograph by Bob Pennisi, Railroad Avenue Enterprises.)

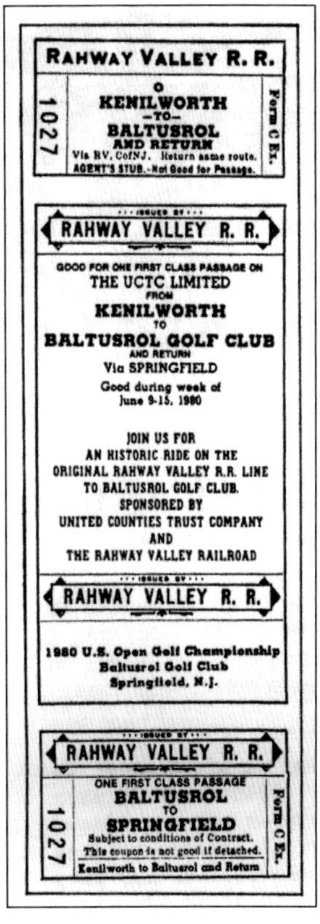

RAHWAY VALLEY R. R.
1027
KENILWORTH
—TO—
BALTUSROL
AND RETURN
Via RV, CofNJ. Return same route.
AGENT'S STUB.–Not Good for Passage.
Form C Ex.

ISSUED BY
RAHWAY VALLEY R. R.
GOOD FOR ONE FIRST CLASS PASSAGE ON
THE UCTC LIMITED
FROM
KENILWORTH
TO
BALTUSROL GOLF CLUB
AND RETURN
Via SPRINGFIELD
Good during week of
June 9-15, 1980

JOIN US FOR
AN HISTORIC RIDE ON THE
ORIGINAL RAHWAY VALLEY R.R. LINE
TO BALTUSROL GOLF CLUB.
SPONSORED BY
UNITED COUNTIES TRUST COMPANY
AND
THE RAHWAY VALLEY RAILROAD

ISSUED BY
RAHWAY VALLEY R. R.
1980 U.S. Open Golf Championship
Baltusrol Golf Club
Springfield, N.J.

ISSUED BY
RAHWAY VALLEY R. R.
1027
ONE FIRST CLASS PASSAGE
BALTUSROL
TO
SPRINGFIELD
Subject to conditions of Contract.
This coupon is not good if detached.
Kenilworth to Baltusrol and Return
Form C Ex.

Special souvenir tickets were printed to commemorate the *UCTC Limited* from Kenilworth to Baltusrol during the U.S. Open in 1980. (Courtesy of Jon Franz.)

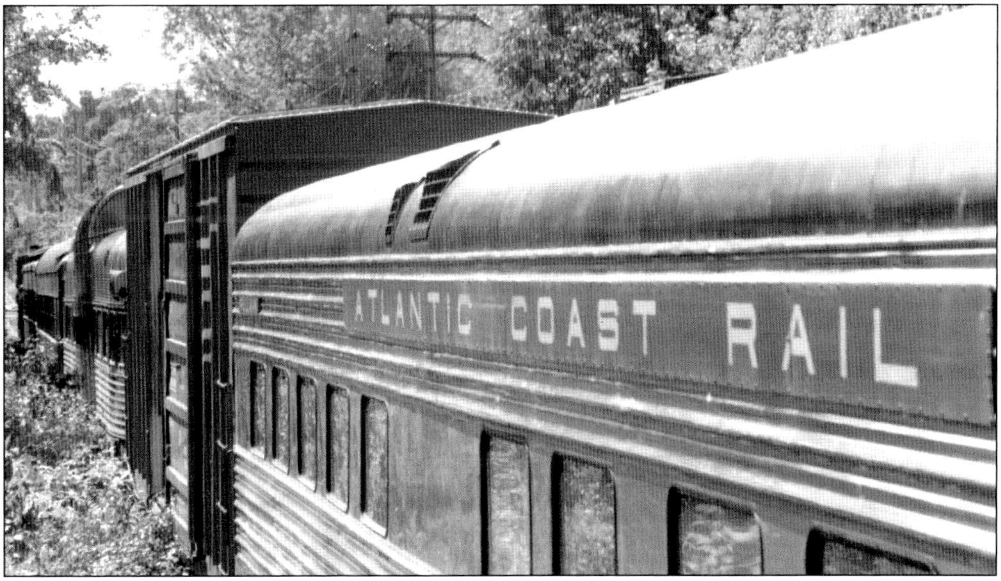

This view from the cab of RV No. 16 provides a close-up look at Atlantic Coast Rail's *Virginia Beach* passenger coach, which could also be seen at the Kenilworth Station, where its owner leased track space. (Photograph by Ronald F. Pietranowicz.)

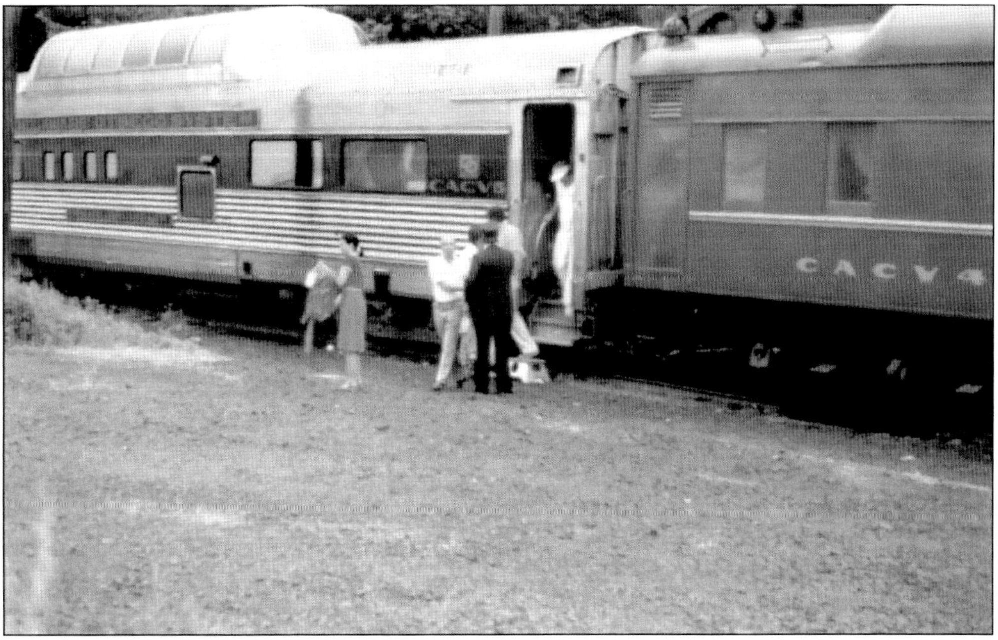

Several passengers disembark from a Cooperstown & Charlotte Valley dome car in Kenilworth following a day at the 1980 U.S. Open and a round trip on the *UCTC Limited*. The passenger cars were leased from the Delaware Otsego Corporation, which would assume freight operations on the Rahway Valley six years later. The names of the cars, which bore Cooperstown & Charlotte Valley reporting marks, were *Otsego Lake*, *Great Sadandaga*, and *Lake Canadarago*. (Photograph by Doug Chieff.)

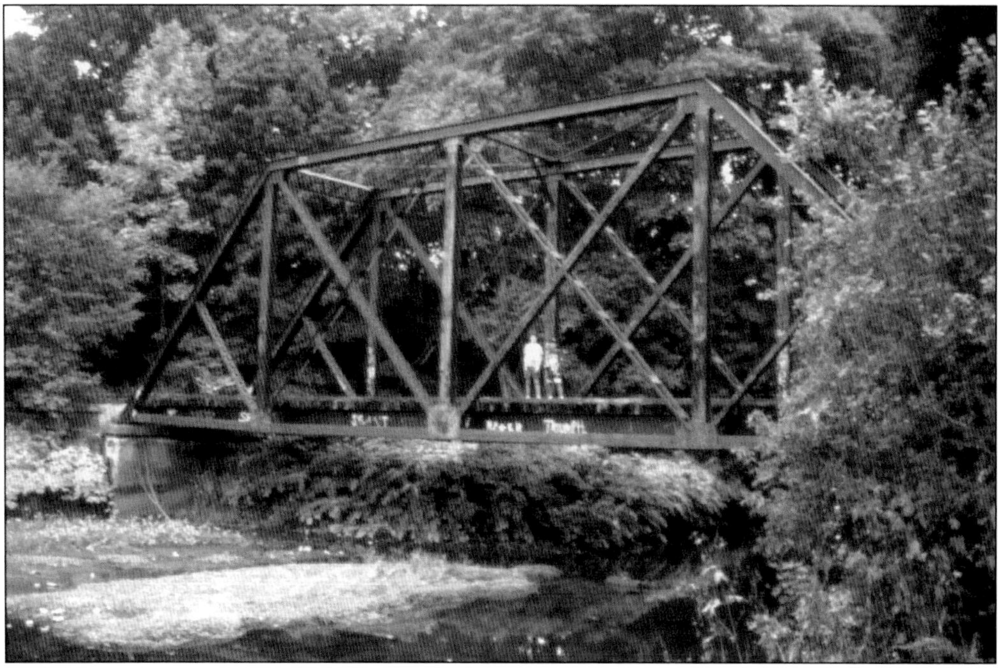

This view of the Rahway River span in Springfield was photographed in October 1991, when the bridge was still visible from Meisel Avenue. After the Springfield Station, this is probably the most impressive surviving structure on the line. (Photograph by John Sheppard.)

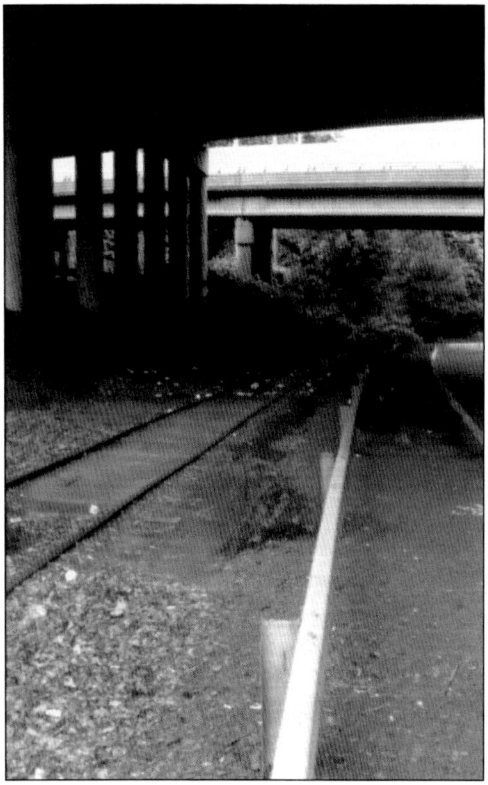

Every day, thousands of drivers traveling on Interstate 78 cross over the Rahway Valley Railroad. During its construction, I-78 bridged the railroad leaving it untouched, but RV trains often halted for heavy construction equipment at this location. (Photograph by John Sheppard.)

Four

Union and Maplewood: "A Great Place for Anthracite"

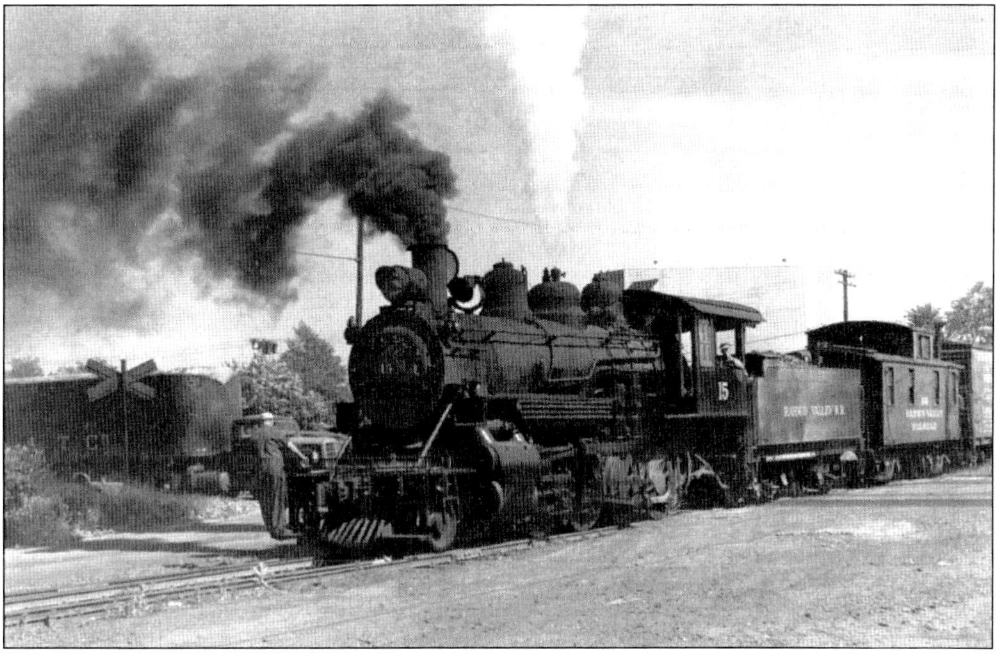

RV No. 15, the railroad's last steam locomotive, crosses New Jersey Route 29 in 1950, generating smoke and steam as it heads toward Branch Junction Station in Union. From Branch Junction, trains would head either toward Springfield and Summit on the mainline or go east through Union and Maplewood. (Photograph by Bruce Nett.)

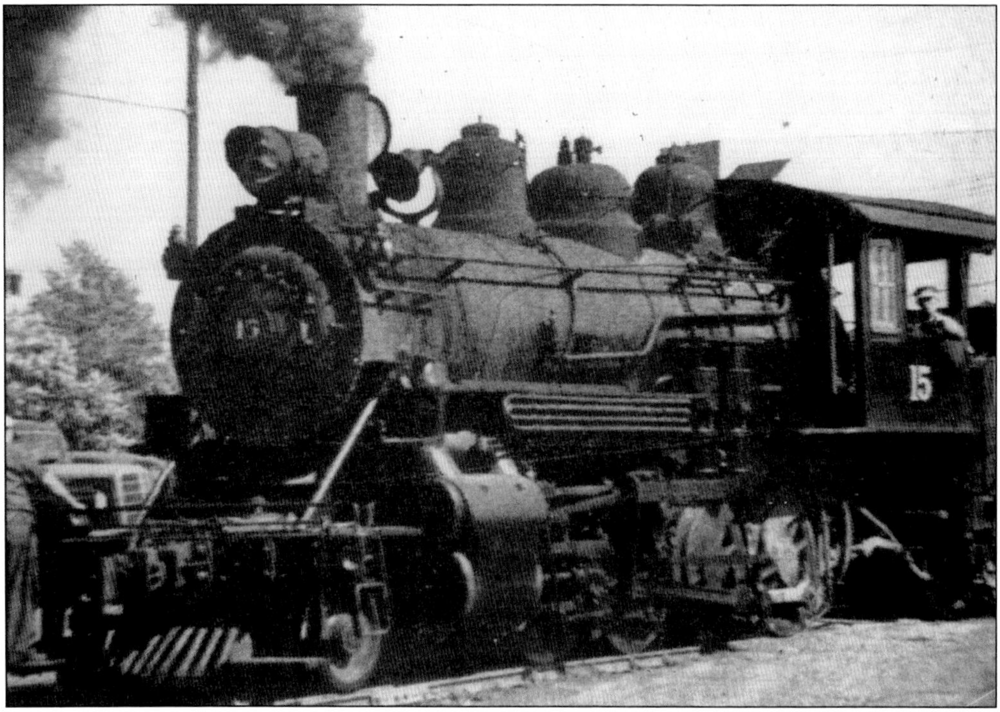

A closer view of the picture on page 83 clearly shows the fireman in the locomotive cab and No. 15's bell ringing away. (Photograph by Bruce Nett.)

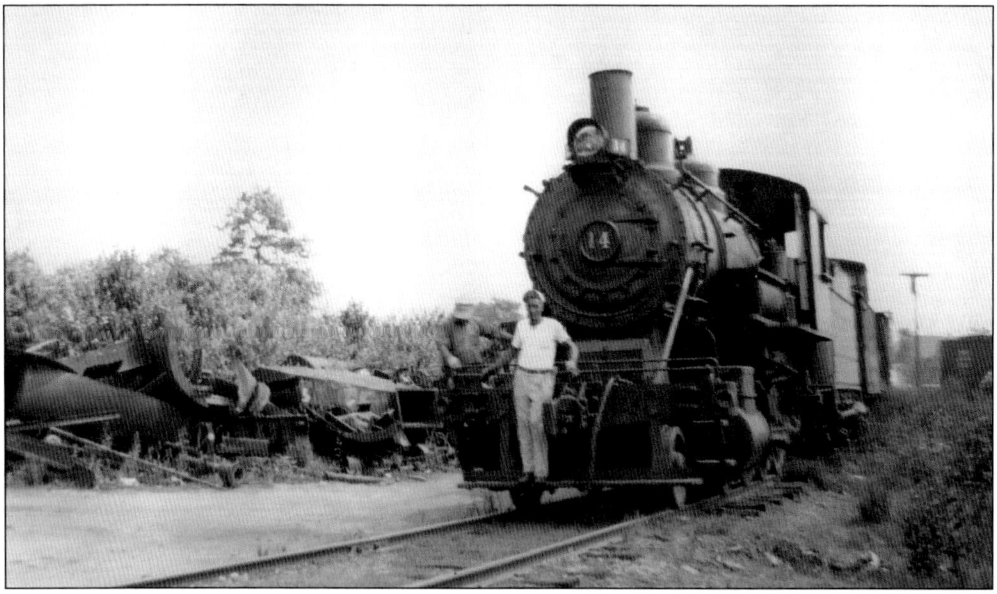

In this 1947 photograph, RV No. 14 has just crossed busy Route 29 (now Route 22) and is heading north through Union, heading for Maplewood. The crew would usually deliver and pick up cars on the main line in Springfield and Summit in the morning and then head back to Kenilworth for lunch. They would cross Route 29 again in the afternoon to drill the line in Union and Maplewood along the Unionbury spur. George Davis can be seen here standing on No. 14's pilot, filling in as the brakeman. (Photograph by Bill Burke.)

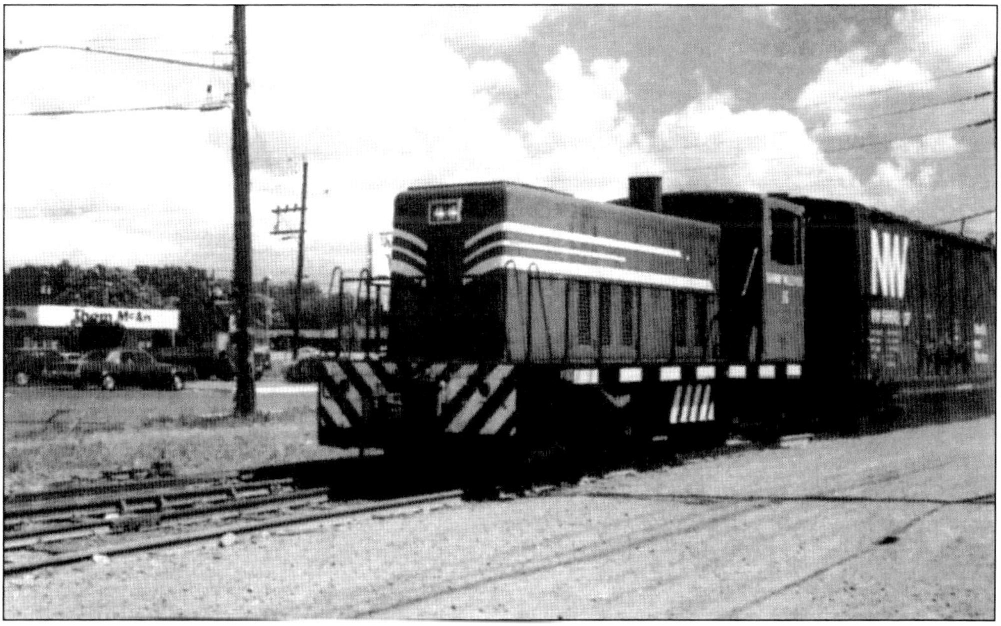

In 1951, the Rahway Valley Railroad purchased its first diesel engine, No. 16. This General Electric 70-tonner is crossing Route 22 (formerly Route 29) in 1986. Traffic on this busy highway in Union made the daily grade crossings hazardous for Rahway Valley crews. President George A. Clark once stated, "That crossing's a son-of-a-gun. We're afraid of it all the time. I sweat to think of what might happen." Minor accidents did occur over the years, the most serious being a derailment of No. 17 in 1969, when a tractor-trailer struck the front of the locomotive. (Courtesy of *Railroad Update* magazine.)

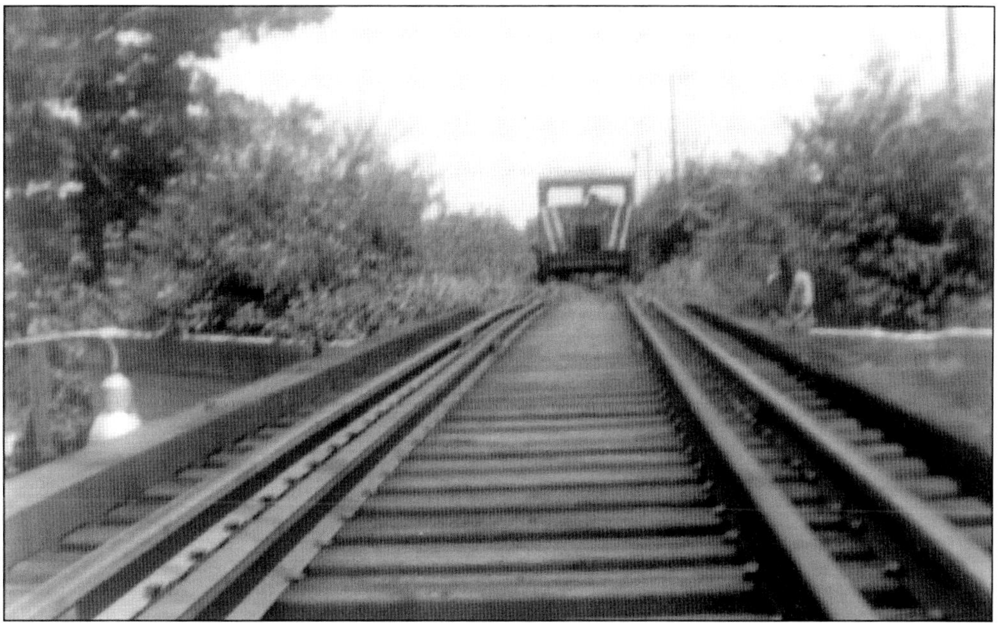

A Rahway Valley maintenance-of-way employee breaks for lunch on the concrete pier of the railroad's bridge over Vauxhall Road in Union c. 1963. His maintenance-of-way vehicle waits directly ahead on the tracks. (Photograph by Bruce Trampler.)

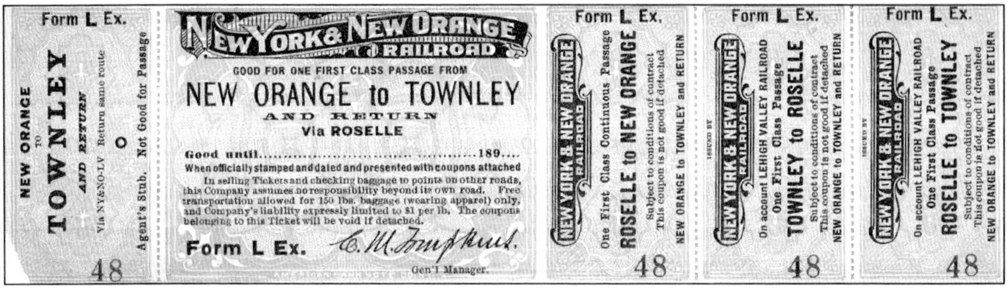

Townley, a section of Union near present-day Kean University, was a destination for many New York & New Orange Railroad passengers in the early 1900s. This ticket was good for a round trip between New Orange (now Kenilworth) and Townley, with the passenger making a connection with a Lehigh Valley Railroad train to complete the journey. (Collection of Donald A. Maxton.)

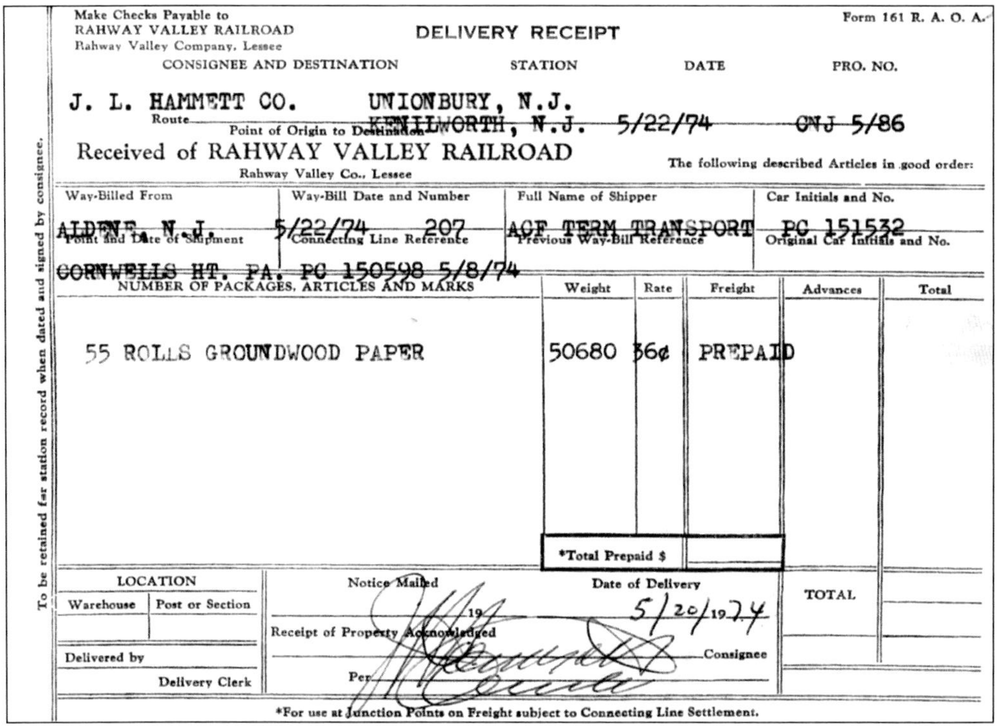
Make Checks Payable to
RAHWAY VALLEY RAILROAD
Rahway Valley Company, Lessee

DELIVERY RECEIPT

Form 161 R. A. O. A.

CONSIGNEE AND DESTINATION	STATION	DATE	PRO. NO.
J. L. HAMMETT CO.	UNIONBURY, N.J.		
Route — Point of Origin to Destination: KENILWORTH, N.J.		5/22/74	CNJ 5/86

Received of RAHWAY VALLEY RAILROAD
Rahway Valley Co., Lessee
The following described Articles in good order:

Way-Billed From	Way-Bill Date and Number	Full Name of Shipper	Car Initials and No.
ALDENE, N.J.	5/22/74 207	ACF TERM TRANSPORT	PC 151532
Point and Date of Shipment	Connecting Line Reference	Previous Way-Bill Reference	Original Car Initials and No.
CORNWELLS HT. PA. PC 150598 5/8/74			

NUMBER OF PACKAGES, ARTICLES AND MARKS	Weight	Rate	Freight	Advances	Total
55 ROLLS GROUNDWOOD PAPER	50680	36¢	PREPAID		
		*Total Prepaid $			

To be retained for station record when dated and signed by consignee.

LOCATION
Warehouse | Post or Section
Delivered by
Delivery Clerk

Notice Mailed 19
Receipt of Property Acknowledged
Date of Delivery 5/20/1974
Consignee
Per

TOTAL

*For use at Junction Points on Freight subject to Connecting Line Settlement.

This is a Rahway Valley receipt for a carload of paper delivered to the J.L. Hammett Company, a producer of school supplies located on the Unionbury spur. This boxcar was picked up at the Rahway Valley's interchange with the Central Railroad of New Jersey at Aldene on May 22, 1974. The number of shippers on the Unionbury spur, later called the Jaeger Industrial Branch, steadily decreased over the years. A short section of the spur between Branch Junction and Morris Avenue remained active until 1991, when the track here was embargoed. (Courtesy of Mary E. McCoy.)

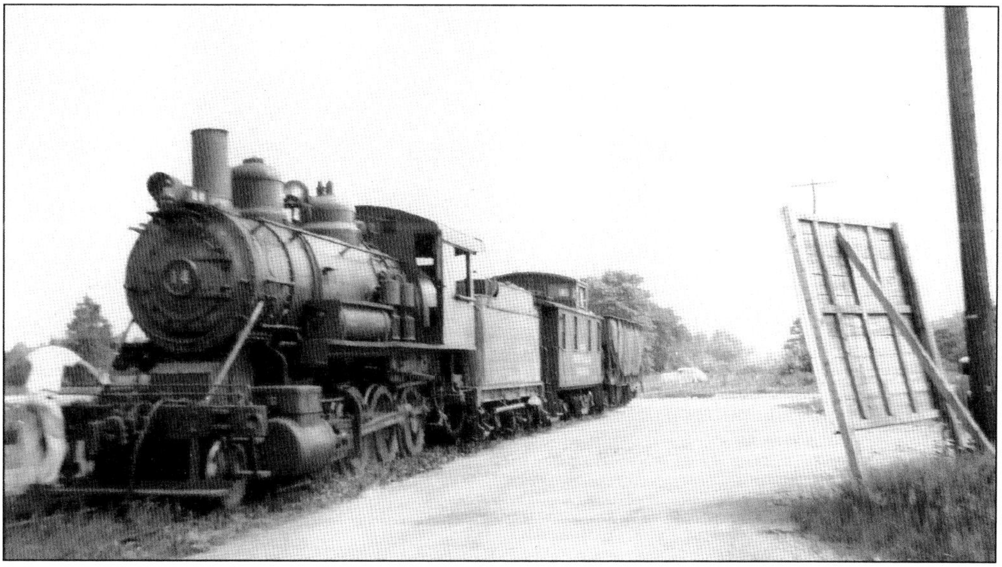

Returning from Branch Junction, RV No. 14 pushes a hopper car and Caboose No. 102 toward the Route 29 crossing in 1947, heading back toward Kenilworth. This crossing grew more dangerous over the years as automobile and truck traffic steadily increased. (Photograph by Bill Burke.)

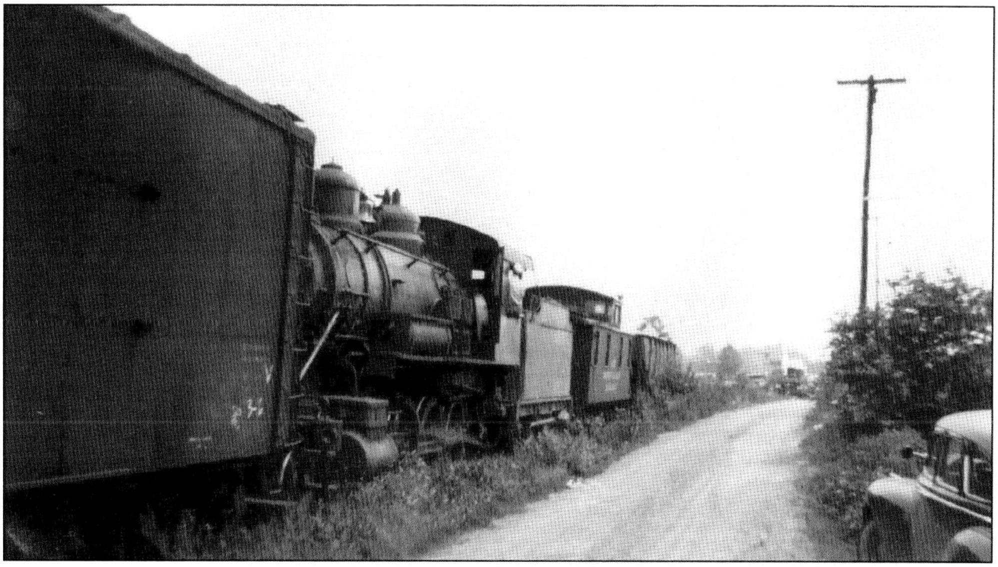

No. 14 steams through an industrial section of the Rahway Valley mainline, handling a boxcar, hopper, and Caboose No. 102 in this view from the late 1940s. (Photograph by Bill Burke.)

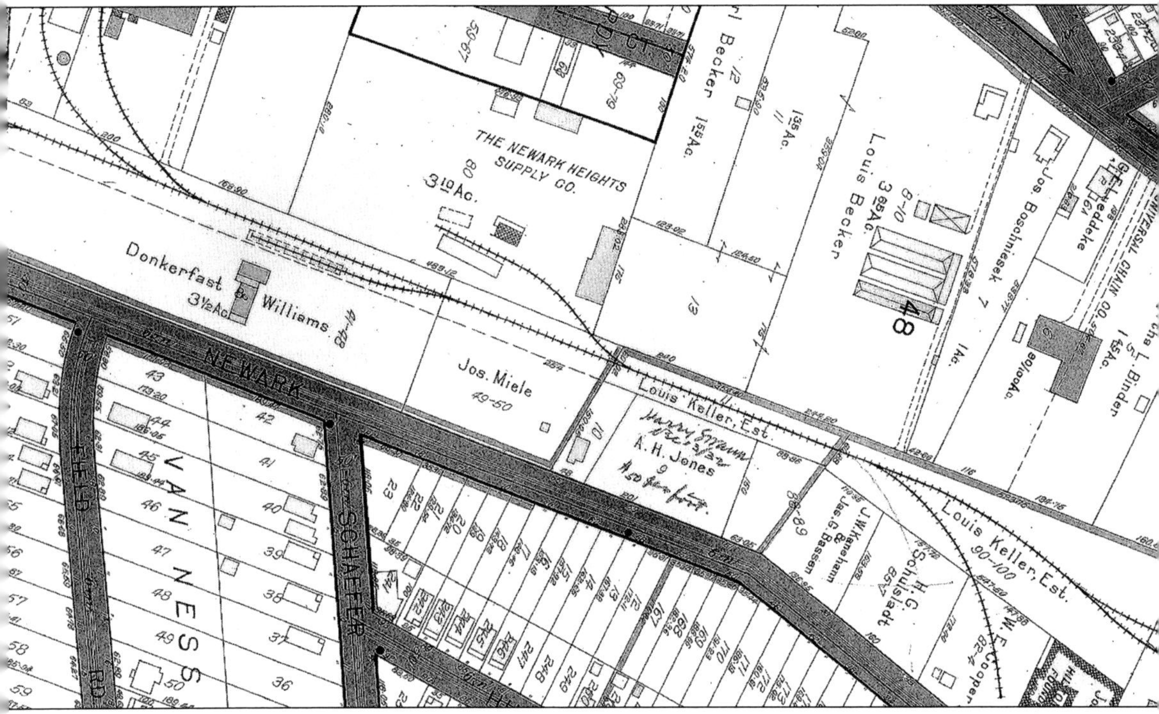

This 1928 Sanborn map shows the Rahway Valley Line tracks that served Maplewood's industrial section. Once part of a country estate, this land was sold to several industries by the Menzel family in the early 1900s. In 1914, Louis Keller created the Rahway Valley Line, a separate company, to build a three-mile branch into Union and this burgeoning industrial district, also known as "Newark Heights." There were three elevated crossings on this branch: Morris Avenue, Vauxhall Road, and Stanley Terrace in Union; and one grade crossing, Rutgers Street in Maplewood. The three bridges have all been dismantled. Freight customers in the Newark Heights section included, at various times, H. Boker and Company, a cutlery manufacturer; the Newark Heights Supply Company; the Hilton Brass Foundry; and the Woolley Coal and Fuel Oil Company. A passenger station was planned at the junction of Newark Way and Tuscan Road, but it was never constructed. (Collection of Donald A. Maxton.)

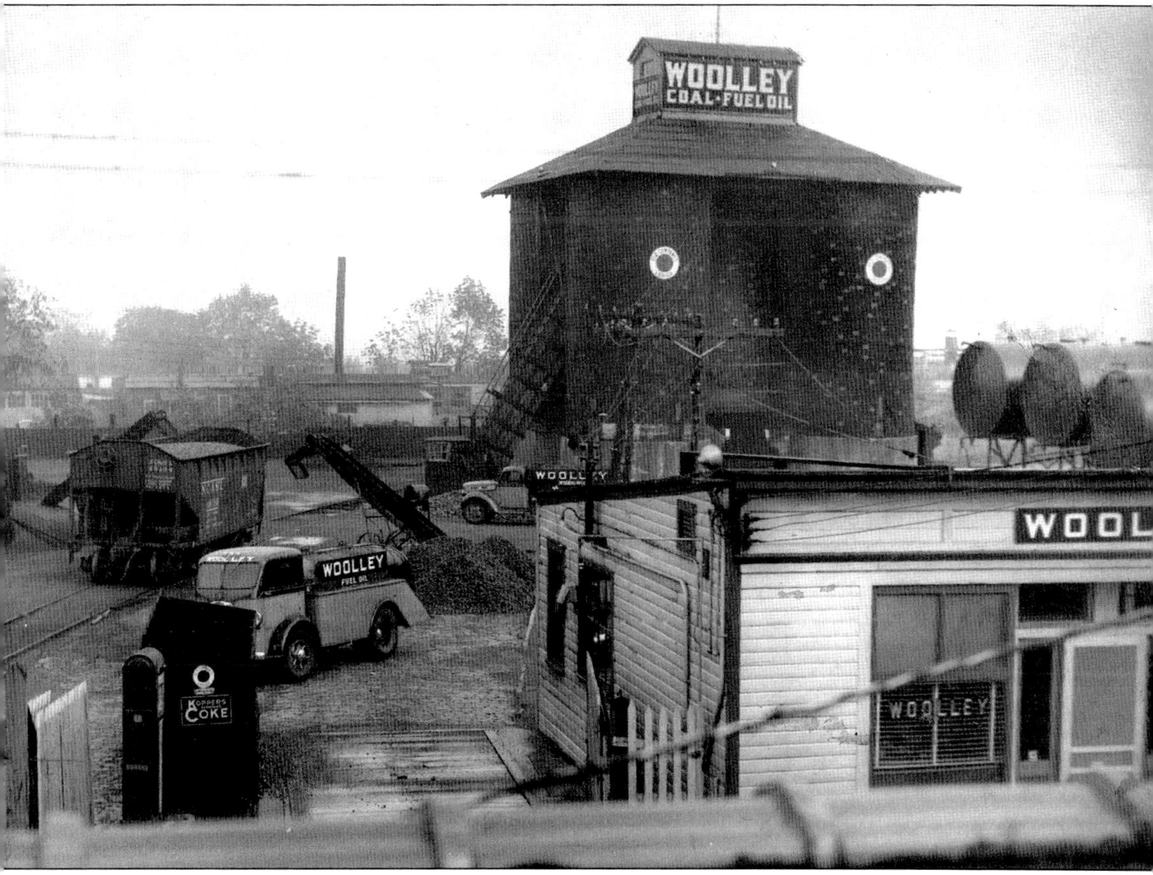

This 1942 photograph of the Woolley Coal and Fuel Oil Company in "Newark Heights" reveals a Nashville, Chattanooga, & St. Louis Railroad hopper filled with anthracite coal on a siding near the company's storage silos. The Rahway Valley Line—constructed 1914-1918—saw a steady decline in coal shipments over the years, as oil became the preferred heating fuel. The Rahway Valley Railroad moved only three cars on this branch spur in 1971 and filed for abandonment of the spur soon after. In the local newspaper, Rahway Valley president George A. Clark wistfully called the branch line, "a great place for anthracite." (Courtesy of Norman W. Woolley.)

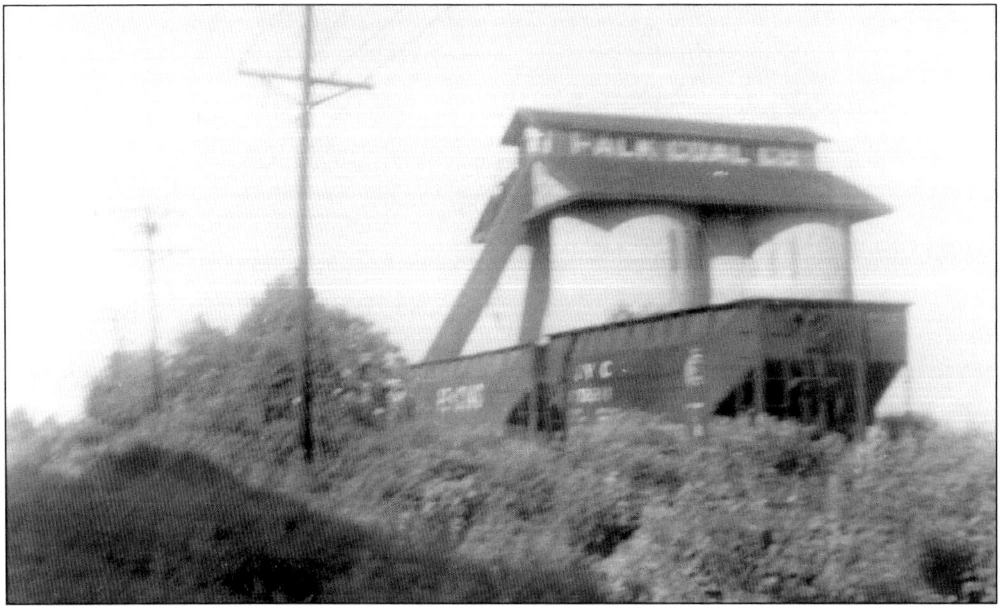

The Falk Coal Company, near Vauxhall Road in Union, was one of many fuel dealers served by the Rahway Valley Railroad on the Unionbury spur. Two hoppers rest on a siding near the Falk Coal storage silos in this scene from the early 1960s. Other nearby customers were the Elastic Stop Nut Corporation, Griffith Laboratories, and Hazel Bishop, a cosmetics company. (Photograph by Bruce Trampler.)

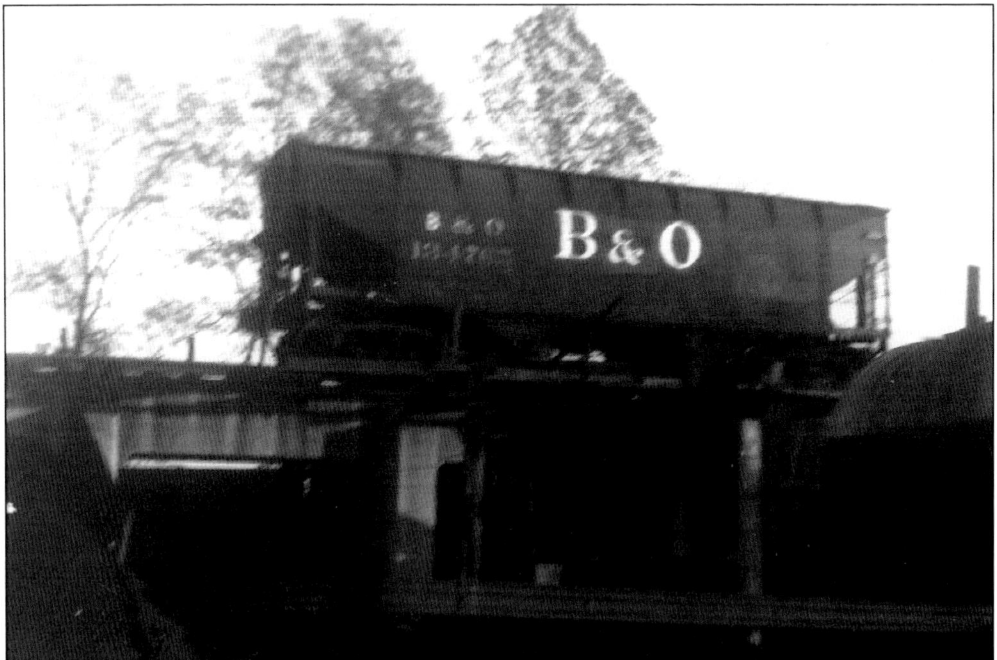

A Baltimore & Ohio Railroad hopper has just dumped a load of coal into the Falk Coal Company's pit in this 1963 photograph. Until the mid-1960s, hoppers filled with anthracite coal were a common sight along the Unionbury spur. (Photograph by Bruce Trampler.)

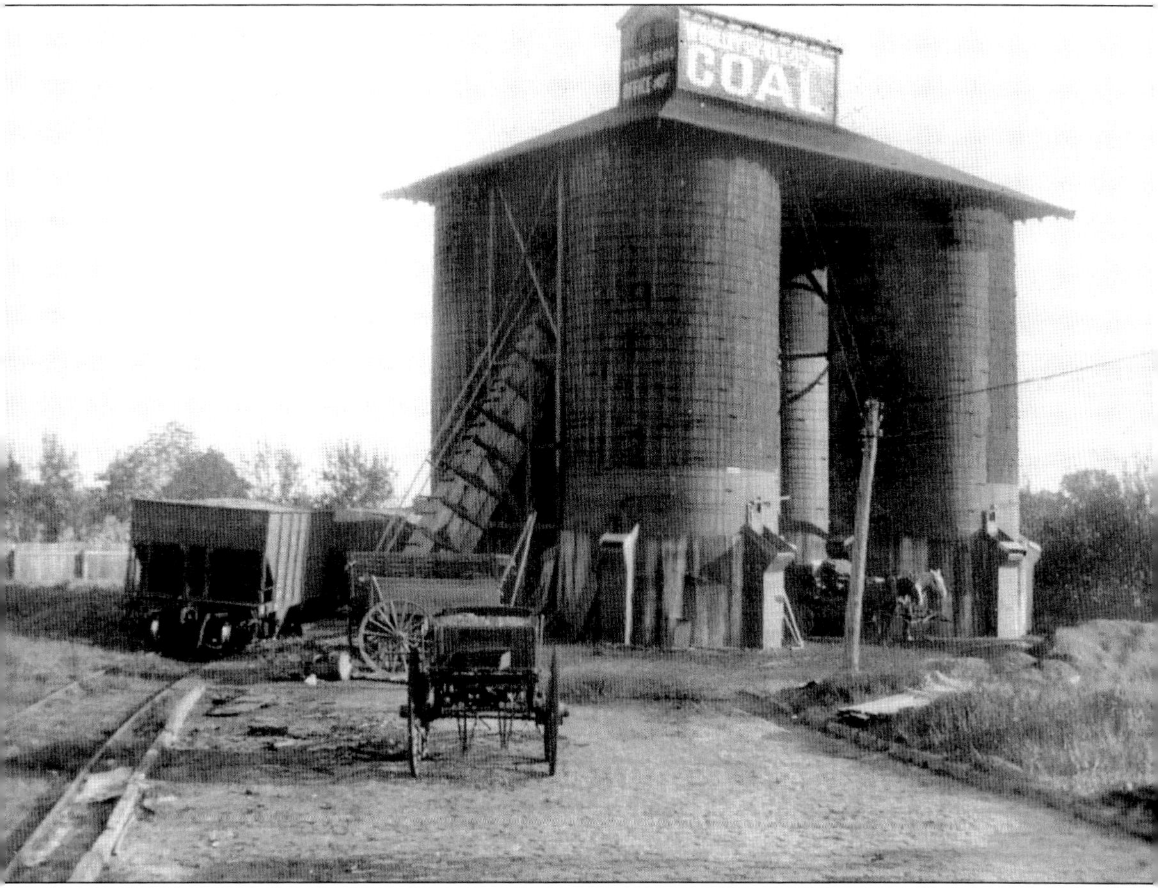

This 1928 view of the Woolley Coal and Fuel Oil property provides a closer look at the conveyor system that carried coal up from a pit under the tracks for storage in the silos. (Courtesy of Norman W. Woolley.)

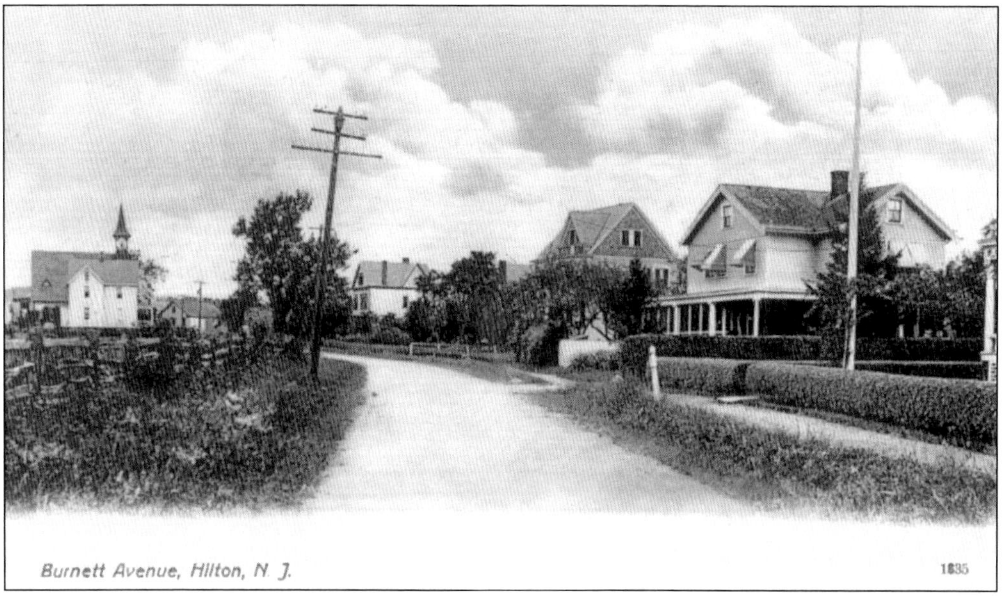

This 1910 postcard provides a tranquil view along Burnett Avenue in Maplewood's Hilton section. Most of these houses are still standing on what is now a very busy street. The Woolley Coal and Fuel Oil Company is out of sight but just down the block on the right-hand side. (Collection of Donald A. Maxton.)

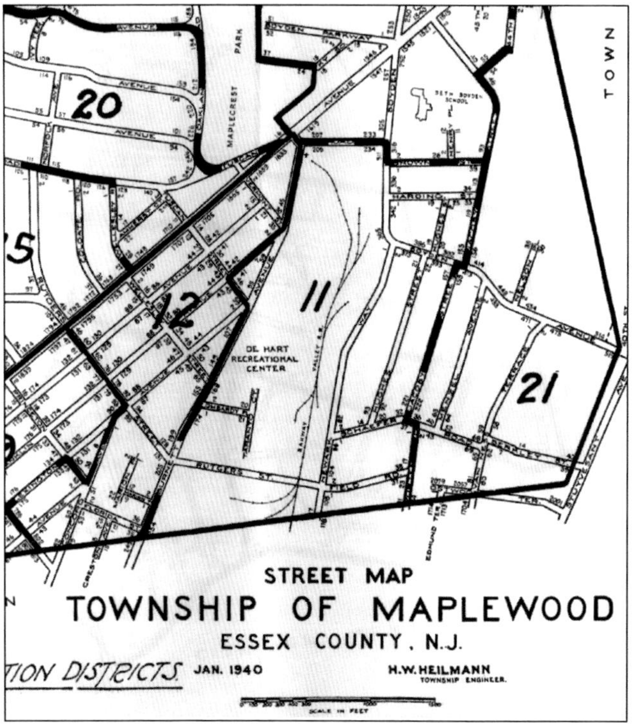

This 1941 map from *Know Your Town: A Survey of Maplewood, New Jersey* reveals that a large section of the industrial district along the Maplewood branch has become the De Hart Recreational Center. The Rahway Valley branch still served a number of customers in Maplewood at this time, and children playing in the park would often run toward the tracks when they heard the train whistle at the Rutgers Street grade crossing and wave to the friendly crew. By the early 1970s, Maplewood Building Specialties was the only customer left on the spur, shipping in an occasional load of slate from the southern United States. (Collection of Donald A. Maxton.)

These freight schedules published between 1972 and 1973 in *The Official Guide of the Railways* show that freight service has been abandoned on the Newark Heights (Maplewood) spur. At this time, Robert G. Clark took over the helm as president, secretary, general manager, and auditor from his father, George A. Clark, who passed away in 1969. Robert G. Clark directed operations until his untimely death in 1975. (Collection of Donald A. Maxton.)

September, 1971.

RAHWAY VALLEY RAILROAD

(*Rahway Valley Company, Lessee*).

RAHWAY VALLEY LINE.

ROBERT G. CLARK, President, Secretary,
General Manager and Auditor, Kenilworth, N. J. 0703
LOUIS S. WEEKS, Jr., Vice-President, "
MARGARET P. ROSEBAULT, Treasurer, "
HORATIO P DINGLEBERRY, Superintendent, "
R. N. SOHOR, Assistant Car Accountant, "

....	....	....	Mls	*September*, 1971.	Connections
....	....	....	0	........**Roselle Park**........	At Aldene, N. J. With Central R. Co. of New Jerse At Roselle Par N. J. - With Lehi Valley R. R. Summit, N. J. With Erie Lack wanna Ry.
....	Freight Service only.		0	...........**Aldene**...........	
....			1.7	.... Kenilworth	
....			2.8	......**Branch Junction**......	
....			4.4	.... Springfield	
....	....	....	5.0	.... Baltusrol	
....	....	....	7.1	.... **Summit**	
....	....	....	Mls	**RAHWAY VALLEY LINE.**	
....	Freight Service only.		0	......**Branch Junction**......	
....			0.9	**Unionbury**(Union, Union County)	
....			2.9	.. Newark Heights (Maplewood) ..	

November, 1972.

RAHWAY VALLEY RAILROAD

(*Rahway Valley Company, Lessee*).

RAHWAY VALLEY LINE.

ROBERT G. CLARK, President, Secretary,
General Manager and Auditor, Kenilworth, N. J. 07033
LOUIS S. WEEKS, Jr., Vice-President, "
MARGARET P. ROSEBAULT, Treasurer, "
HORATIO P. DINGLEBERRY, Superintendent, "
————————, Assistant Car Accountant, "

....	....	....	Mls	**Table 1**—STATIONS.	Connections
....	....	....	0	........**Roselle Park**........	At Aldene, N. J.— With Central R.R Co. of New Jersey At Roselle Park N.J. With Lehigh Valley R. R. A Summit, N. J.— With Erie Lacka wanna Ry.
....	Freight Service only.		0	...........**Aldene**...........	
...			1.7	.... Kenilworth	
....			2.8	......**Branch Junction**......	
....			4.4	.... Springfield	
....	....	....	5.0	.... Baltusrol	
....	....	....	7.1	.... **Summit**	
....	....	....	Mls	**RAHWAY VALLEY LINE.**	
....	Freight Service only.		0	......**Branch Junction**......	
....			0.9	**Unionbury**(Union, Union County)	
....			....	....	*October*, 1972.

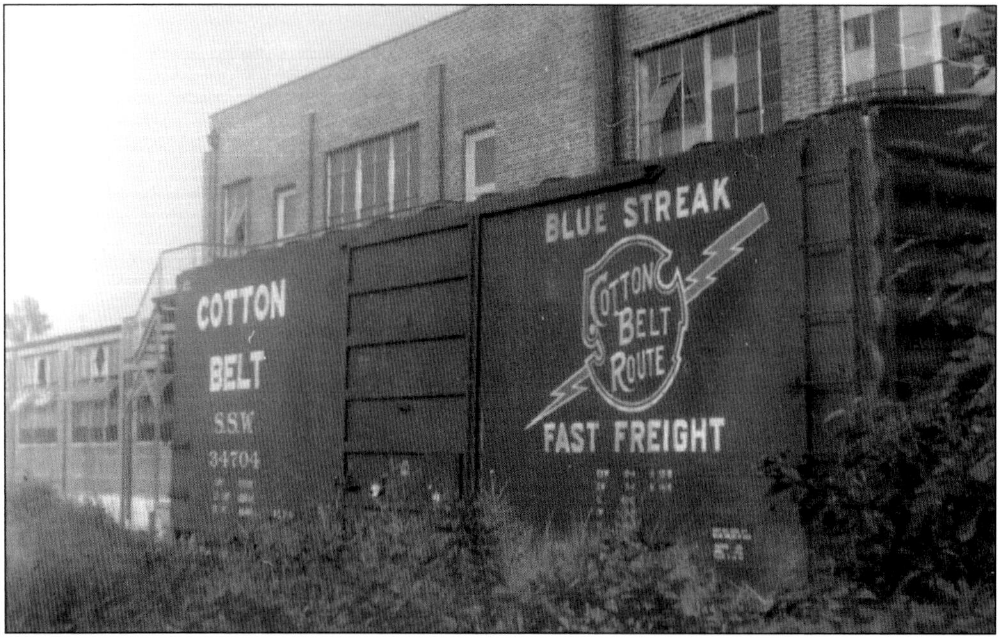

A Cotton Belt "Blue Streak Fast Freight" car rests on the Menner Packing Company siding on the Rahway Valley Railroad's Maplewood branch. Menner Packing was just a stone's throw from Rutgers Street, the railroad's only grade crossing in Maplewood. Menner specialized in Spanish rice, beef stew, and other food products, and residents still remember the fragrant aromas that filled the air in this neighborhood. (Photograph by Bruce Trampler.)

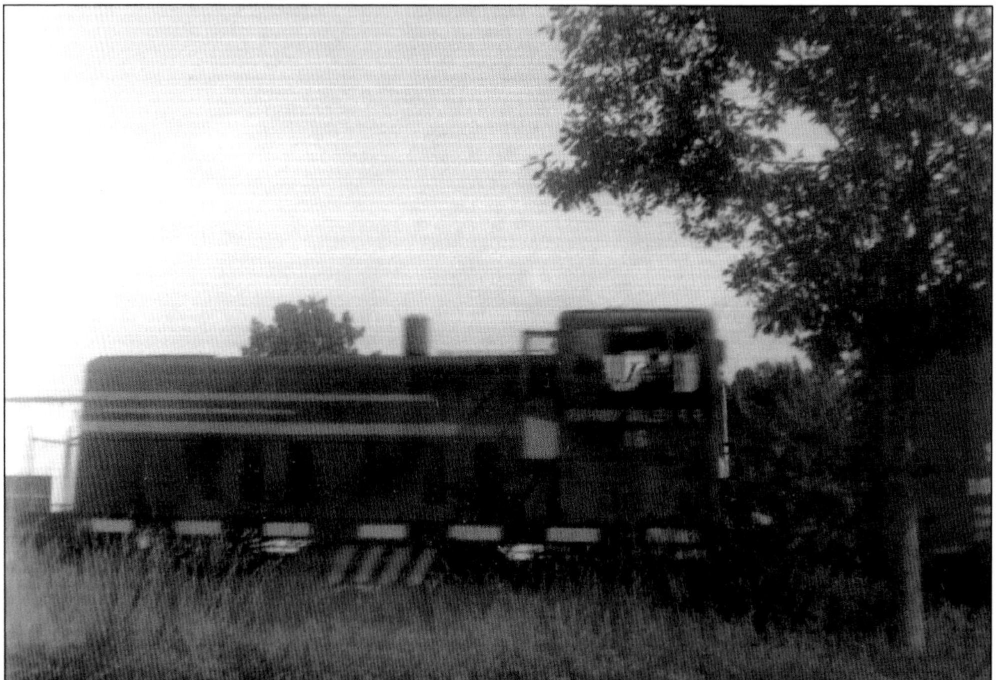

RV No. 16 has just crossed Rutgers Street and is heading toward the Menner Packing Company siding in this 1962 view. (Photograph by Bruce Trampler.)

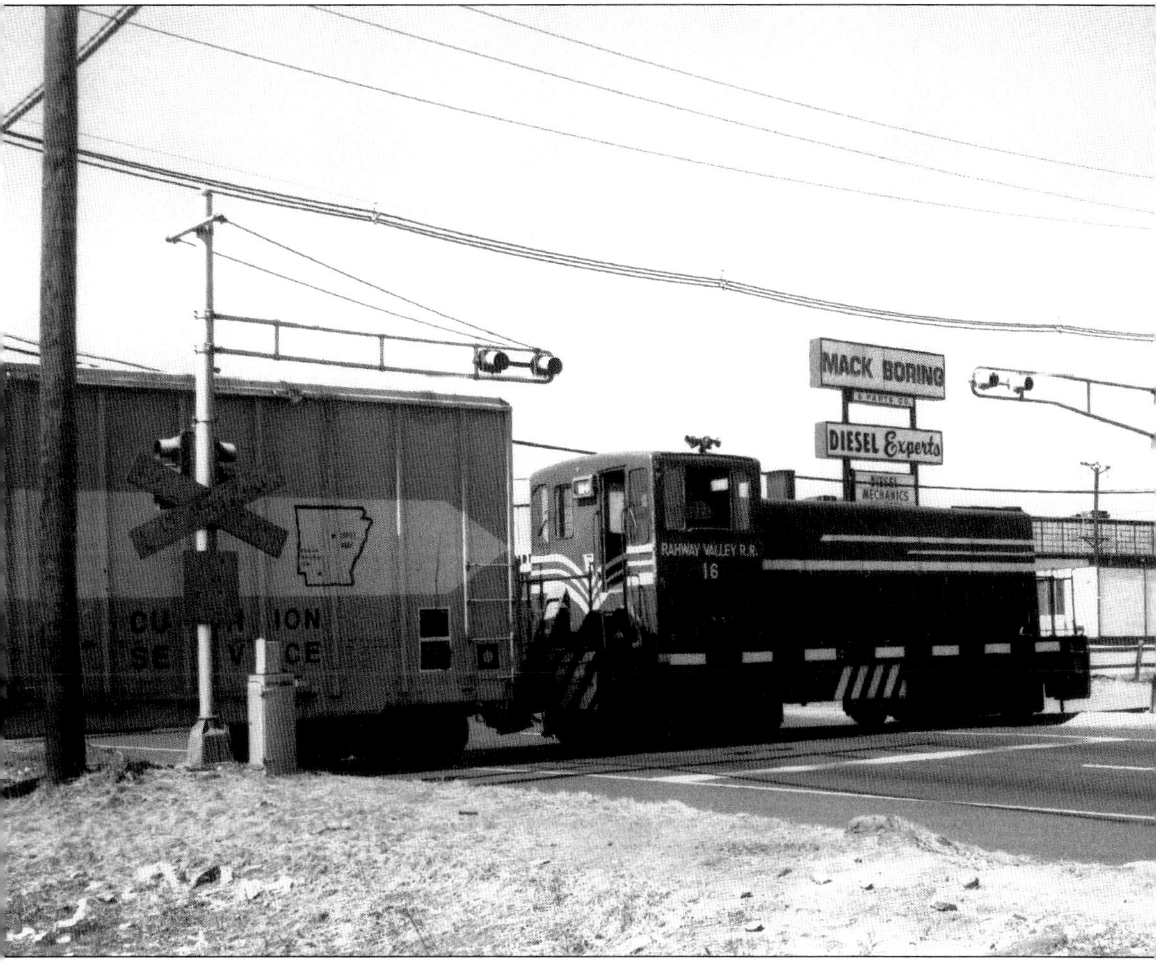

A Rahway Valley Railroad crew runs the Route 22 gauntlet, with No. 16 pulling a boxcar across the busy highway in Union. Many vehicles often ignored the Rahway Valley's signaling system, installed in an attempt to improve the level of safety on this dangerous crossing. (Photograph by Jon Franz.)

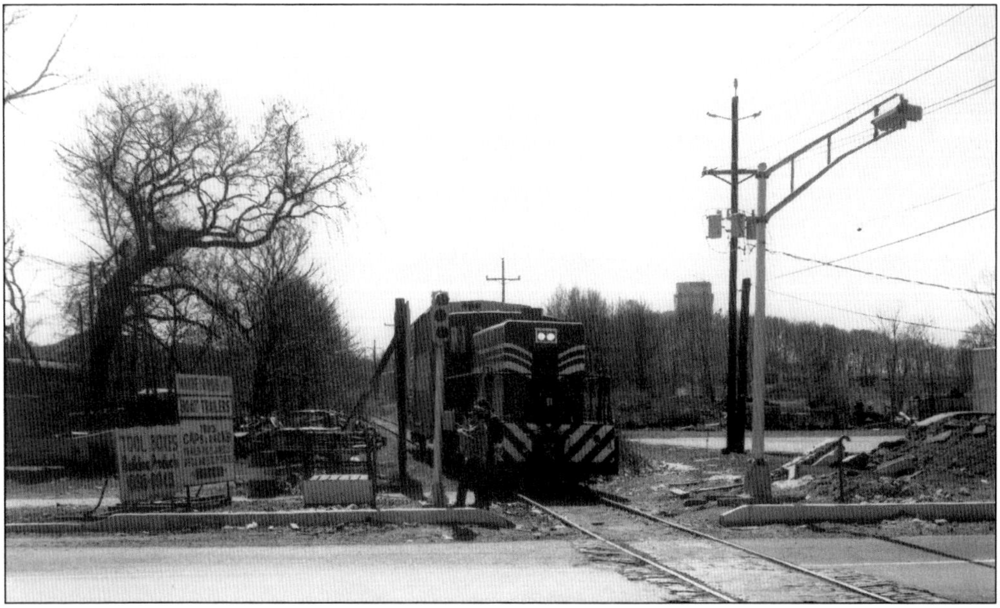

RV No. 16 approaches the railroad's grade crossing at Route 22 in Union on March 28, 1986, in this view looking south toward Kenilworth. This scene was photographed just days after operations were assumed by the Delaware Otsego Corporation. Part of the Unionbury spur, which Delaware Otsego renamed the Jaeger Industrial Branch, remained active until 1990. (Photograph by Jon Franz.)

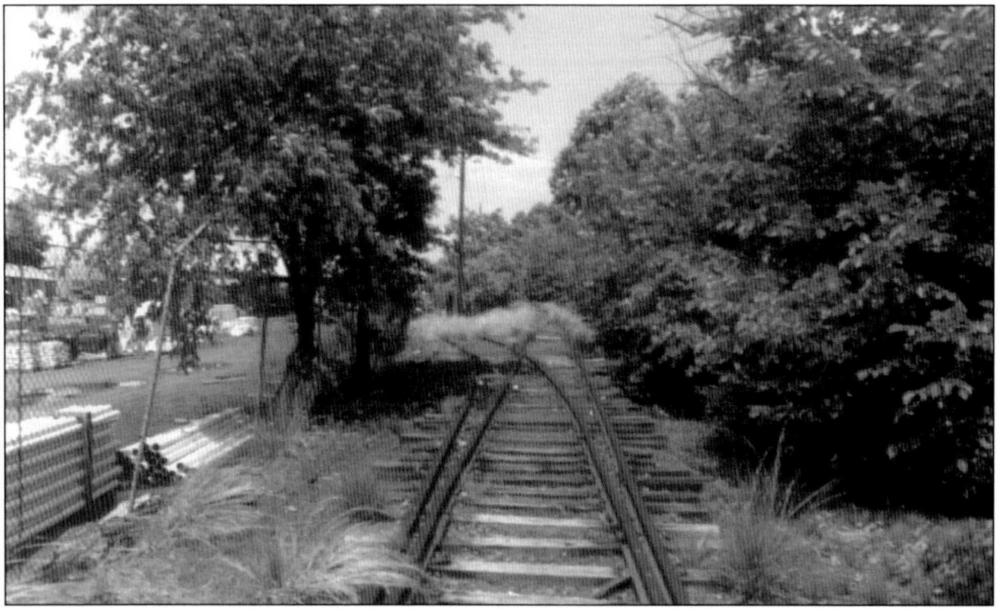

This is an August 1992 view of Jaeger Lumber's siding near the Rahway Valley bridge over Morris Avenue in Union—about two years after the lumber company took its last delivery by rail and four months after formal abandonment of the Rahway Valley Railroad. The thick vegetation visible on the rails past the siding shows that a train had not traveled past the siding in quite some time. The railroad also had a siding nearby where it stored boxcars. (Photograph by Donald A. Maxton.)

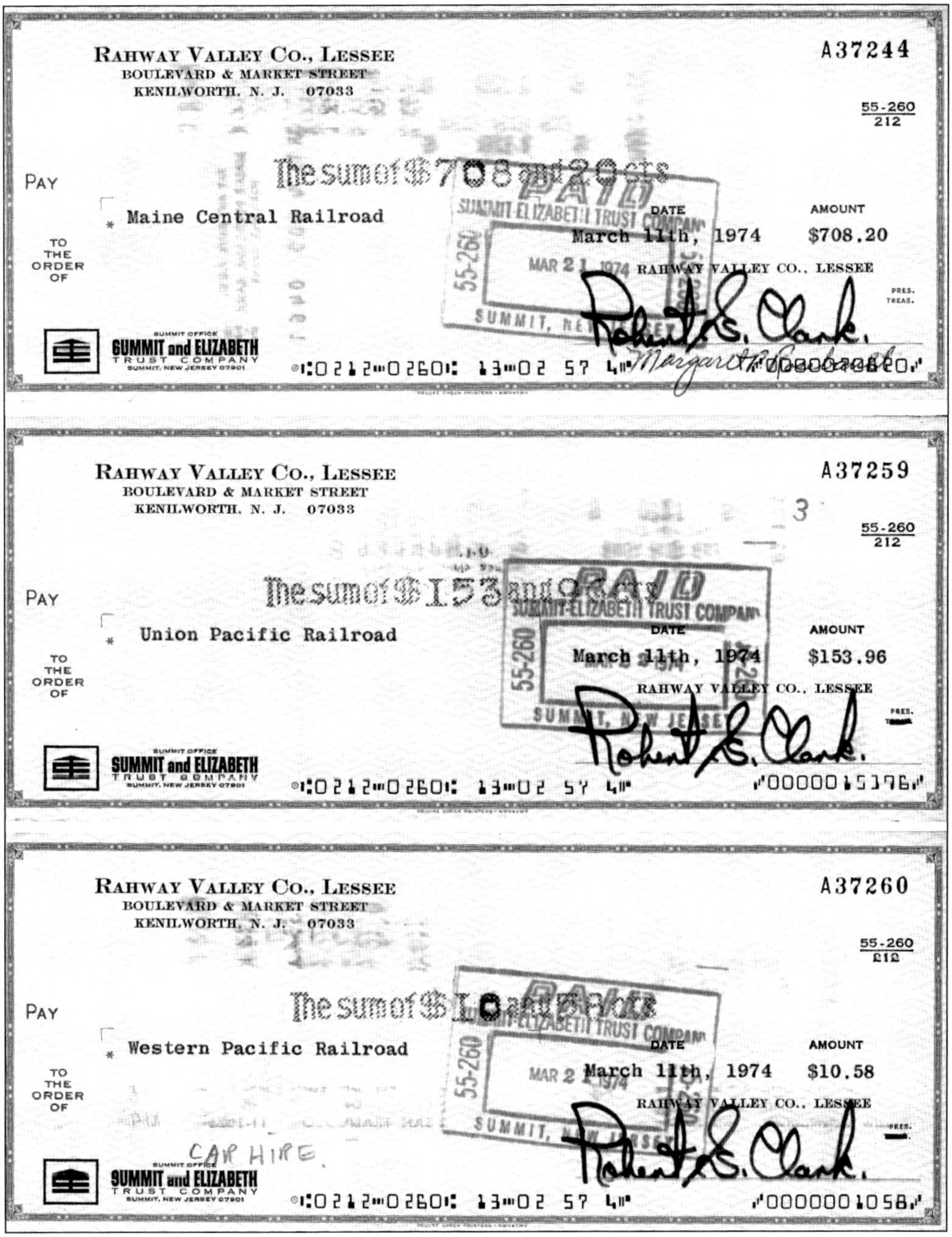

RAHWAY VALLEY CO., LESSEE
BOULEVARD & MARKET STREET
KENILWORTH, N. J. 07033
A37244
55-260
212
PAY The sum of $708 and 20 cts
TO THE ORDER OF * Maine Central Railroad
DATE March 11th, 1974
AMOUNT $708.20
RAHWAY VALLEY CO., LESSEE
PRES. TREAS.
Robert S. Clark
PAID SUMMIT-ELIZABETH TRUST COMPANY MAR 21 1974 55-260 SUMMIT, NEW JERSEY
SUMMIT OFFICE SUMMIT and ELIZABETH TRUST COMPANY SUMMIT, NEW JERSEY 07901

RAHWAY VALLEY CO., LESSEE
BOULEVARD & MARKET STREET
KENILWORTH, N. J. 07033
A37259
55-260
212
PAY The sum of $153 and 96 cts
TO THE ORDER OF * Union Pacific Railroad
DATE March 11th, 1974
AMOUNT $153.96
RAHWAY VALLEY CO., LESSEE
PRES.
Robert S. Clark
PAID SUMMIT-ELIZABETH TRUST COMPANY 55-260 SUMMIT, NEW JERSEY
SUMMIT OFFICE SUMMIT and ELIZABETH TRUST COMPANY SUMMIT, NEW JERSEY 07901
⑈0000015396⑈

RAHWAY VALLEY CO., LESSEE
BOULEVARD & MARKET STREET
KENILWORTH, N. J. 07033
A37260
55-260
212
PAY The sum of $10 and 58 cts
TO THE ORDER OF * Western Pacific Railroad
DATE March 11th, 1974
AMOUNT $10.58
RAHWAY VALLEY CO., LESSEE
PRES.
Robert S. Clark
CAR HIRE.
PAID SUMMIT-ELIZABETH TRUST COMPANY MAR 2 1974 55-260 SUMMIT, NEW JERSEY
SUMMIT OFFICE SUMMIT and ELIZABETH TRUST COMPANY SUMMIT, NEW JERSEY 07901
⑈0000001058⑈

Following the death of George A. Clark, his son Robert assumed the duties of president, secretary, general manager, and auditor, as shown by his signature on these checks from 1974. They are payable to a variety of different railroads. (Courtesy of Bruce Trampler.)

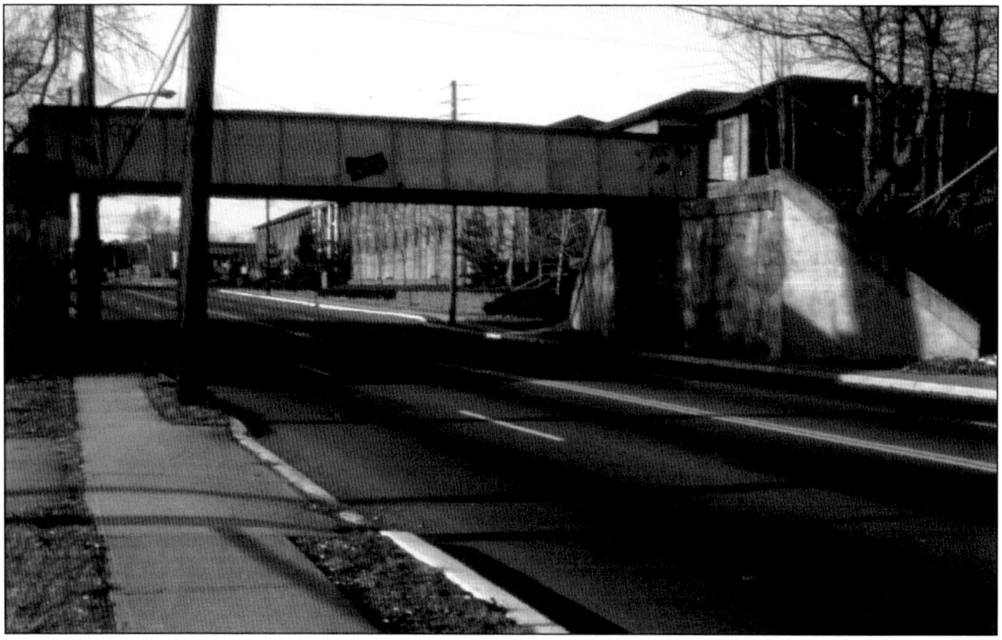

The Rahway Valley's bridge over Morris Avenue, located near Jaeger Lumber on the Unionbury spur, is seen here. Other bridges along the spur spanned Vauxhall Road and Stanley Terrace. This photograph was taken in January 1992; the bridge was removed in 2007. (Photograph by Donald A. Maxton.)

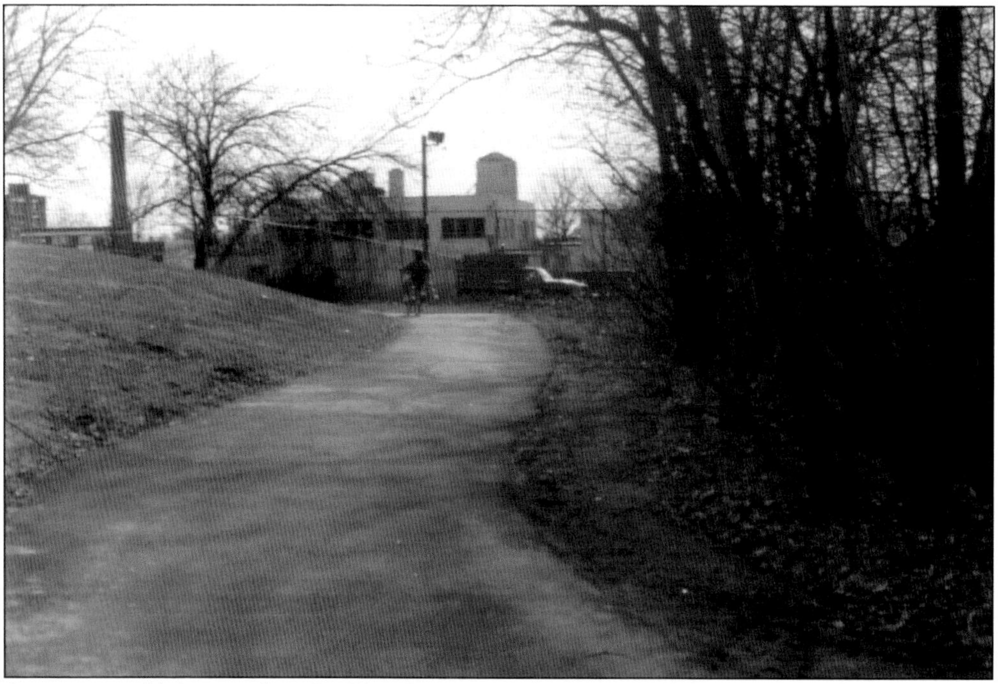

A jogging and biking path at De Hart Recreational Center is all that remains of the once busy Rahway Valley right of way in Maplewood. This view looks toward factory buildings once served by the railroad. (Photograph by Donald A. Maxton.)

Five

Aldene and Roselle Park: Making Connections

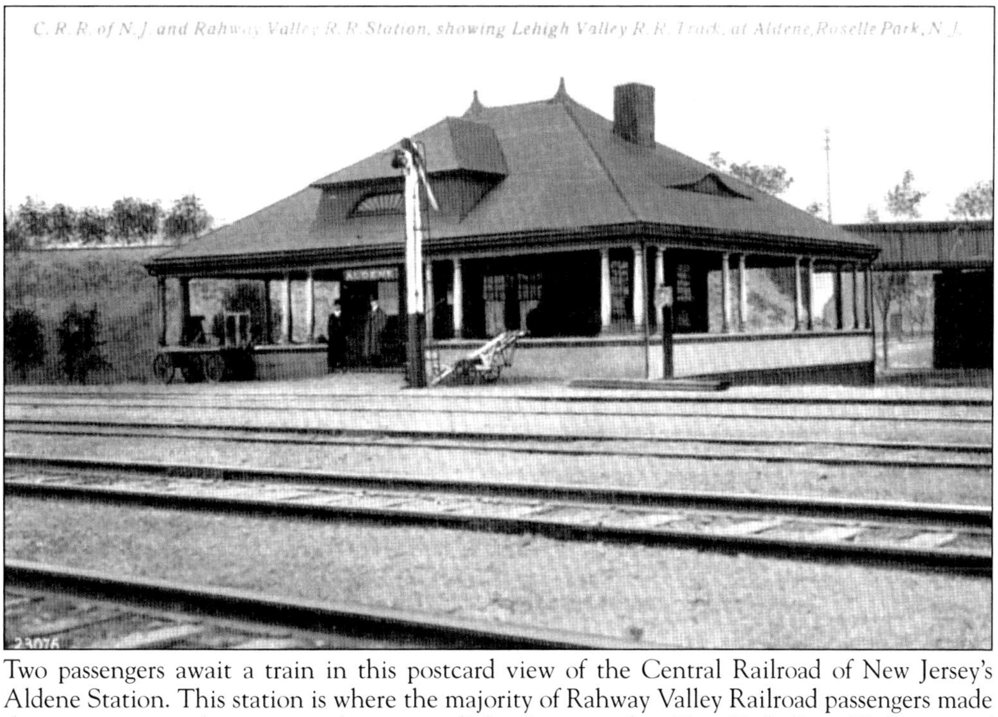

Two passengers await a train in this postcard view of the Central Railroad of New Jersey's Aldene Station. This station is where the majority of Rahway Valley Railroad passengers made their connections for trips to other parts of New Jersey and to New York City. (Collection of Donald A. Maxton.)

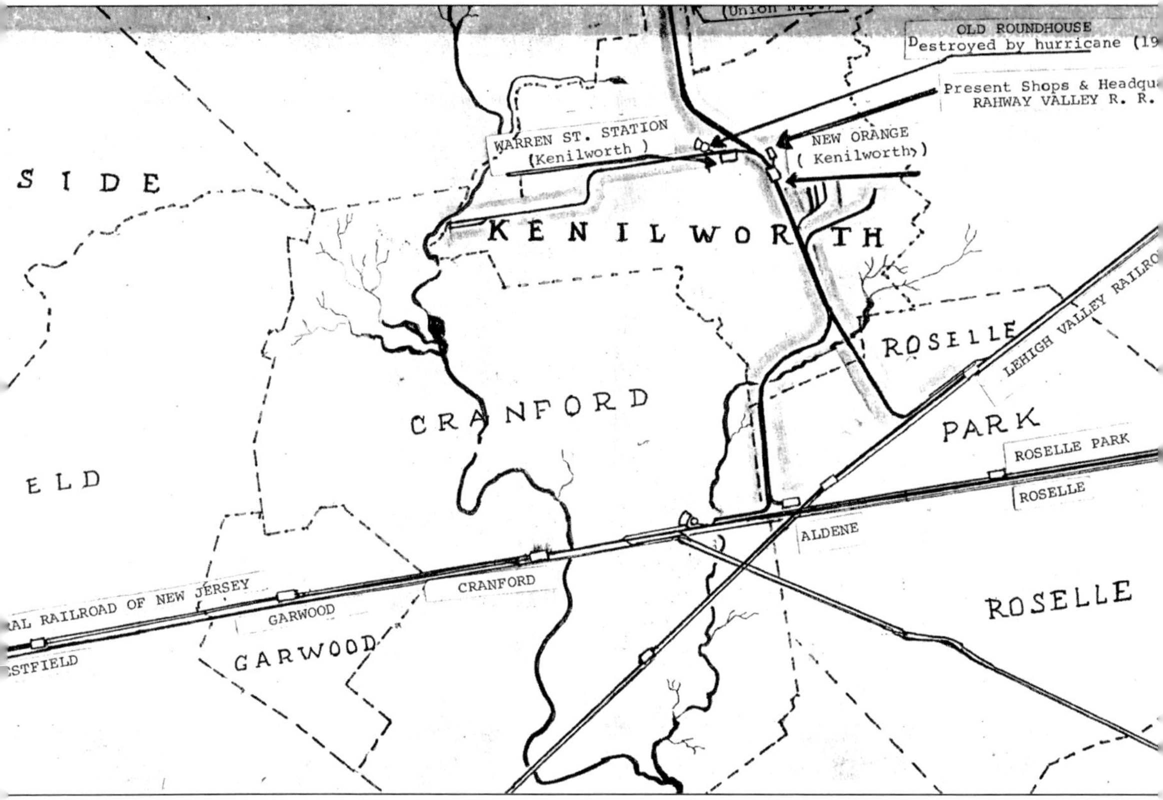

This map shows the Rahway Valley Railroad's connections to the two major railroads crossing through "Rahway Valley Territory:" the Central Railroad of New Jersey and the Lehigh Valley Railroad. Links to these major carriers provided Rahway Valley passengers access to a number of destinations and enabled businesses along the Rahway Valley line to reach markets throughout the United States. (Courtesy of Mary E. McCoy.)

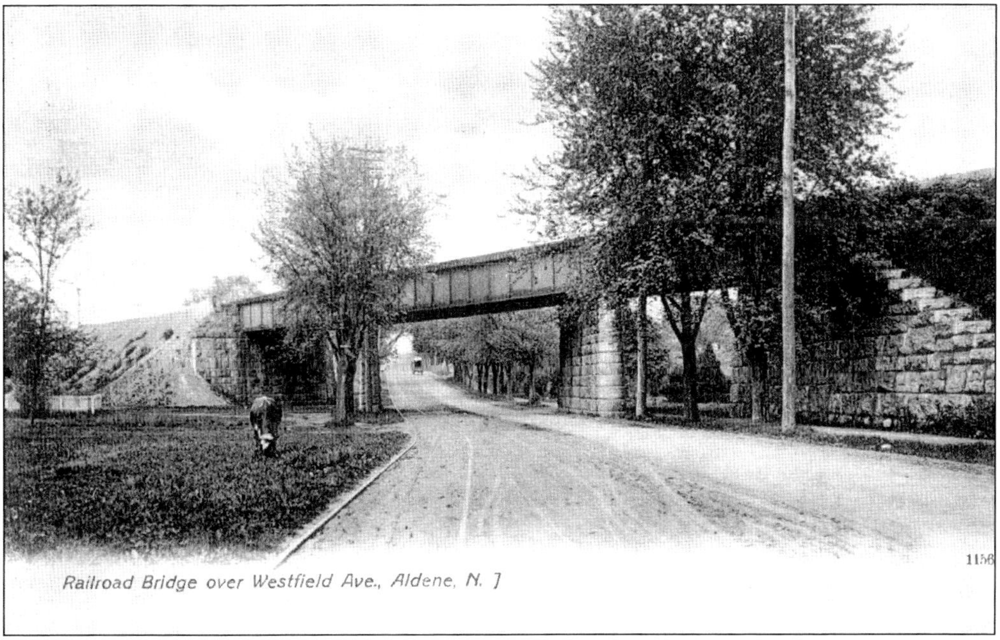

The Lehigh Valley Railroad trestle spanning Westfield Avenue near Aldene is still a landmark in the area, but the station itself is gone. Busy Westfield Avenue was little more than a country road when this postcard view was photographed, with a grazing cow munching contentedly on the roadside. One lonely vehicle is just visible in the distance. (Courtesy of Scott Schnipper.)

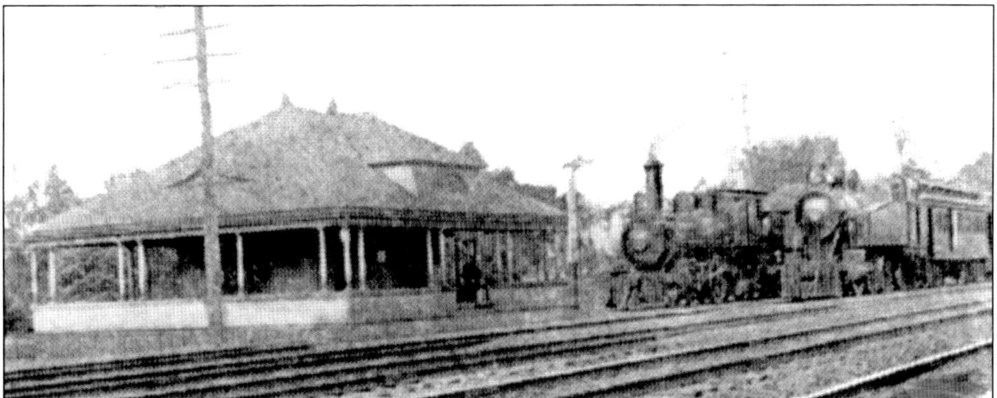

In this rare photograph, a Rahway Valley locomotive waits at Aldene for passengers arriving on a Central Railroad of New Jersey train. Passengers changed here for stations at Kenilworth, Springfield, Summit, and other stops along the Rahway Valley line. (Courtesy of Mary E. McCoy.)

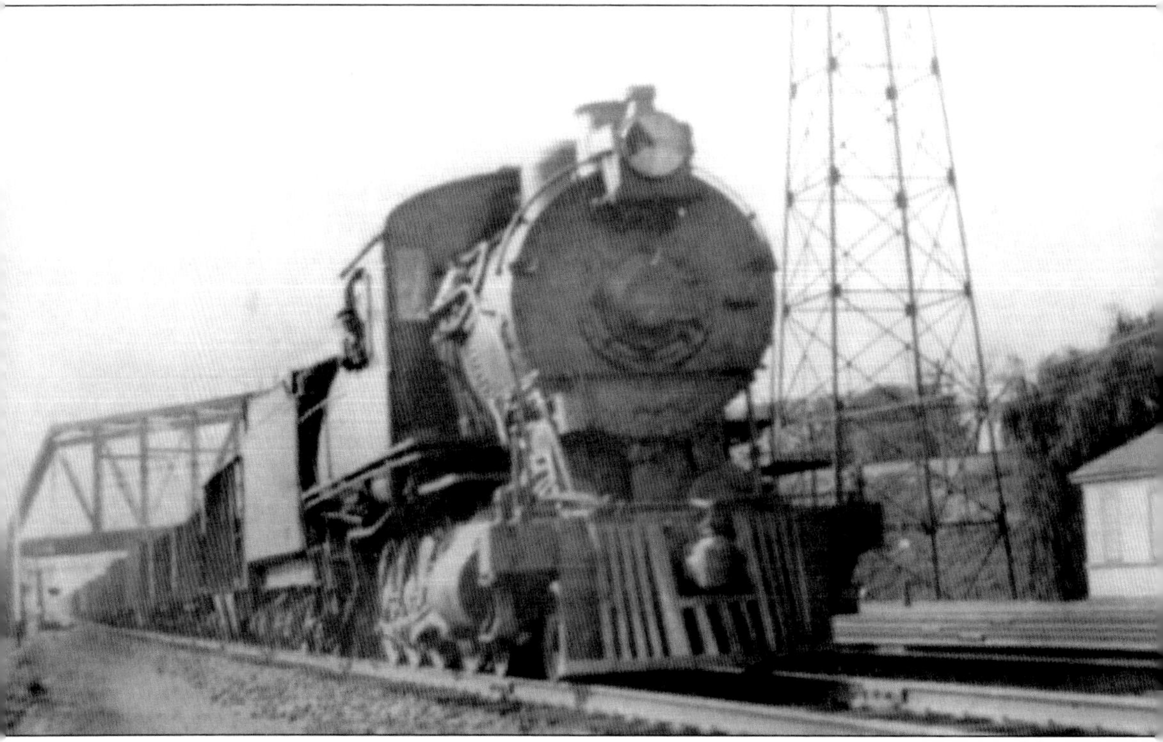

In this *c.* 1902 photograph, a Central Railroad of New Jersey Camelback steam locomotive has just passed under the Lehigh Valley as it pulls an eastbound freight through Aldene. (Courtesy of the Roselle Park Historical Society.)

Most Rahway Valley passengers most likely would have carried a Central Railroad of New Jersey timetable—probably not much different from this one from 1931—to coordinate their local trains with the arrival of Central Railroad of New Jersey trains at Aldene. (Courtesy of the Roselle Park Historical Society.)

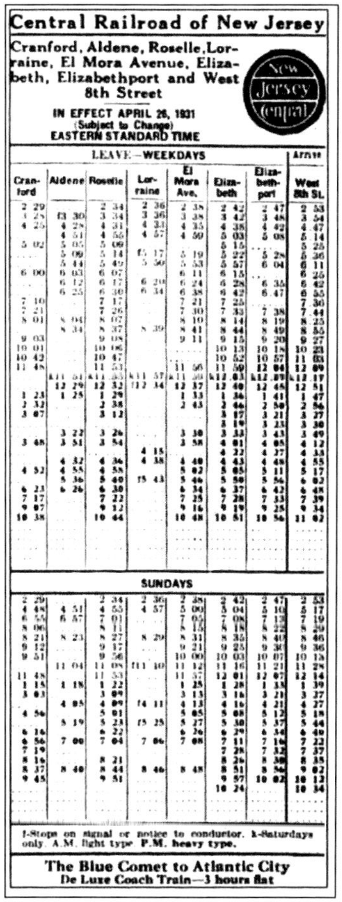

Central Railroad of New Jersey

Cranford, Aldene, Roselle, Lorraine, El Mora Avenue, Elizabeth, Elizabethport and West 8th Street

IN EFFECT APRIL 26, 1931
(Subject to Change)
EASTERN STANDARD TIME

LEAVE—WEEKDAYS

Cranford	Aldene	Roselle	Lorraine	El Mora Ave.	Elizabeth	Elizabethport	Arrive West 8th St.
2 29		2 34	2 36	2 38	2 42	2 47	2 53
3 28	f3 30	3 34	3 36	3 38	3 42	3 48	3 54
4 25	4 28	4 31	4 33	4 35	4 38	4 42	4 47
	4 51	4 55	4 57	4 59	5 03	5 08	5 14
5 02	5 05	5 09			5 15		5 25
	5 09	5 14	f5 17	5 19	5 22	5 28	5 36
	5 44	5 49	5 50	5 53	5 57	6 04	6 11
6 00	6 03	6 07		6 11	6 15		6 25
	6 12	6 17	6 20	6 24	6 28	6 35	6 42
	6 25	6 30	6 34	6 38	6 42	6 47	6 55
7 10		7 17		7 21	7 25		7 30
7 21		7 26		7 30	7 33	7 38	7 44
8 01	8 04	8 07		8 10	8 14	8 19	8 25
	8 34	8 37	8 39	8 41	8 44	8 49	8 55
9 03		9 08		9 11	9 15	9 20	9 27
10 01		10 06			10 13	10 18	10 23
10 42		10 47			10 52	10 57	11 03
11 48		11 53		11 56	11 59	12 04	12 09
	k11 51	k11 55	k11 57	k11 59	k12 03	k12 09	k12 17
	12 29	12 32	f12 34	12 37	12 40	12 45	12 51
1 23	1 25	1 29		1 33	1 36	1 41	1 47
2 32		2 38		2 43	2 46	2 50	2 56
3 07		3 12			3 17	3 21	3 27
					3 19	3 23	3 30
	3 22	3 26		3 30	3 33	3 43	3 49
3 48	3 51	3 54		3 58	4 01	4 05	4 12
			4 15		4 22	4 27	4 33
	4 32	4 36	4 38	4 40	4 43	4 48	4 55
4 52	4 55	4 58		5 02	5 05	5 11	5 17
	5 36	5 40	f5 43	5 46	5 50	5 56	6 02
6 23	6 26	6 30		6 34	6 37	6 42	6 48
7 17		7 22		7 25	7 28	7 33	7 39
9 07		9 12		9 16	9 19	9 25	9 34
10 38		10 44		10 48	10 51	10 56	11 02

SUNDAYS

Cranford	Aldene	Roselle	Lorraine	El Mora Ave.	Elizabeth	Elizabethport	Arrive West 8th St.
2 29		2 34	2 36	2 38	2 42	2 47	2 53
4 48	4 51	4 55	4 57	5 00	5 04	5 10	5 17
6 55	6 57	7 01		7 05	7 08	7 13	7 19
8 06		8 11		8 15	8 18	8 22	8 29
8 21	8 23	8 27	8 29	8 31	8 35	8 40	8 46
9 12		9 17		9 21	9 25	9 30	9 36
9 51		9 56		10 00	10 03	10 07	10 15
	11 04	11 08	f11 10	11 12	11 16	11 21	11 28
11 48		11 53		11 57	12 01	12 07	12 14
1 15	1 18	1 22		1 25	1 28	1 33	1 39
3 03		3 09		3 13	3 16	3 21	3 27
	4 05	4 09	f4 11	4 13	4 16	4 21	4 27
4 56		5 01		5 05	5 08	5 12	5 18
	5 19	5 23	f5 25	5 27	5 30	5 37	5 44
6 16		6 22		6 26	6 29	6 34	6 40
6 56	7 00	7 04	7 06	7 08	7 11	7 16	7 22
7 19					7 28	7 32	7 37
8 16		8 21			8 26	8 30	8 35
8 37	8 40	8 44	8 46	8 48	8 51	8 56	9 02
9 45		9 51			9 57	10 02	10 12
					10 24		10 34

f-Stops on signal or notice to conductor. k-Saturdays only. A.M. light type. P.M. heavy type.

The Blue Comet to Atlantic City
De Luxe Coach Train—3 hours flat

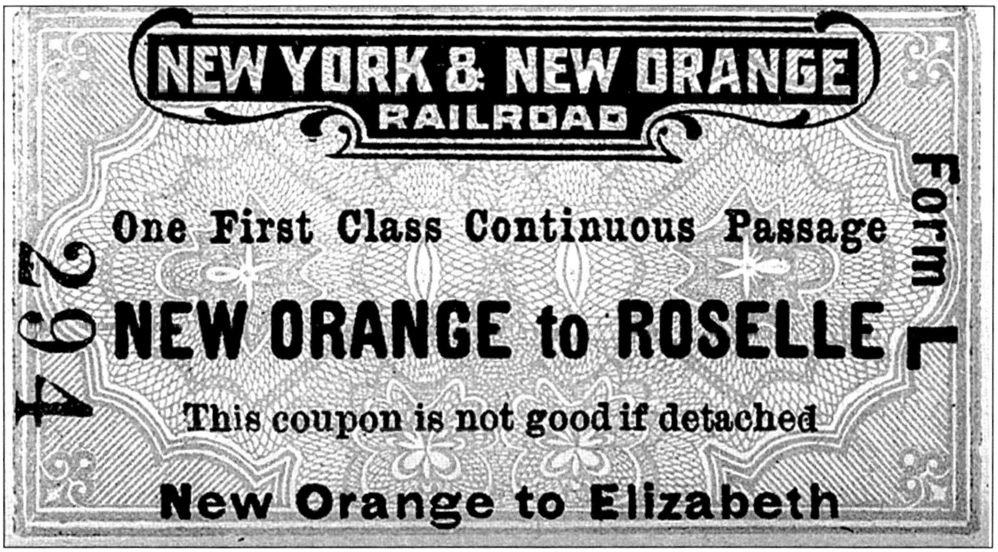

This New York & New Orange Railroad stub was detached from a first-class ticket, good for one passage between New Orange and Roselle. The Roselle Station, on the Central Railroad of New Jersey, was one stop away from the Aldene Station. (Collection of Donald A. Maxton.)

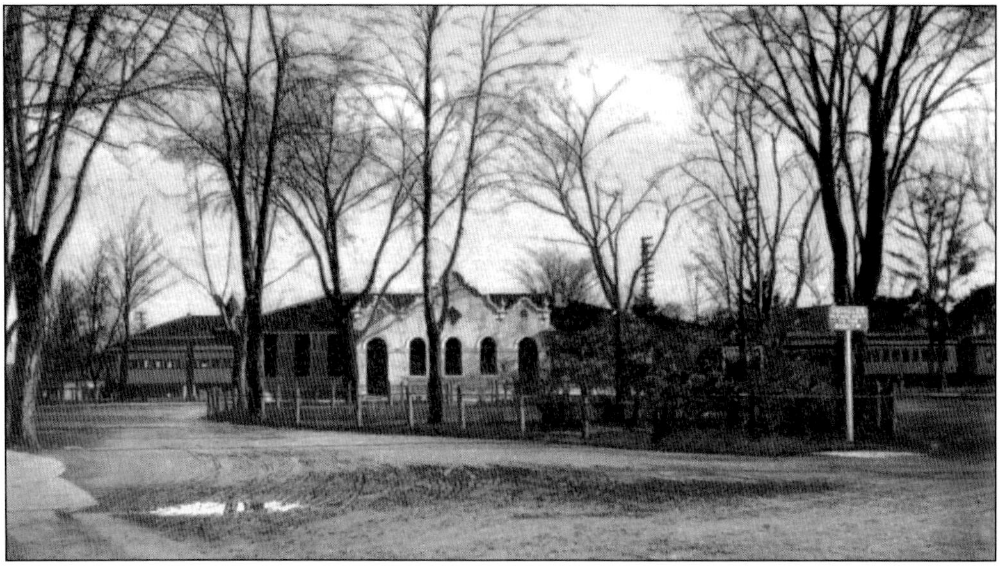

Passengers traveling from towns along the New York & New Orange Railroad (later, the Rahway Valley Railroad) to Roselle would detrain at the Central Railroad of New Jersey's Roselle Station, shown here in an early postcard view. (Collection of Donald A. Maxton.)

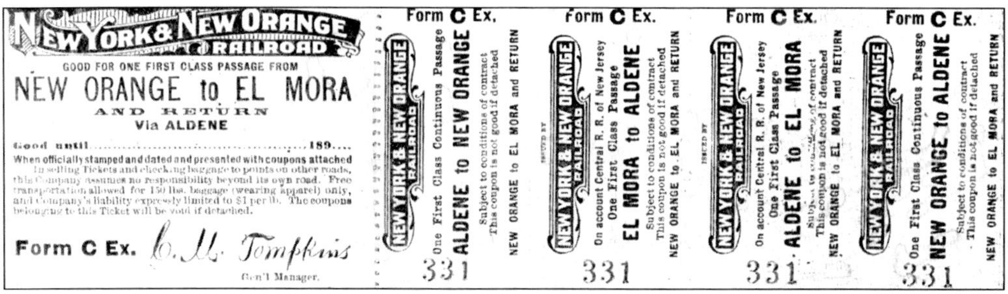

The distance between New Orange (now Kenilworth) and the Elmora section of Elizabeth is only a few miles, but a train was the most convenient way of making that journey in the early 1900s. This New York & New Orange Railroad ticket provided a first-class return passage between those two points. (Collection of Donald A. Maxton.)

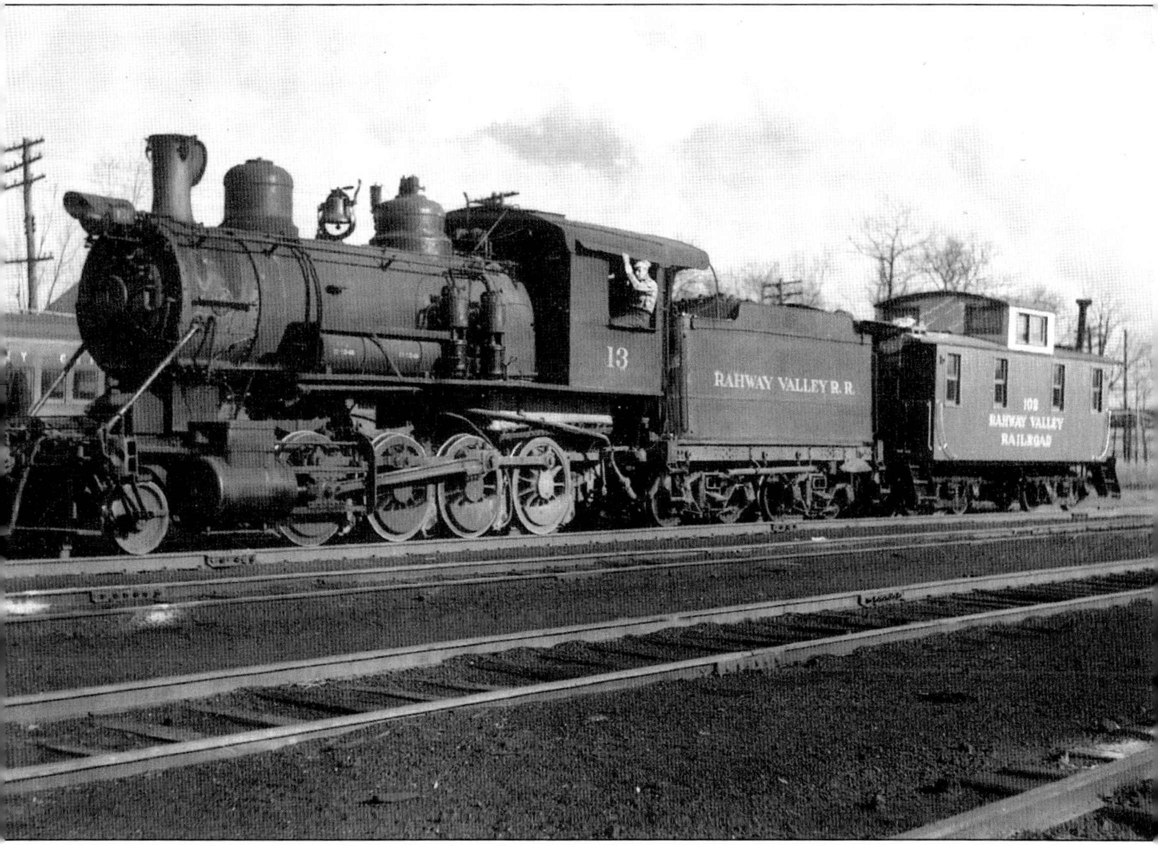

Aldene was a favorite spot for railroad enthusiasts, who took many excellent photographs here over the years. In this one, a Rahway Valley fireman Bob Hoeft waves and the brakeman stands at the front of No. 13 as it gets ready to move down the line with Caboose No. 102 in tow on December 9, 1950. Part of a Central Railroad of New Jersey passenger coach is just visible on the left. (Courtesy of Mary E. McCoy.)

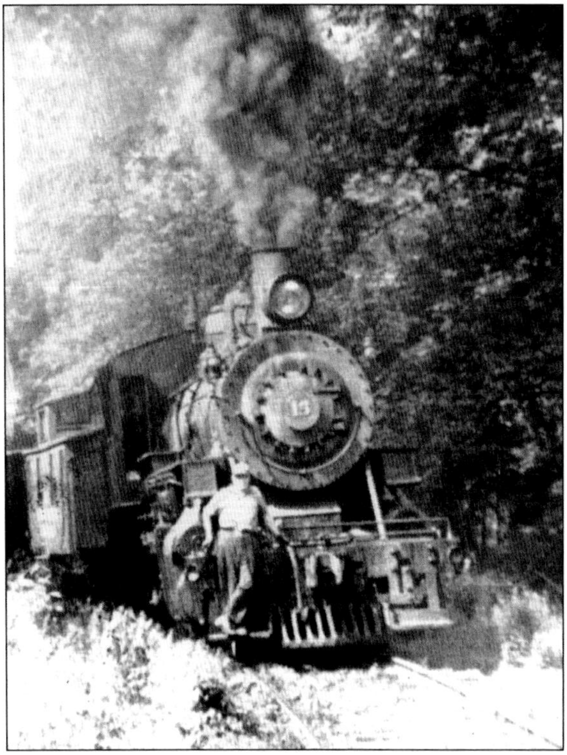

RV No. 15 hauls a train into Kenilworth from the Central Railroad of New Jersey interchange at Aldene in 1950, with John Enright standing on the pilot. By 1950, the RV was competing vigorously with the trucking industry, moving as many as 40 cars a day. In the October 1950 issue of *Trains* magazine, Clark pointed out, "35 are about what we can handle nicely." (Photograph by Bruce Nett.)

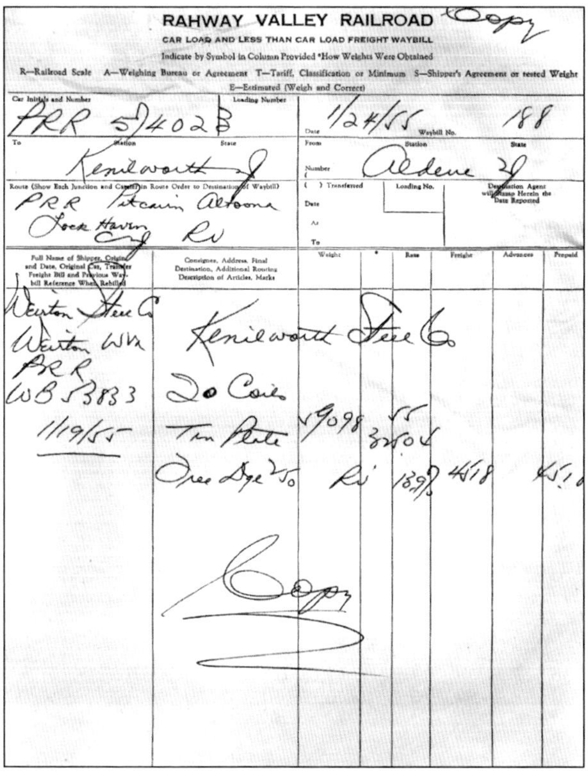

RAHWAY VALLEY RAILROAD Copy

CAR LOAD AND LESS THAN CAR LOAD FREIGHT WAYBILL

Indicate by Symbol in Column Provided *How Weights Were Obtained

R—Railroad Scale A—Weighing Bureau or Agreement T—Tariff, Classification or Minimum S—Shipper's Agreement or tested Weight E—Estimated (Weigh and Correct)

Car Initials and Number: PRR 517402B
Loading Number
Date: 1/24/55
Waybill No.: 188
To Station: Kenilworth State: NJ
From Station: Aldene State: NJ
Number
Route (Show Each Junction and Carrier in Route Order to Destination of Waybill): PRR Pitcairn Altoona Lock Haven CNJ RV
( ) Transferred Date At To
Loading No.
Destination Agent will Stamp Herein the Date Reported

Full Name of Shipper, Origin and Date, Original Car, Transfer Freight Bill and Previous Waybill Reference When Rebilled	Consignee, Address, Final Destination, Additional Routing Description of Articles, Marks	Weight	*	Rate	Freight	Advances	Prepaid
Weirton Steel Co Weirton WVa PRR WB 53833 1/19/55	Kenilworth Steel Co 20 Coils Tin Plate	9098					

Copy

The Rahway Valley Railroad picked up a wide variety of freight at the Aldene interchange. Here is a 1955 waybill for a carload of steel picked up for the Kenilworth Steel Company. This load was shipped from the Weirton Steel Company of Weirton, West Virginia, on the Pennsylvania Railroad. Once it reached Aldene, the Rahway Valley Railroad handled the rest of the job, delivering it directly to the customer's freight siding. (Courtesy of Mary E. McCoy.)

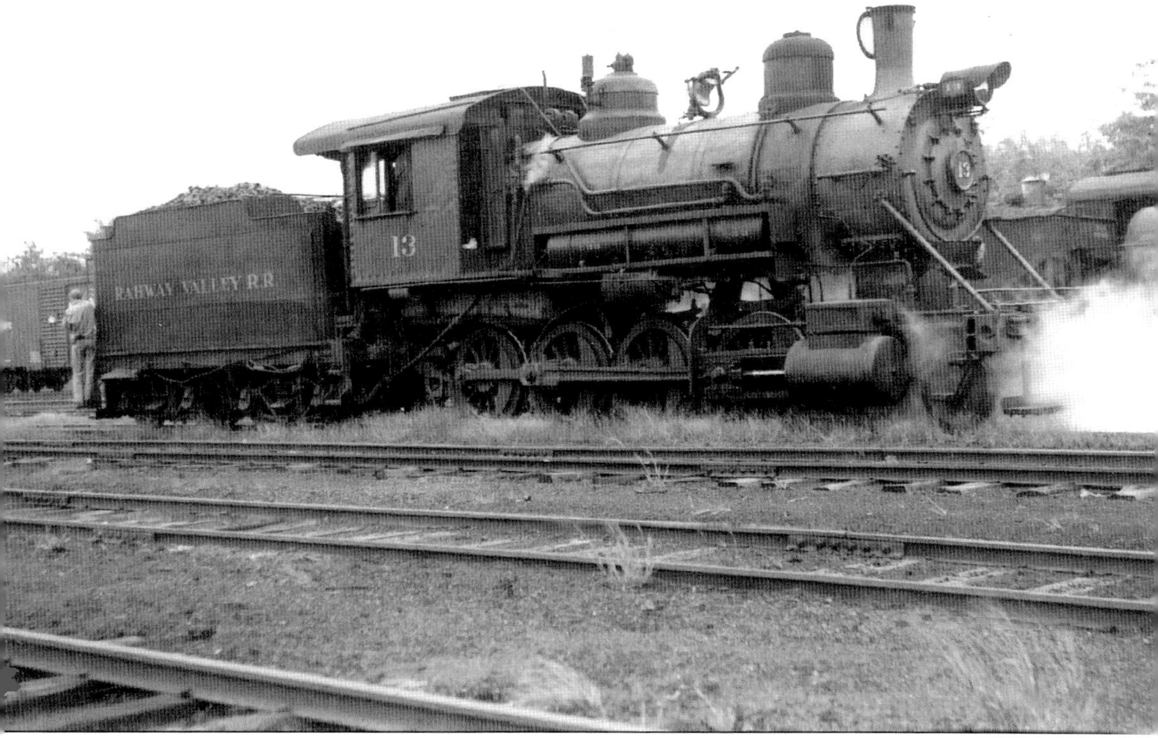

Here is another view of RV No. 13 in action at the Aldene interchange, on August 28, 1950. Nos. 13 and 14 handled the lion's share of chores on the Rahway Valley Railroad, even after the line acquired No. 15, its last steam locomotive. (Courtesy of Mary E. McCoy.)

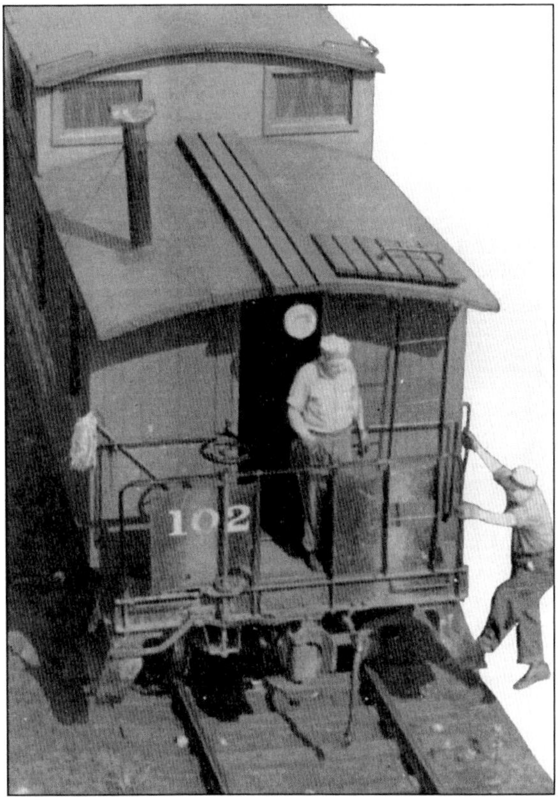

A Rahway Valley crew works on Caboose No. 102 at the Aldene interchange in this photograph, which illustrated an article in *Trains* magazine. This nationwide publication focused a lot of attention on the little Rahway Valley Railroad. (Photograph by Bruce Nett.)

On another occasion, the Rahway Valley Railroad picked up a less typical load for the Kenilworth Steel Company: a Pennsylvania Railroad dining car for an industrial show. As described in this letter forwarded to Rahway Valley president and general manager George A. Clark, it was moved by the Pennsylvania Railroad to Oak Island Junction in Newark. From there, the Central Railroad of New Jersey delivered it to Aldene, where the Rahway Valley Railroad picked it up and brought it to Kenilworth Steel. (Courtesy of Mary E. McCoy.)

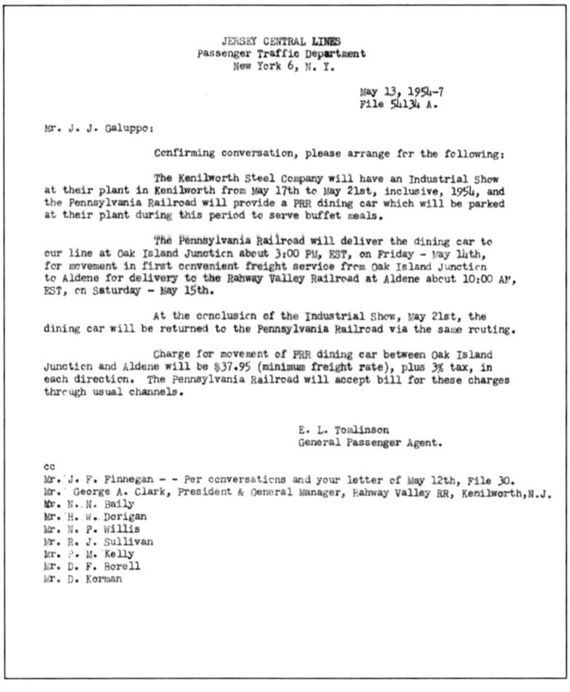

JERSEY CENTRAL LINES
Passenger Traffic Department
New York 6, N. Y.

May 13, 1954-7
File 54134 A.

Mr. J. J. Galuppo:

Confirming conversation, please arrange for the following:

The Kenilworth Steel Company will have an Industrial Show at their plant in Kenilworth from May 17th to May 21st, inclusive, 1954, and the Pennsylvania Railroad will provide a PRR dining car which will be parked at their plant during this period to serve buffet meals.

The Pennsylvania Railroad will deliver the dining car to our line at Oak Island Junction about 3:00 PM, EST, on Friday - May 14th, for movement in first convenient freight service from Oak Island Junction to Aldene for delivery to the Rahway Valley Railroad at Aldene about 10:00 AM, EST, on Saturday - May 15th.

At the conclusion of the Industrial Show, May 21st, the dining car will be returned to the Pennsylvania Railroad via the same routing.

Charge for movement of PRR dining car between Oak Island Junction and Aldene will be $37.95 (minimum freight rate), plus 3% tax, in each direction. The Pennsylvania Railroad will accept bill for these charges through usual channels.

E. L. Tomlinson
General Passenger Agent.

cc
Mr. J. F. Finnegan - - Per conversations and your letter of May 12th, File 30.
Mr. George A. Clark, President & General Manager, Rahway Valley RR, Kenilworth,N.J.
Mr. N. N. Baily
Mr. H. W. Dorigan
Mr. N. P. Willis
Mr. R. J. Sullivan
Mr. P. M. Kelly
Mr. D. F. Borell
Mr. D. Korman

SUBJECT TO TARIFF OF INCREASED RATES AND CHARGES No. X-175-B, AGENT C. W. BOIN'S I.C.C. No. A-955, P.U.C.-N.J. No. A-62, SUPPLEMENTS TO OR SUCCESSIVE ISSUES THEREOF.

Supplements Nos. †1 and 2 contain all changes.

† - Special Supplement Ex Parte No. 175

Supplement No. 2 to
I.C.C. No. 178
Supplement No. 2 to
P.U.C.-N.J. No. 9

RAHWAY VALLEY COMPANY

(RAHWAY VALLEY COMPANY, LESSEE)

LOCAL AND PROPORTIONAL FREIGHT TARIFF

APPLYING ON

COMMODITIES

BETWEEN STATIONS ON

RAHWAY VALLEY COMPANY
(RAHWAY VALLEY COMPANY, Lessee)

(AS SHOWN HEREIN)

Governed, except as otherwise provided by the Official Classification, No. 64, Agent W. S. Flint's I.C.C.-O.C. No. 64, P.U.C.-N.J.-O.C. No. 64, by exceptions thereto as published in Agent C. W. Boin's Freight Tariff No. 90-K I.C.C. No. A 848, P.U.C.-N.J. No. A-30, and by supplements to and successive issues of said publications.

ISSUED JUNE 29, 1954 EFFECTIVE AUGUST 1, 1954

This supplement contains changes in rates resulting in increases and reductions, specific indication of which, as required by Rule 2(a) of Tariff Circular No. 20, is omitted under Permission of the Interstate Commerce Commission No. 60971, dated May 13, 19[illegible]

GEORGE A. CLARK
President and General Manager
Boulevard and Market Street
KENILWORTH, NEW JERSEY

Issued by
A. T. MOSCA
General Freight Agent
Boulevard and Market Street
KENILWORTH, NEW JERSEY

(100)

5692-A

This 1954 supplement to a Rahway Valley Railroad freight tariff was issued by A.T. Mosca, the railroad's general freight agent. The reverse side shows the commodity rates (given in cents) for shipping various grades of coal—still widely used as heating fuel in the 1950s—from the Rahway Valley interchanges at Aldene and Roselle Park to Kenilworth, Baltusrol, Springfield, Unionbury, Newark Heights, and Summit. The highest rate was for shipping anthracite coal to Summit, at $1.13 per ton. Coal was a mainstay of the Rahway Valley's business until the 1960s. (Courtesy of Mary E. McCoy.)

COMMODITY RATES--- In Cents.

ITEM NO.	COMMODITY	BETWEEN	AND	RATE
				Per ton 2,000 lbs.
35-A Cancels 35	Coal, Anthracite, Including Anthracite Briquettes and Boulettes, C.L. Minimum 44,800 lbs............... (In straight or mixed carloads)	Aldene.........N.J. Roselle Park...N.J.	Kenilworth......N.J. Baltusrol.......N.J. Springfield.....N.J. Unionbury.......N.J. Newark Heights (Maplewood)....N.J. Summit..........N.J.	92 92 92 92 113 113
		BETWEEN	AND	Per ton 2,000 lbs.
40-A Cancels 40	Coal, Bituminous, C.L. Minimum weight 44,800 pounds..	Aldene.........N.J. Roselle Park...N.J.	Kenilworth......N.J. Balustrol.......N.J. Springfield.....N.J. Unionbury.......N.J. Newark Heights (Maplewood)....N.J. Summit..........N.J.	79 79 79 79 100 100
		BETWEEN	AND	Per ton 2,000 lbs.
42-A Cancels 42	Coal, cannel, C.L., Minimum weight 44,800 pounds.....	Aldene.........N.J. Roselle Park...N.J.	Kenilworth......N.J. Balustrol.......N.J. Springfield.....N.J. Unionbury.......N.J. Newark Heights (Maplewood)....N.J. Summit..........N.J.	79 79 79 79 100 100

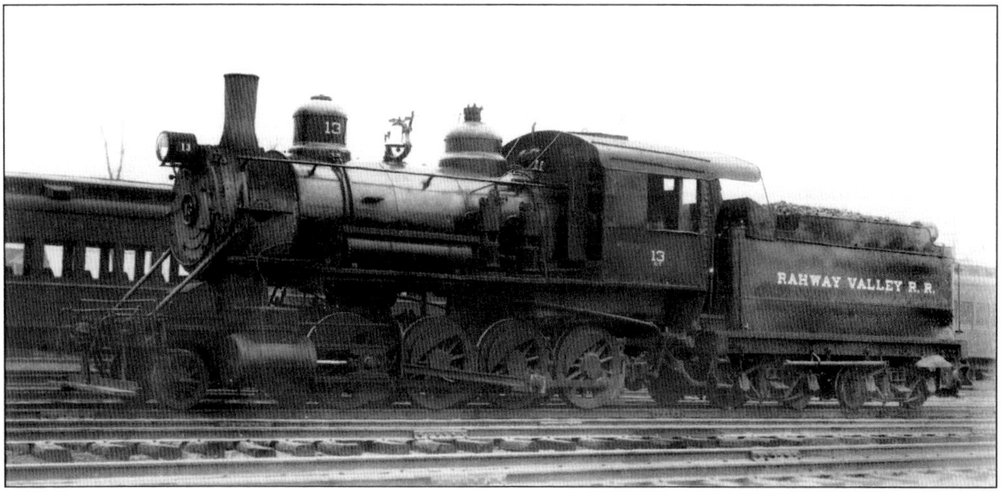

Here is RV No. 13 in action on the border of Roselle Park and Cranford, just down the line from the Aldene Station. (Photograph by R.P. Morris, courtesy of Edward H. Weber.)

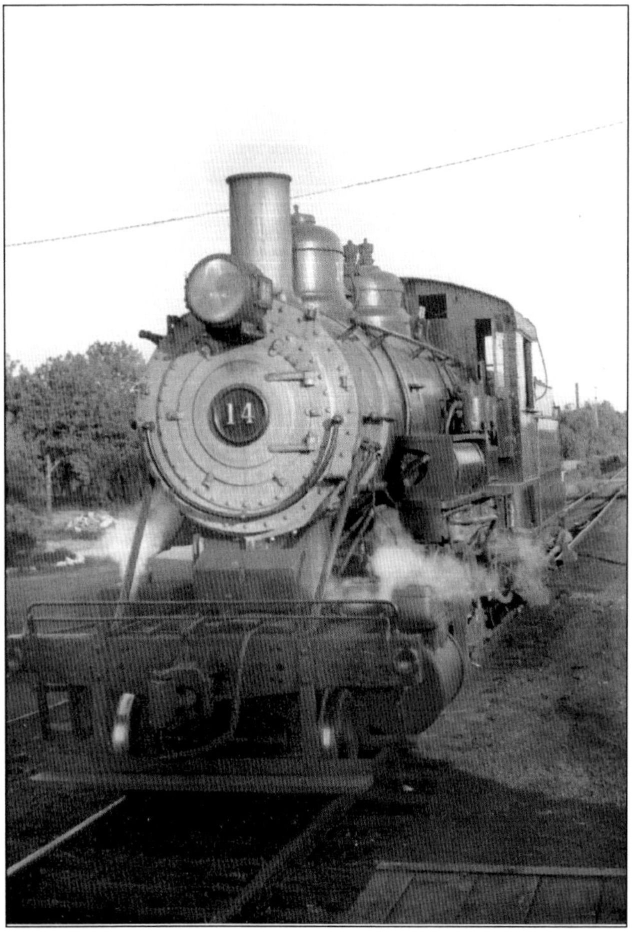

Here is a striking view of RV No. 14 in action. Nos. 13 and 14, twins built in 1905, were steady, reliable workhorses on the short line for many years. No. 14 was retired in 1951, the year the Rahway Valley purchased its first diesel engine, a General Electric 70-tonner. No. 13 was kept in running condition for a short while longer. (Courtesy of Mary E. McCoy.)

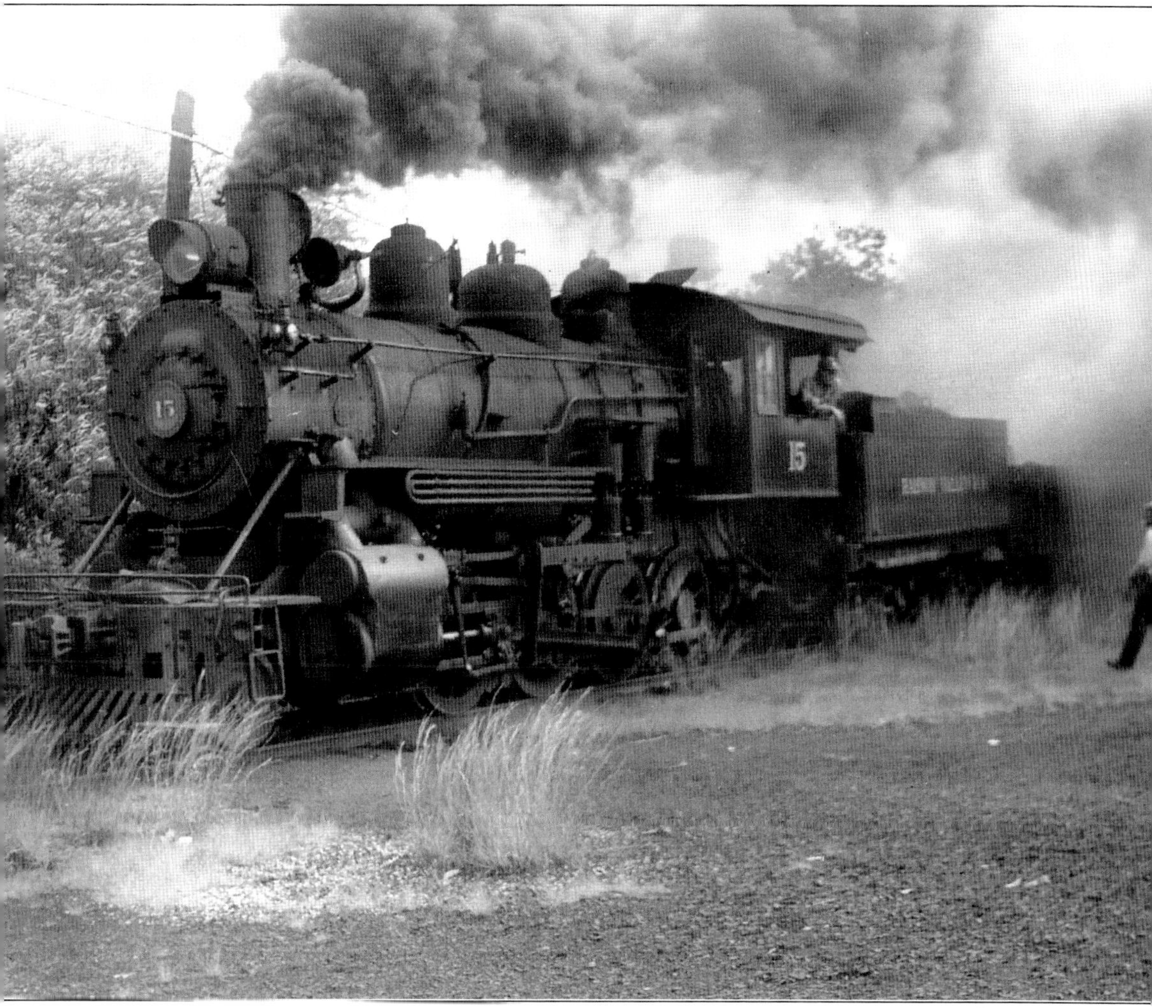

RV No. 15 is an impressive sight as it generates a fine plume of smoke at the Aldene interchange, sometime during the 1940s. The days of steam were numbered on the Rahway Valley Railroad and other railroads by this time, but photographers managed to document these magnificent machines for future generations to enjoy. (Railroad Avenue Enterprises.)

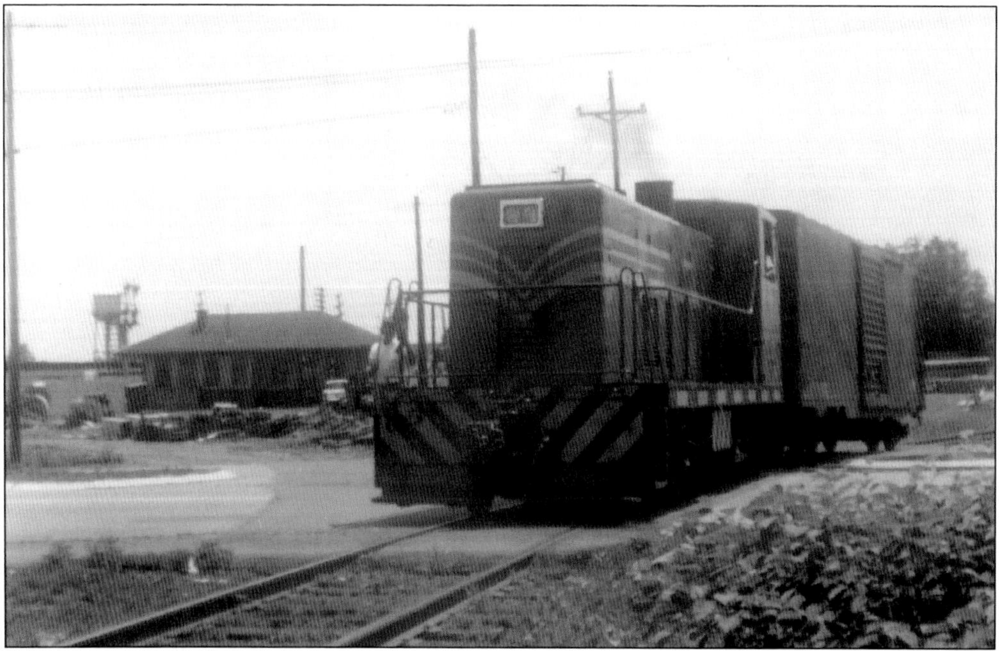

A Rahway Valley diesel engine crosses Westfield Avenue, on the border of Roselle Park and Cranford, with a single boxcar in 1963. It is heading north toward Kenilworth. The second Aldene passenger station may be seen on the left, across the avenue, and the elevated tracks of the Lehigh Valley are visible behind the station. (Photograph by Bruce Trampler.)

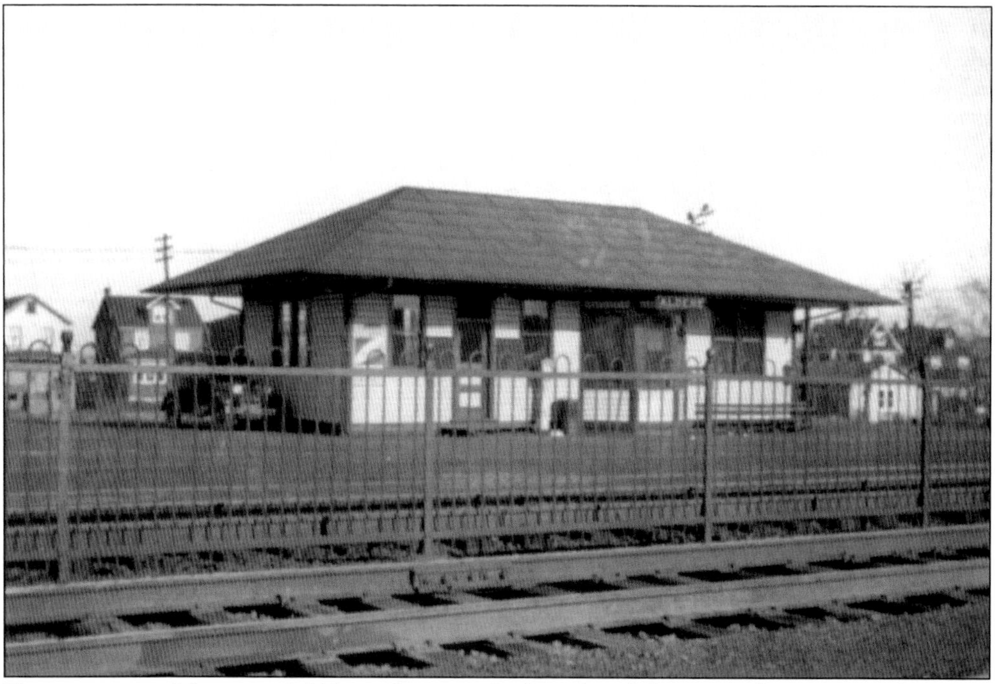

Here is a view of the second Aldene Station, which replaced the original one pictured on page 99. This building has also been razed and is now the site of the Sun Tavern. (Courtesy of the Roselle Park Historical Society.)

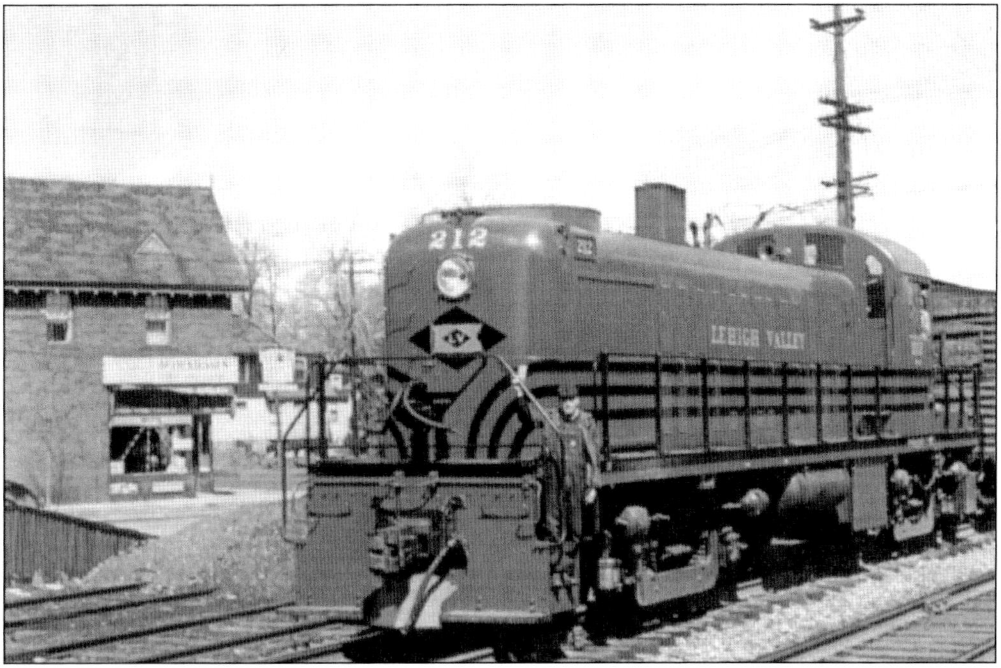

Lehigh Valley No. 212 pulls a freight train past the Chestnut Street grade crossing in Roselle Park, heading toward the railroad's interchange with the Rahway Valley Railroad. (Courtesy of the Roselle Park Historical Society.)

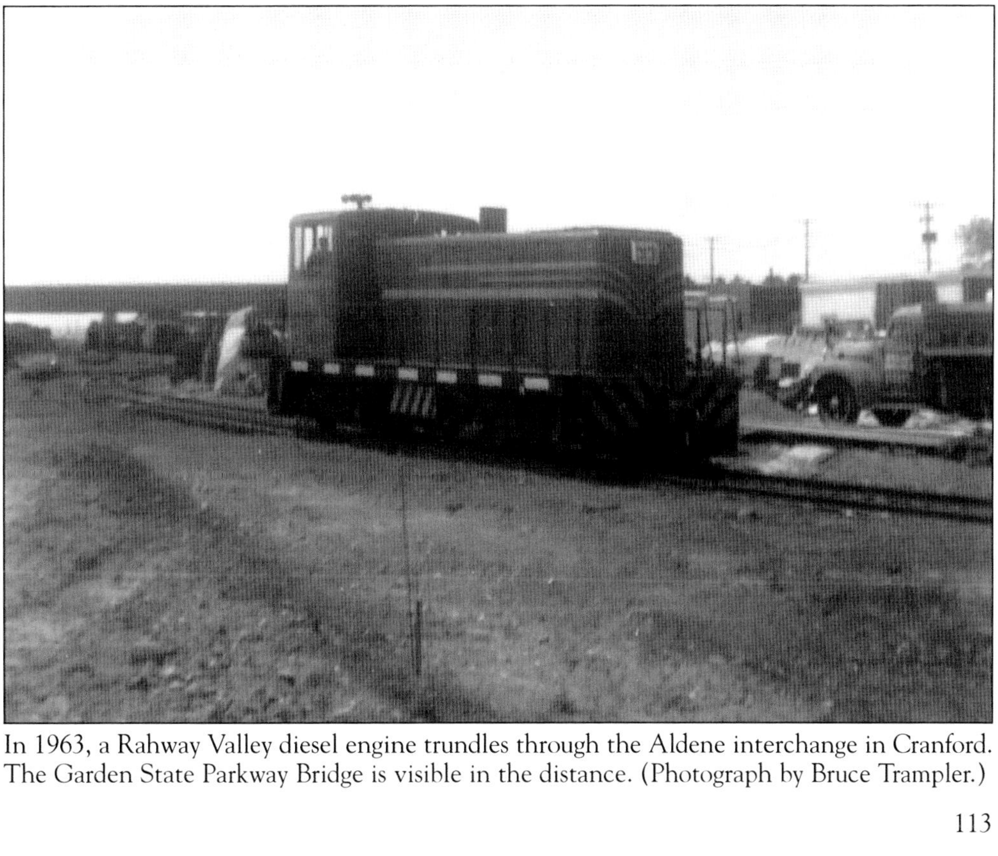

In 1963, a Rahway Valley diesel engine trundles through the Aldene interchange in Cranford. The Garden State Parkway Bridge is visible in the distance. (Photograph by Bruce Trampler.)

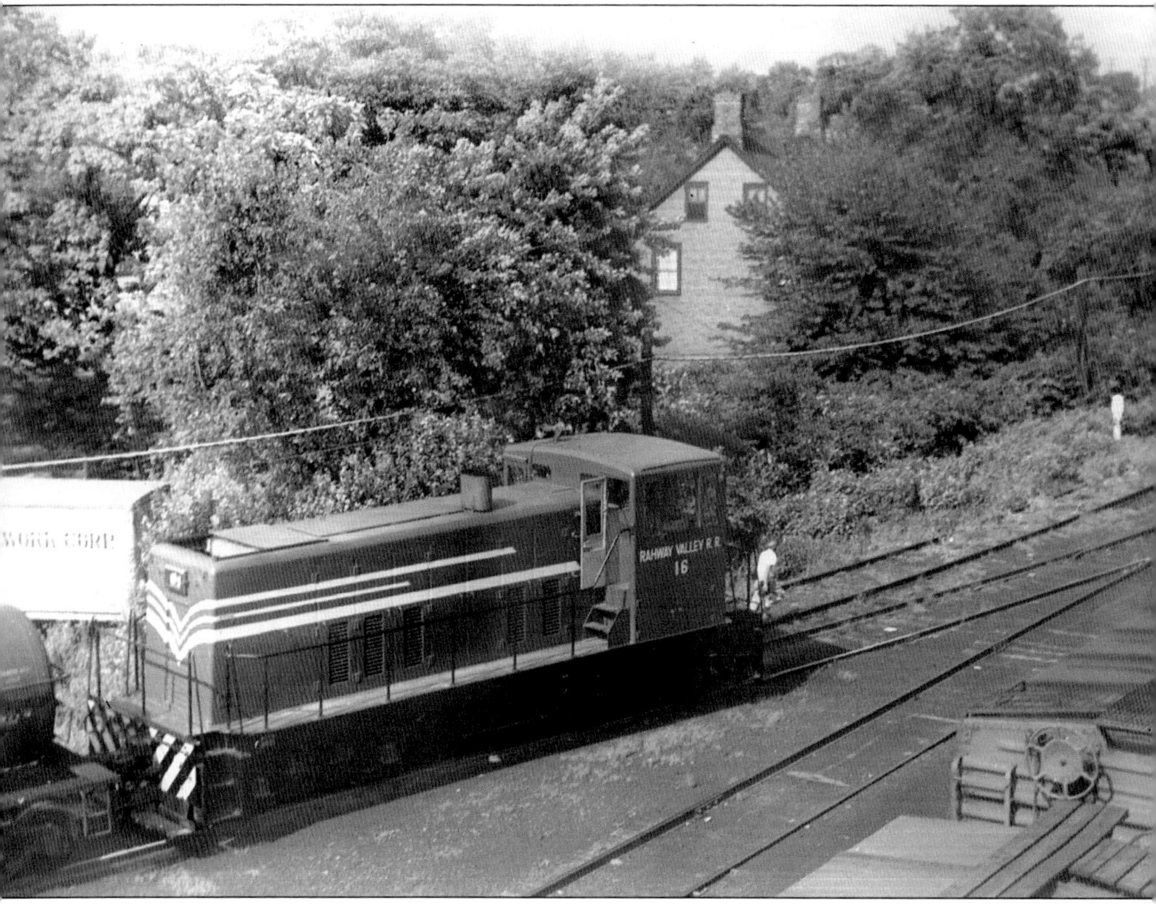

The Rahway Valley Railroad's first diesel engine arrived in 1951. RV No. 16 was still pretty new when this photograph was taken at the Aldene interchange. (Railroad Avenue Enterprises.)

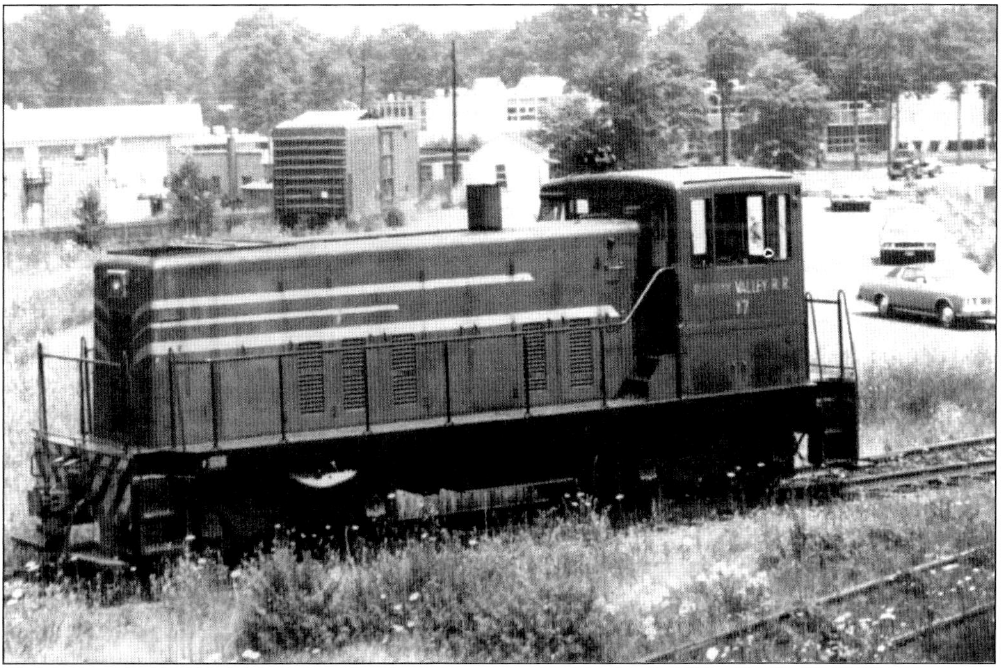

The Rahway Valley Railroad's interchange with the Lehigh Valley Railroad was the short line's other major connection in the Roselle Park area. Here, No. 17 waits for freight cars to be dropped off by the Lehigh Valley Railroad in July 1974. The General Electric 70-tonner looks the worse for wear in this photograph. Both diesels were repainted in their handsome red and white colors during Bernard J. Cahill's tenure as president and general manager of the Rahway Valley Railroad. (Photograph by Richard Hyer and John Zec.)

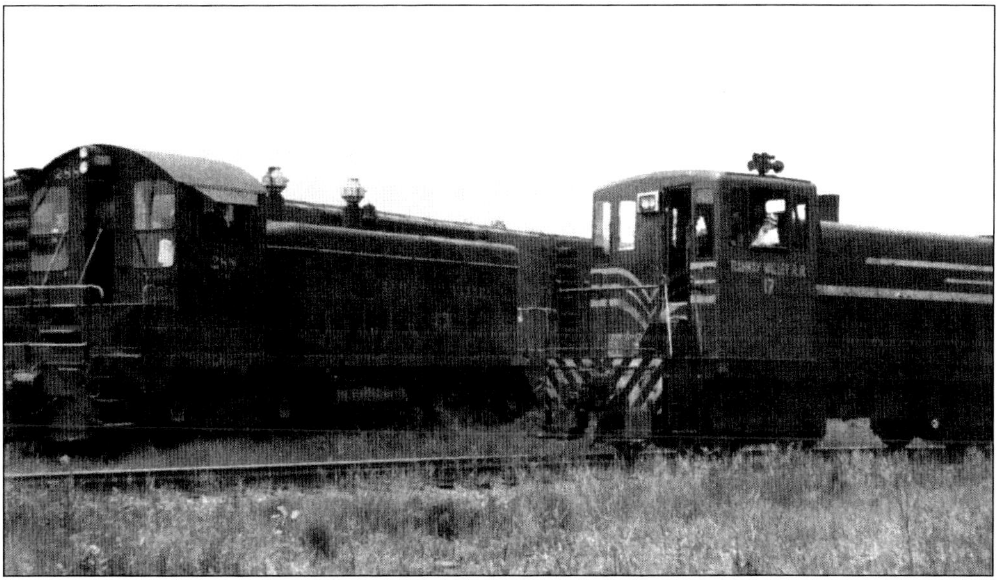

RV No. 17 handles a transfer of cars at the Lehigh Valley Railroad interchange in Roselle Park on a warm day in June 1973. (Photograph by Richard Hyer and John Zec.)

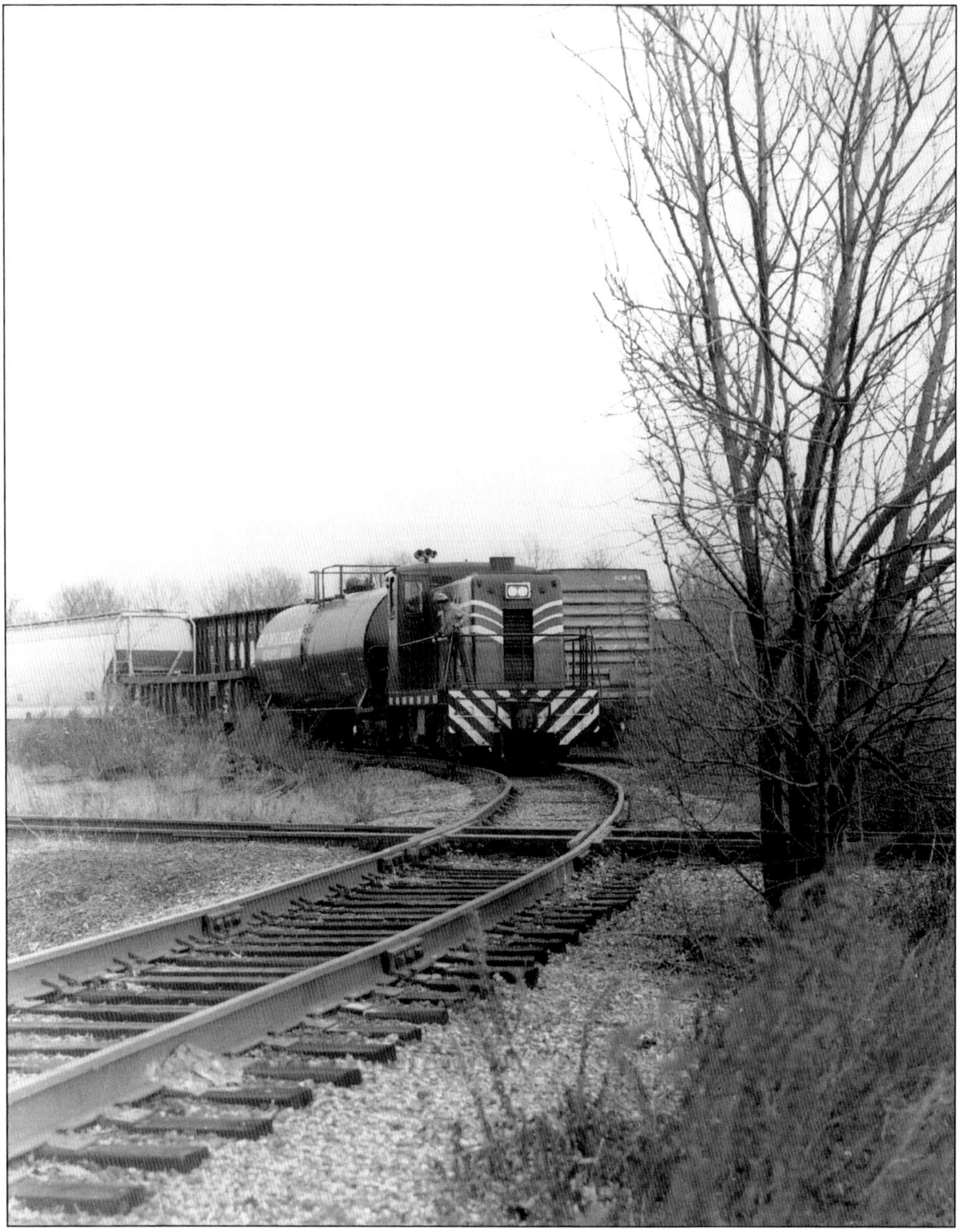

RV No. 17 approaches the "diamond" at the Conrail (former Lehigh Valley) interchange in December 1985. A covered hopper, lumber car, and boxcar stand on a siding behind the short train. By this time, Bernard J. Cahill had upgraded the track in this interchange and freight yard. (Photograph by Bob Pennisi, Railroad Avenue Enterprises.)

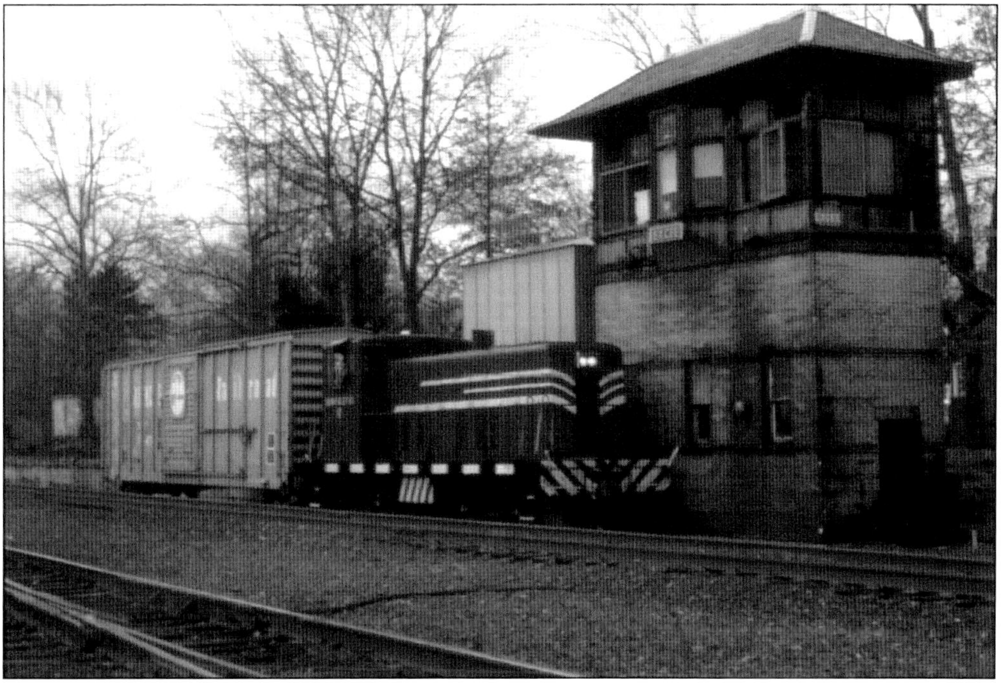

RV No. 17 trundles past New Jersey Transit's tower at Aldene with a single boxcar on December 3, 1988, in the waning years of the Rahway Valley Railroad. (Photograph by Carl G. Perelman.)

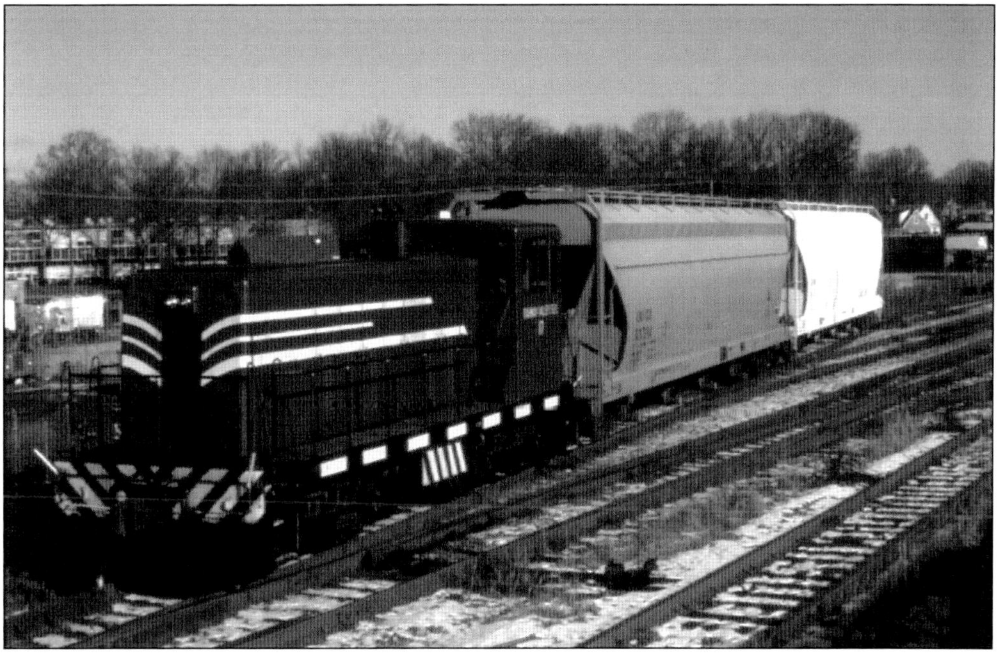

RV No. 17 switches two covered hoppers at the Conrail interchange in Roselle Park on a bright winter's day in January 1987. (Photograph by Carl G. Perelman.)

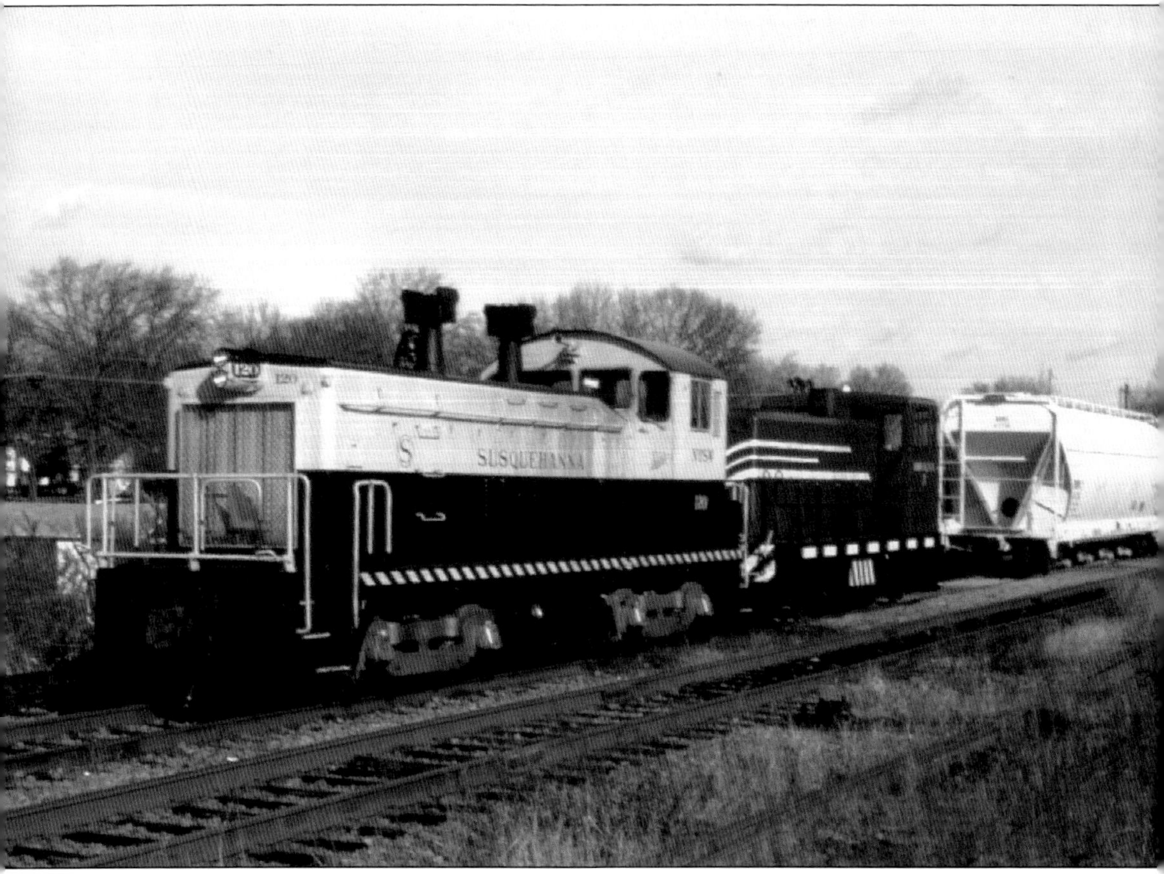

RV No. 17 is joined by NYSW SW9 120 to switch two covered hoppers at the Conrail interchange in Roselle Park. When the Rahway Valley Railroad was acquired by the Delaware Otsego Corporation in 1986, NYSW SW9 120 gradually assumed most of the short line's chores, although it sometimes worked in tandem with a Rahway Valley diesel. New York, Susquehanna & Western crews also used this engine to operate the Staten Island Railway, a short line acquired by Delaware Otsego in 1985. (Photograph by Carl G. Perelman.)

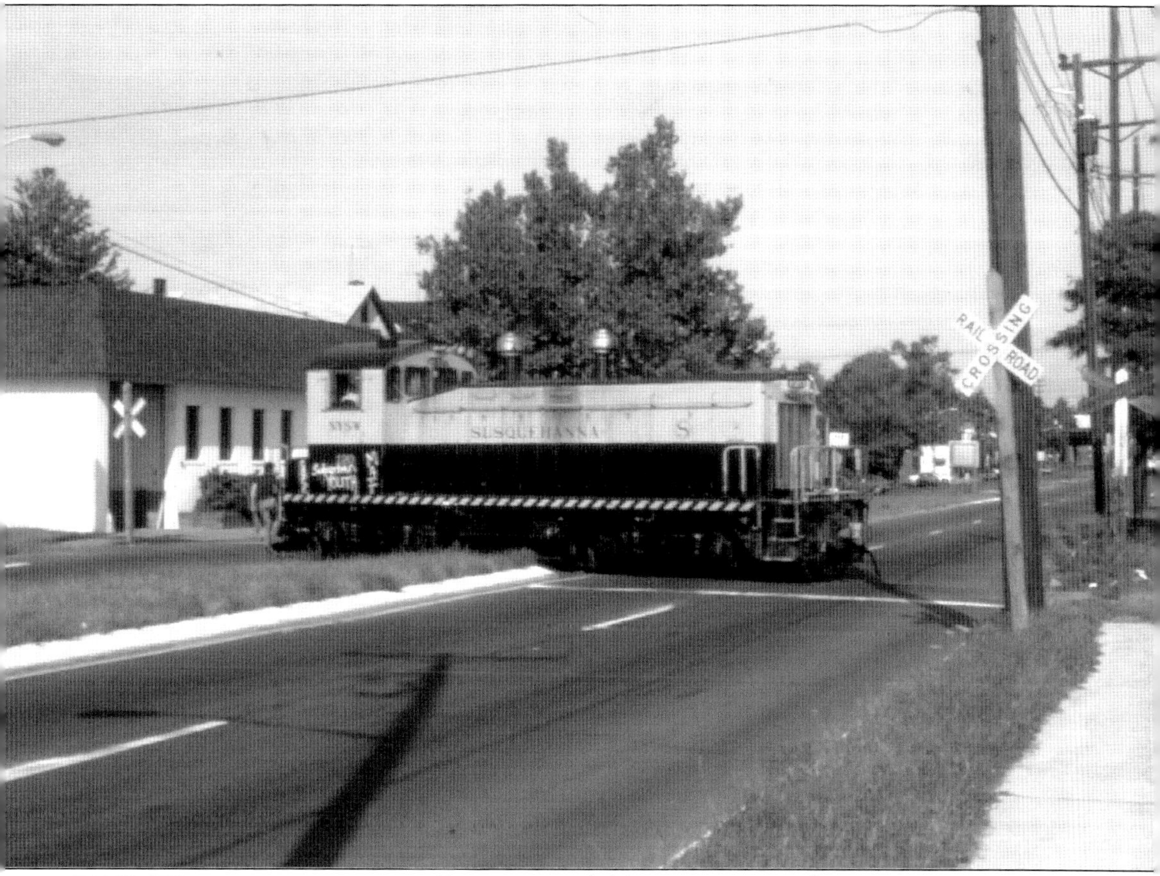

NYSW SW9 120 crosses an unusually quiet Westfield Avenue in Roselle Park, returning from Cranford. After the Delaware Otsego Corporation closed the Roselle Park interchange, the Rahway Valley Railroad would connect at the Staten Island Railway interchange in nearby Cranford. This photograph was taken in 1991, the last full year of service on the Rahway Valley Railroad. (Photograph by Doug Chicff.)

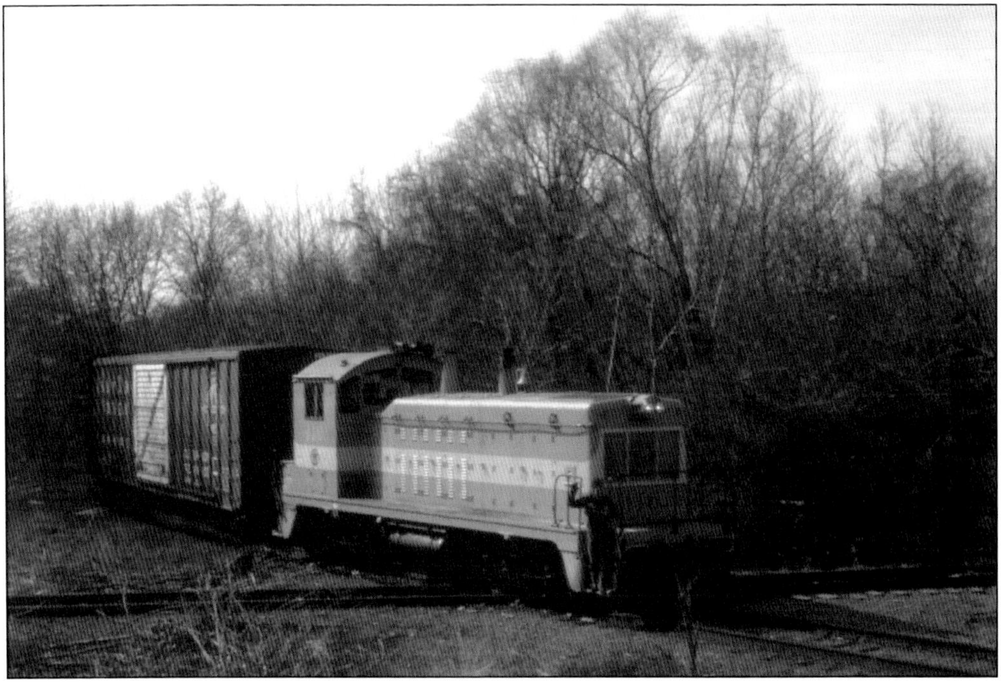

New York Ontario & Western NW2 No. 116 was another visitor to the Rahway Valley Railroad during the Delaware Otsego years. Here, the train crosses the diamond near the Conrail interchange with a boxcar on March 23, 1988. One month later, Delaware Otsego closed this interchange, and the tracks were eventually torn up. (Photograph by Carl G. Perelman.)

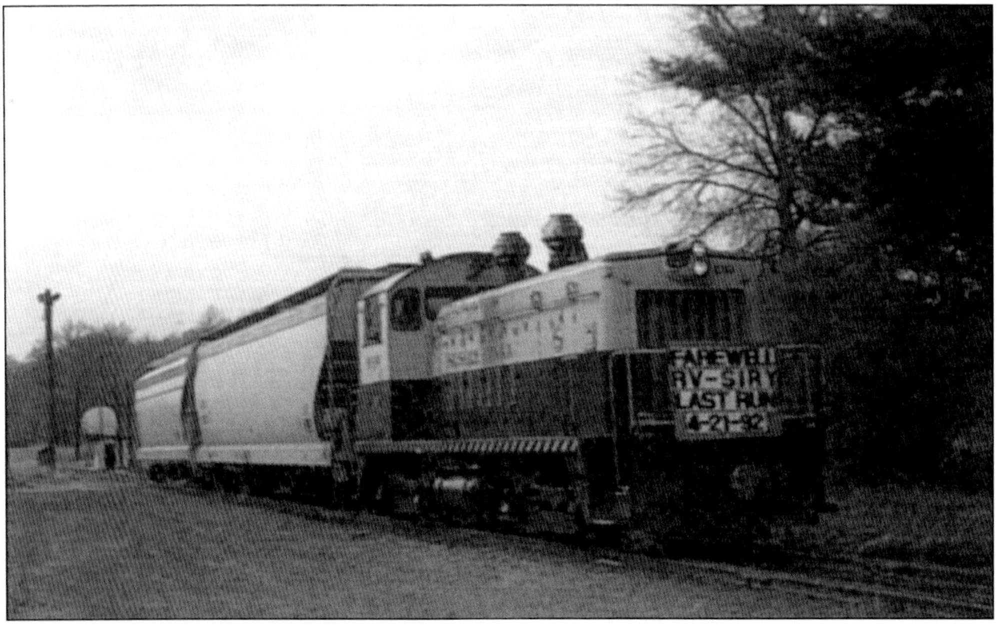

On April 21, 1992, NYSW No. 120 had the honor of being motive power for the Rahway Valley Railroad's last train. On this day, it hauled two of Christie Enterprises' empty covered hoppers to the Conrail interchange in Cranford. This day also marked the end of the Staten Island Railway. (Photograph by Carl G. Perelman.)

Six

STEAMTOWN AND BEYOND: RAHWAY VALLEY CODA

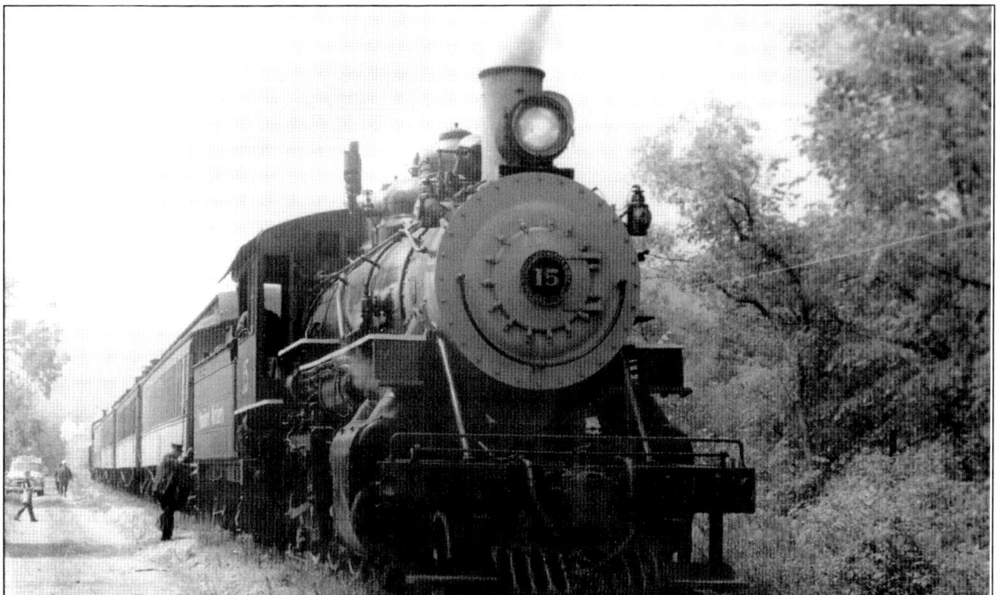

F. Nelson Blount, president of a steam-operated excursion line in South Carver, Massachusetts, purchased RV No. 15 in 1959 for use as an exhibit at Pleasure Island Park in Wakefield, Massachusetts. Eventually, he had the locomotive overhauled and put it into service on his Monadnack, Steamtown and Northern Railroad, an excursion line in Bellows Falls, Vermont. Here is former RV No. 15 getting ready to leave Bellow Falls for its destination in Chester, which was 13 miles away, on June 7, 1964. No. 15 was a favorite of rail fans and came to be called "Faithful Fifteen" in honor of its reliability. (Photograph by Bill Burke.)

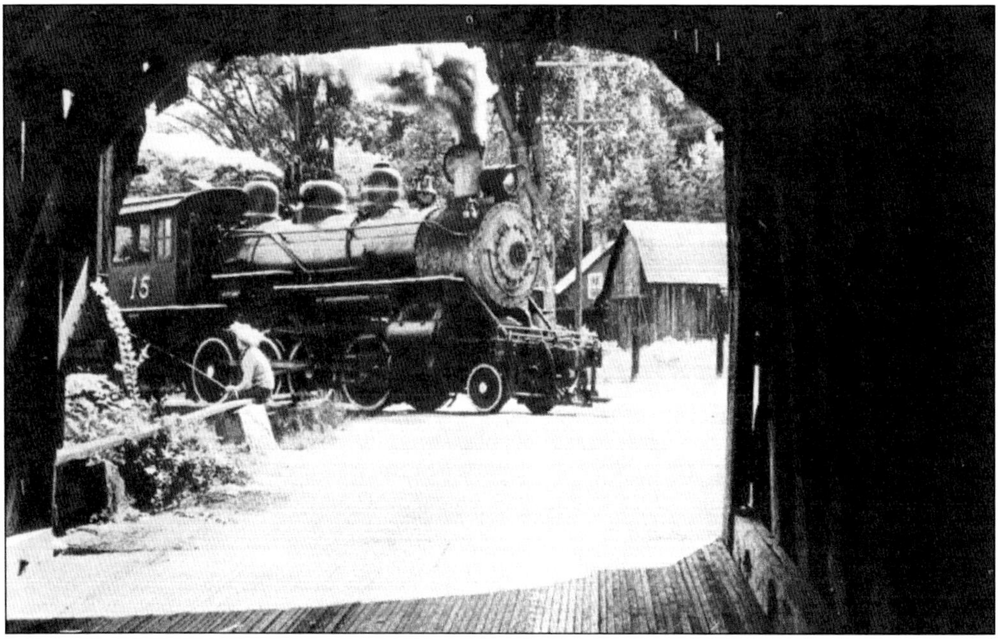

Former RV No. 15 passes a quaint covered bridge in Brockway Mills, Vermont. The little boy sitting near the bridge seems more focused on fishing than on the old steam locomotive! (Photograph by Richard E. Towle, courtesy of Ruth Blount.)

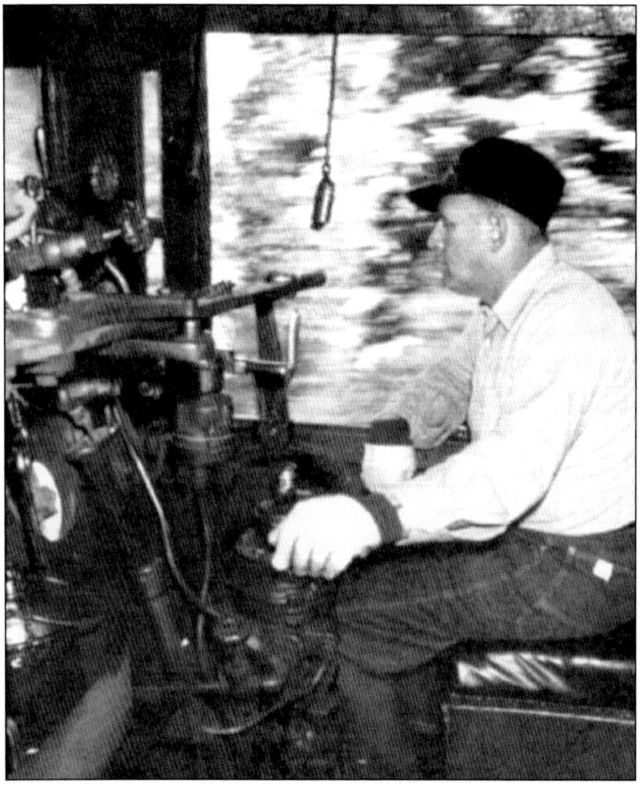

F. Nelson Blount enjoyed working at the throttle of former RV No. 15. Blount, a New Englander who grew wealthy in the seafood business, pursued a wide range of interests in his lifetime, including hunting, fishing, and aviation. He also developed a passion for steam locomotives. At Steamtown in Bellows Falls, he had some 50 of them on display. (Courtesy of Ruth Blount.)

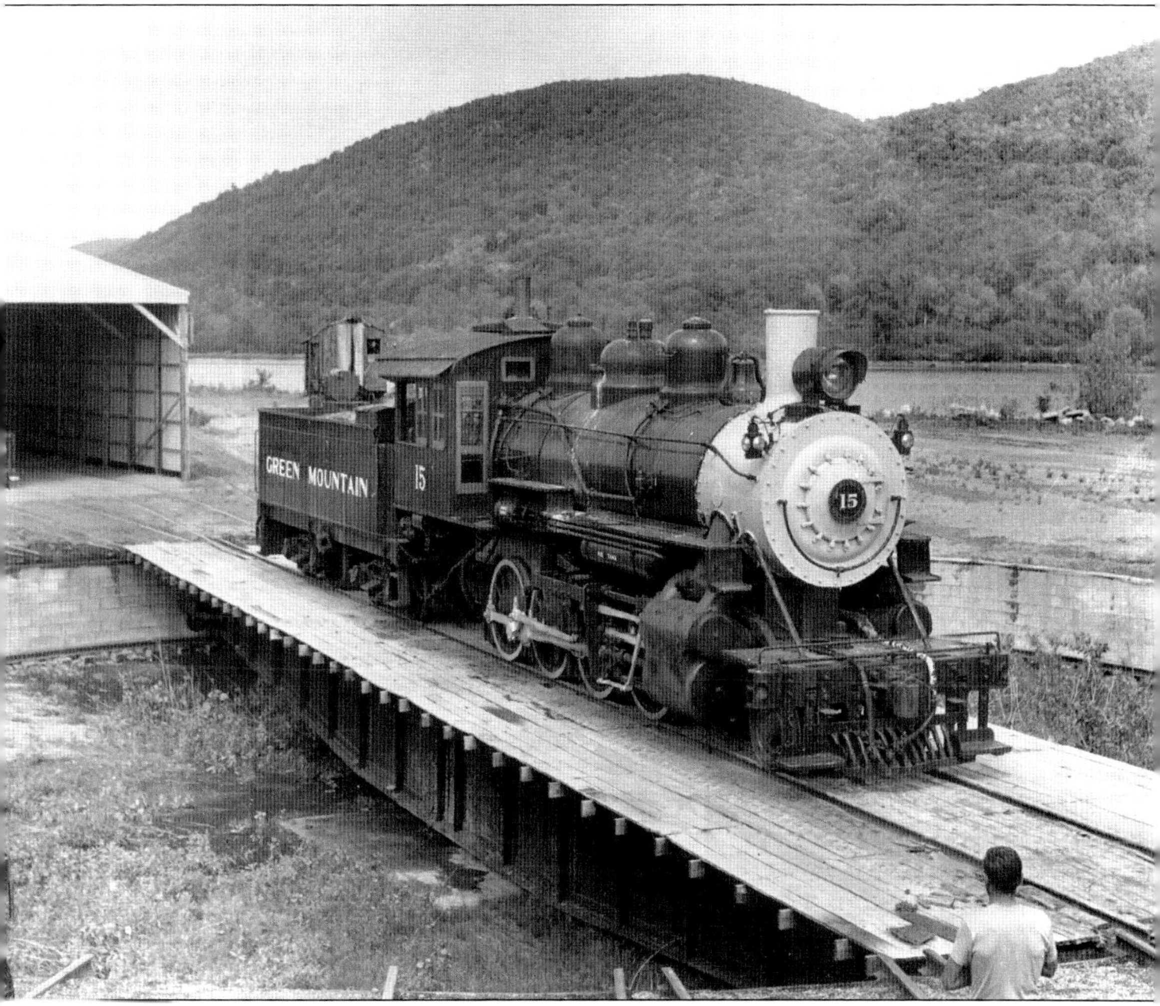

In 1968, following the death of F. Nelson Blount, the Steamtown Foundation put former RV No. 15 into service on Vermont's Green Mountain Railroad excursion line. Suffering from mechanical troubles, after it blew a flue, it made only a few runs here and was placed in storage until 1973. Here, Faithful Fifteen rests on the Green Mountain turntable. (Courtesy of Mary E. McCoy.)

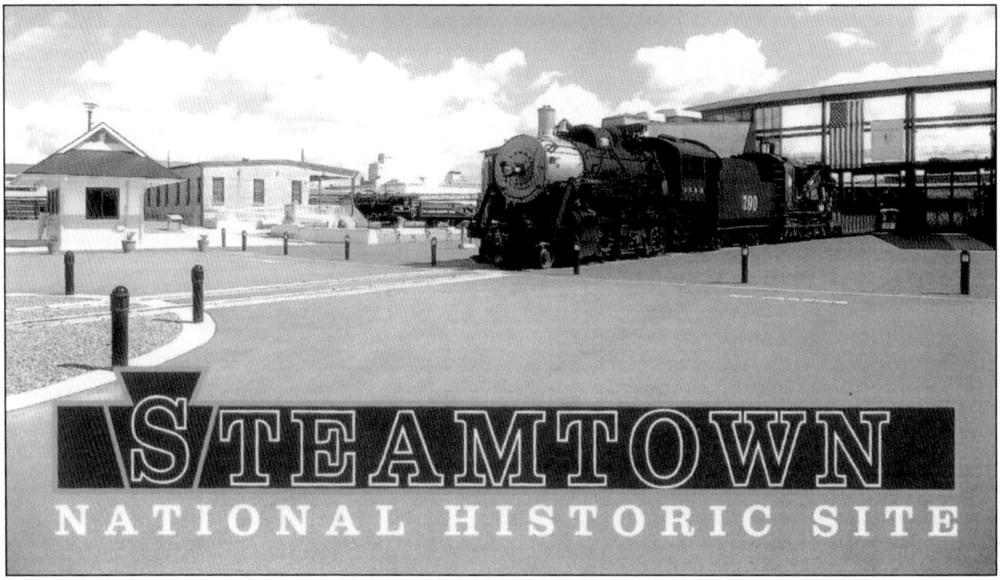

The Steamtown National Historic Site in Scranton, Pennsylvania, home of former RV No. 15, is a great place to see steam locomotives up close and personal. (Collection of Donald A. Maxton.)

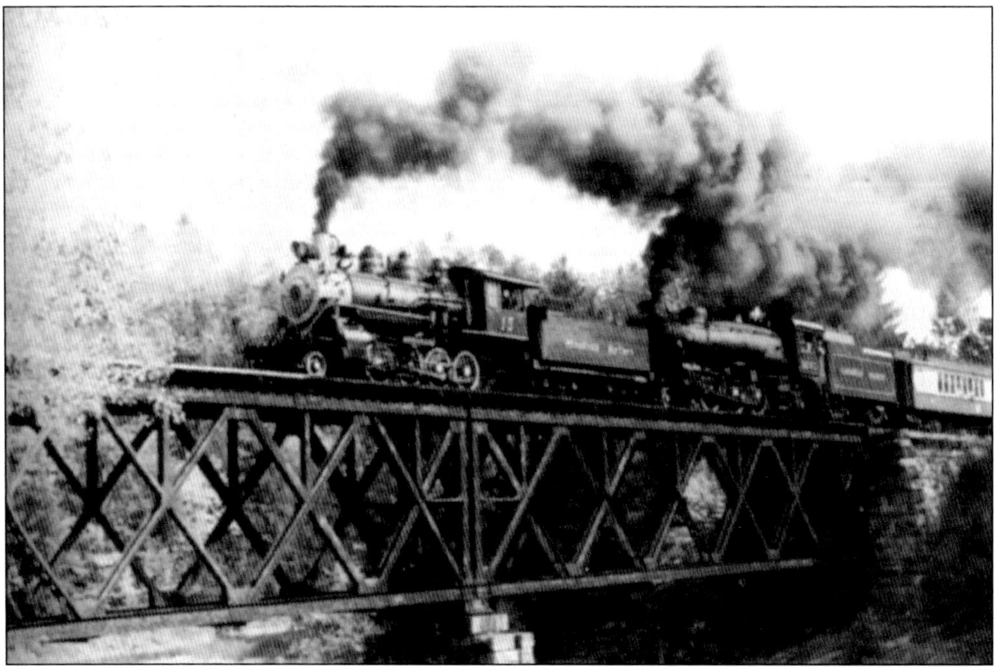

In this photograph, former RV No. 15 steams toward Chester, Vermont, in tandem with another vintage locomotive. From Chester, No. 15 will take a train by itself to Summit, 20 miles farther down the line. (Photograph by Donald S. Robinson, courtesy of Ruth Blount.)

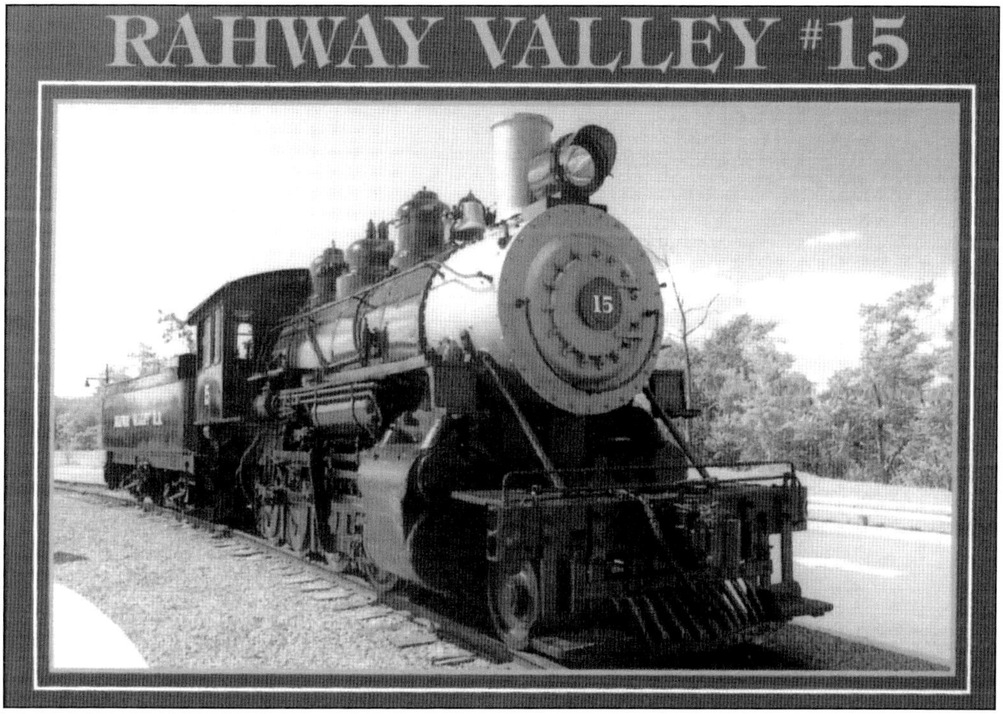

The Rahway Valley Railroad's faithful No. 15, its last steam locomotive, is a top attraction at the Steamtown National Historic Site. This handsome postcard is readily available at the Steamtown Museum Shop. (Collection of Donald A. Maxton.)

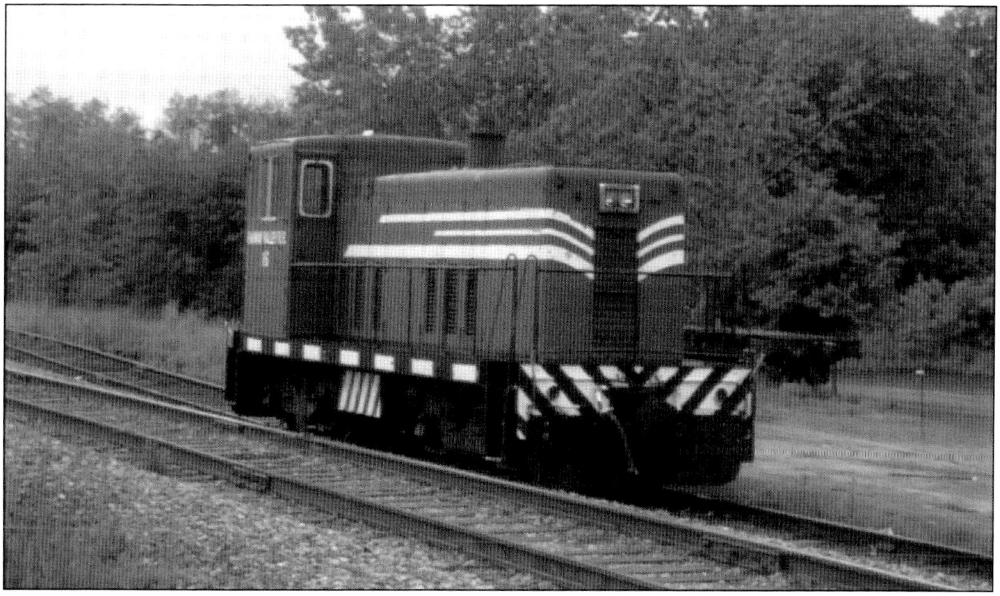

RV No. 16 stands solitary on the New York, Susquehanna & Western right of way near the railroad's interchange with Conrail's Bergen County Line in northern New Jersey. After assuming operation of the Rahway Valley Railroad in 1986, the Delaware Otsego Corporation used Nos. 16 and 17 for service in Passaic and Binghamton, New York. Later, they were sold to the United Railroad Historical Society. (Photograph by Doug Chieff.)

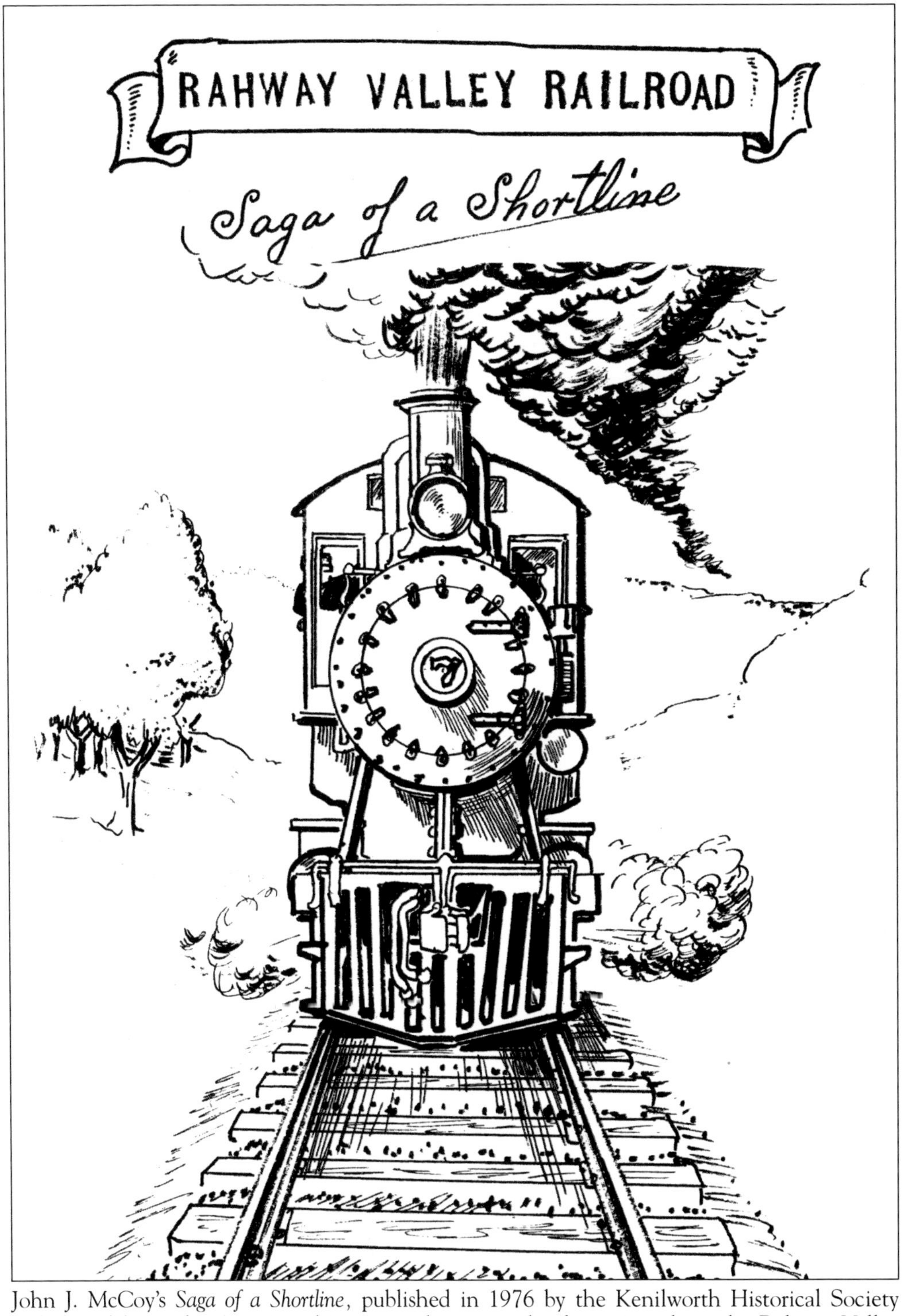

John J. McCoy's *Saga of a Shortline*, published in 1976 by the Kenilworth Historical Society to help celebrate the American bicentennial, preserved information about the Rahway Valley Railroad that might otherwise have been lost forever. It is a treasure trove of information about Rahway Valley history up to 1976. (Art by John J. McCoy.)

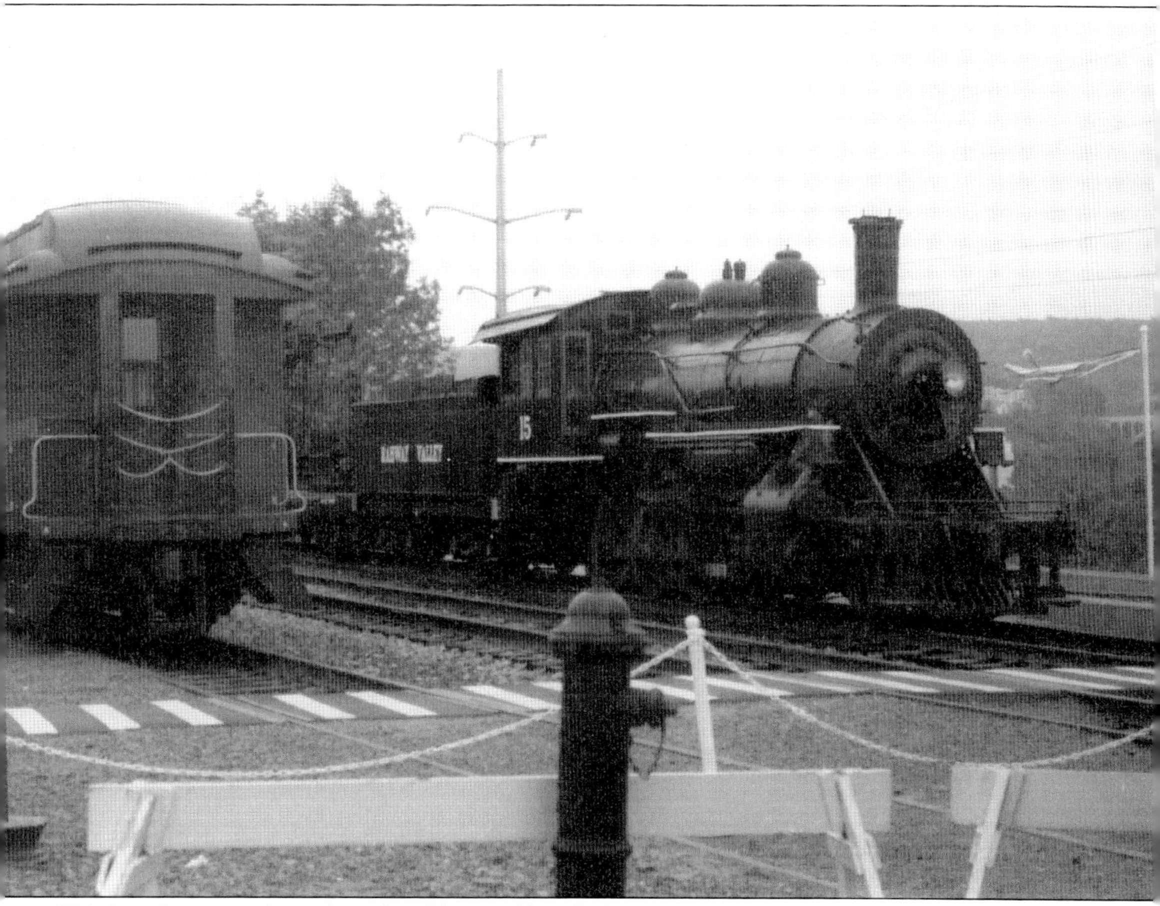

RV No. 15 rests, with its short-lived lowered headlight appearance, at the Steamtown National Historic Site near a vintage passenger coach. No. 15 is not currently employed on excursions, but it is one of the most popular sites at Steamtown, even as a static display. (Photograph by Ronald F. Pietranowicz.)

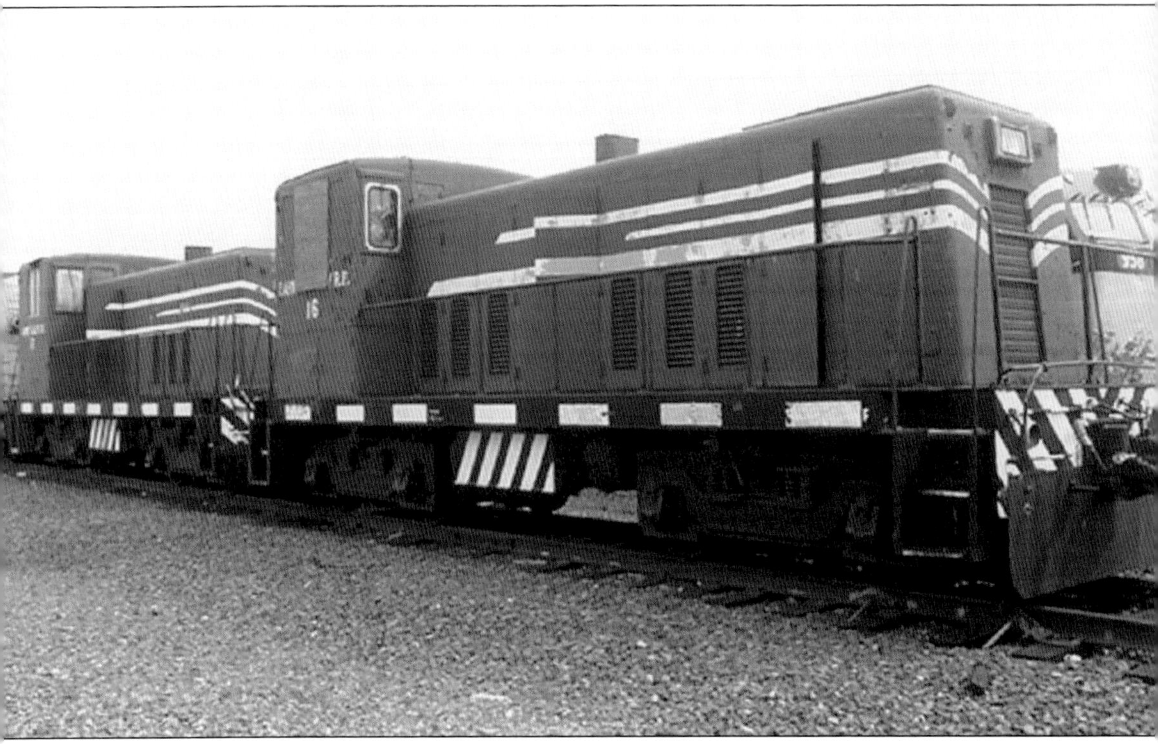

RV Nos. 16 and 17, seen here at the New Jersey Transit's Meadowlands Maintenance Center in South Kearny, are now on display at the Whippany Railway Museum in Whippany, NJ. They are owned by the United Railroad Historical Society. (Photograph by Jeffrey A. Lubchansky.)